BIODIVERSITY
OF
INDONESIA

TANAH AIR

THE PUBLISHER WOULD LIKE TO EXTEND THANKS
TO IBU SITI HEDIATI PRABOWO, CHAIRPERSON OF
PT MAHARANI PARAMITRA AND TO MR HARRY SAPTO, WITHOUT THEIR
GENEROUS SUPPORT AND INTEREST THIS PROJECT
WOULD NOT HAVE BEEN POSSIBLE.

FOREWORD BY
M SOEHARTO
PRESIDENT OF THE
REPUBLIC OF INDONESIA

BOOK INITIATOR
H E MINISTER OF TOURISM, POST
AND TELECOMMUNICATIONS
JOOP AVÉ

AUTHOR
DR DAVID STONE

SPECIAL FEATURES WRITERS
JANET COCHRANE
DR CHRISTOPHER HAILS
DESI HARAHAP
DR SOEDARSONO RISWAN
FELIA SALIM
DR JATNA SUPRIATNA

PRINCIPAL PHOTOGRAPHERS
MICHAEL AW
ALAIN COMPOST
JEAN-PAUL FERRERO
RIO HELMI
MIKE SEVERNS

ADVISERS
DR IVAN POLUNIN
PAUL SPENCER SOCHACZEWSKI
DR TONY WHITTEN

READER
SYARIL NURSAL

SENIOR EDITOR
VIVIEN CRUMP

ART DIRECTOR
TAN TAT GHEE

DESIGNERS
TAN SEOK LUI
NORREHA BT SAYUTI
DORINE SAM

ILLUSTRATORS
BRUCE GRANQUIST
ANUAR BIN ABDUL RAHIM

PRODUCTION MANAGER
EDMUND LAM

ADMINISTRATION
(JAKARTA OFFICE)
SETI-ARTI KAILOLA

The Biodiversity of Indonesia: Tanah Air
© Editions Didier Millet 1994
593 Havelock Road, #02-01/02, Isetan Office Building, Singapore 169641
Reprinted 1995, 1997

Printed in Singapore by Tien Wah Press

ISBN 981-3018-36-4

THE PUBLISHER WOULD LIKE TO EXTEND THANKS TO
THE SAHID JAYA HOTEL & TOWER FOR THEIR GENEROUS SPONSORSHIP OF THIS PROJECT

BIODIVERSITY
OF
INDONESIA
TANAH AIR

FOREWORD
PRESIDENT SOEHARTO

TEXT
DR DAVID STONE

SPECIAL FEATURES
JANET COCHRANE
DR CHRISTOPHER HAILS
DESI HARAHAP
DR SOEDARSONO RISWAN
FELIA SALIM
DR JATNA SUPRIATNA

PHOTOGRAPHY
MICHAEL AW
ALAIN COMPOST
MIKE SEVERNS

ARCHIPELAGO PRESS

CONTENTS

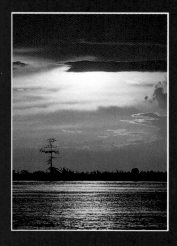

FOREWORD

We thank God for his blessings on Indonesia, our beloved Homeland, with its very great biological diversity and rich plant and animal life. We are stewards of ten per cent of the world's remaining forests. Our seas teem with life. Our people rely on the nation's biological diversity for many of the practical essentials of life. Nature is part of our spiritual life as well as our material existence, and many of our traditional cultures place a great emphasis on respect for Nature's wisdom.

We attach the greatest importance to the preservation and conservation of the environment, as mandated by the guidelines of state policy. We are strongly committed to promoting national development with a view to improving the people's prosperity and well-being. The preservation of the environment is an integral part of our many development endeavours.

The ultimate goal of our development is the creation of a just and prosperous society founded on our fundamental state philosophy, Pancasila. In our efforts at sustainable development, we try hard to strike a better balance between man and his fellow beings, man and his society, man and his environment and man and God the Creator.

Through a series of Five-Year Development Plans (REPELITA), we have been implementing programmes based on what is known as the "Trilogy of Development", namely; stability, growth and equitable distribution of the fruits of development. Indonesia has achieved encouraging results in many areas over the past 25 years. We are determined to continue to fight against poverty, ignorance and backwardness as the principal causes of environmental degradation.

Moreover, we adhere consistently to our motto "development without destroying the environment". It is imperative to preserve the environment – both for present and for future generations – and to use it sustainably, so as to achieve development and conservation goals.

In 1993 the villagers of Keluru, near Kerinci Seblat National Park in Sumatra, received the first Kalapataru Environment Award, which I gave them myself. These men and women, working in association with conservation groups like WWF, have taken responsibility to conserve their environment. I see similar recognition of Nature's importance growing throughout our vast country.

In our forests and our seas we regularly discover new wonders. We invite others to visit our national parks and see for themselves. You will learn why Indonesians describe their country by referring to *Tanah Airku*, 'our land and water'.

It is with such a spirit I warmly welcome this important and beautiful book on some of Indonesia's finest flora and fauna. I hope that it will be a major contribution to encourage understanding and appreciation of Nature and all the efforts that we are making to preserve the environment.

BY PRESIDENT SOEHARTO

INTRO

TAMPAK LAH HUTAN
RIMBA DAN NGARAI
LAGIPUN SAWAH,
SUNGAI YANG PERMAI
SERTA GERANGAN,
LIHAT LAH PULA
LANGIT YANG HIJAU
BERTUKAR WAMA
OLEH PUCUK,
DAUN KELAPA
ITU LAH TANAH,
TANAH AIRKU

Mohamad Yamin, 1920

LOOK ON THE BEAUTY
OF VERDANT FOREST,
OF JUNGLES, GORGES,
RICEFIELDS AND RIVERS TOO
AND VIEW WITH WONDER
THE SKY'S COLOUR
CHANGING TO GREEN
WITH THE WAVING
OF COCONUT FRONDS.
YES, THIS IS MY LAND.
MY MOTHERLAND

Translation,
John McGlynn, 1994

INTRODUCTION

Preceding page: Gunung Kerinci, Sumatra.

Above: a sulphur collector carrying a load of 70 kilograms, Gunung Welerang, East Java.

Below: Anak Krakatau.

Tanah air kita means 'Our land and water'. If ever a nation had the right to feel proud of its natural wealth and beauty, surely it is Indonesia. Descriptions of the country command superlatives; the natural history of others pales beside that of Indonesia. The range of its natural resources is only rivalled by its cultural diversity, the roots of which can be traced back to some of the earliest settlers of the Asian region, some million years ago.

Indonesia is the world's largest archipelago, located between the continents of Asia and Australia, extending for some 5000 square kilometres along the Equator between 4°N and 11°S and 95° and 141°E. The archipelago consists of over 17,000 islands, of which only 600 are inhabited. From the boundaries of this vast expanse of islands and water, the land stretches across some 1,770 kilometres from north to south and 5,152 kilometres from east to west, a total area of 1,948,700 square kilometres. A rugged and varied landscape typifies the region; in part, a constant reminder of its turbulent geological history. The land is dominated by a chain of high mountains and volcanoes extending in an arc from the northwestern tip of Sumatra, through the central area and south coast of Java, to Timor in Nusa Tenggara. Other impressive mountain formations reach through the centre of Sulawesi and the central and northern parts of Irian Jaya. Kalimantan, the largest part of the great island of Borneo, is geologically older than much of the rest of the country and is a more stable landmass with no volcanoes.

Indonesia's great oceans are no less dramatic or spectacular in the range of features on display, and contain many, as yet unexplored, wonders. The flamboyant forms of Indonesia's coral reefs and underwater gardens abound with life – a myriad of shapes, sizes and colours blending together to produce one of the greatest natural spectacles on Earth. An equally great range of atolls provides some of the most beautiful scenery within the seas. Underwater volcanoes and deep trenches create spectacular and varied landscapes below the seas.

Indonesia covers only 1.3 per cent of the Earth's surface yet harbours ten per cent of all flowering plants, 12 per cent of the world's mammals, 16 per cent of the world's reptiles and amphibians, 17 per cent of all birds and more than a quarter of known marine and freshwater fish species. Overall, it is one of the richest countries in terms of biological diversity. The many islands of the archipelago support a wide range and variety of habitats; from lowland rain forests and mangroves to savanna grasslands, swamp forests and limestone hills to montane forests, alpine meadows and snow-capped mountains almost on the Equator. About 59 per cent of Indonesia's land area is covered with forest; this represents almost ten per cent of the world's remaining tropical forest. Within the country, natural forest cover varies from a mere seven per cent in Java to 92 per cent in Irian Jaya.

Much of this richness can be attributed to the fact that Indonesia spans two major biogeographical realms (Indo-Malayan and Australasian), which have been long isolated from each other by deep waters. The distinctive flora and fauna of these regions only come together and mingle in a small area of overlap. Flanked by the two great continents of Asia and Australia, the archipelago is of interest not only to naturalists and anthropologists, but to geologists as well.

BIRTH OF THE ARCHIPELAGO

The Earth is a dynamic planet. Despite the solid structure it portrays from the surface, it is in constant turmoil. In addition to the complex series of events which surround the visible solar and tidal systems, other forces of far greater magnitude are constantly at work deep within the Earth's core. The thin, outer crust of the Earth acts like a protective mantle for all life on Earth. The great landmasses rest on strong plates which gradually, but steadily, move over a hot, partially molten layer that lies at a depth of 60 to 70 kilometres beneath the surface, in which turbulent convection currents originate moving the plates about the Earth's surface. Where the crust has been weakened, for example where two plates collide or separate, some of the unimaginable pressure contained within the Earth's core escapes via a volcano, or vent, releasing steam and molten rock.

In the four and a half billion years since the Earth formed, the landmasses have radically changed position and shape on a number of occasions. Some 250 million years ago, scientists believe the Earth was a single continent surrounded by a great ocean, *Panthalassa*. During the Jurassic period (50 to 100 million years later) – a brief span of time in terms of the Earth's history – this large continent called *Pangea* began to break up and drift apart, creating new oceans in the process. The two resulting land components, known as *Laurasia* (which gave rise to North America and Eurasia) and *Gondwanaland* (South America, Africa, Australia and Antarctica), gradually moved towards

their respective poles, changing shape even further in the process.

Amidst this incredibly slow but cataclysmic process of shaping the Earth's surface, scientists have now discovered that some forms of life were present on Earth. Fossil evidence shows that several distinct forms of bacteria-like organism lived even some 3000 million years ago. Living conditions at the time are thought to have resembled those of the hot, acrid atmosphere similar to the many hot springs and volcanoes in Indonesia today. In time, minute algal growths developed, relying on the sun's energy and carbon dioxide in the atmosphere to generate food materials; they created oxygen as a by-product. During the millennia which followed, a gradual build up of oxygen began to change the composition of the Earth's atmosphere, making it possible for air-breathing organisms to evolve.

Life on Earth originated in shallow seas and thrived in these conditions for millions of years. As new species evolved, however, competition for food, shelter and living space forced many creatures to adapt to conditions higher up the shoreline. Here life was somewhat less competitive but new dangers had to be faced and overcome, particularly exposure to air (which was probably deadly to the earliest life forms). To begin with, the first land plants and early animals were probably confined to damp places; but they gradually managed to reduce their dependence on water, and their descendants were able to move into slightly drier habitats. In time, more and more species joined these early pio-

neers until pressures on space and food supplies increased once again. These events have continued during the course of evolution. As these animals moved further inland, gills gave rise to primitive lungs, skin developed a waterproof mantle to reduce evaporation, and fins became modified to bear weight on land. An increasing number of organisms became less reliant on the sea and some eventually severed all attachment to it. The great colonization of the land had begun.

Around 250 million years ago animal life on Earth was still at a very early stage of development. Birds had not yet evolved and the first primitive mammals were just about to put in an appearance. Fossil records show that these were small, shrew-like animals with woolly coats and sweat glands by which they could regulate body temperature. These furtive animals probably lived on the margins of the forests and areas of water, wary of the much larger reptiles of that time. As climatic conditions on Earth changed even further, many of the huge, lumbering dinosaurs died out and were gradually replaced with new lines of mammal and bird.

As to the precise origins of the Indonesian Archipelago, the geological record is somewhat unclear, but it is known

Above: Anak Krakatau about 65 years after it emerged from the sea.

Below: an aerial view into the crater of Gunung Gede, West Java.

Right: Gunung Papan-Dieng, from De Indiesche Archipel (1865).

Below: at the beginning of the twentieth century the concept of continental drift was first developed, though it has only recently been universally accepted. Over the millions of years, the Earth's landmasses are thought to have changed considerably.

that the country as we see it today is the culmination of many breaks and unions of the gradually moving land blocks. About 150 million years ago, what is now Sumatra, Borneo and western Sulawesi split off from Gondwanaland and drifted northwards. Some 70 million years later, India also broke off from the southern block of land and it too drifted northwards, colliding eventually with the Asian landmass, the upthrust giving rise to the Himalayan mountain chain. As Gondwanaland continued to disintegrate, New Guinea was gradually pushed further north, ahead of Australia, into the tropics. More recently, about 15 million years ago, a part of New Guinea went its separate way, drifting westwards until it collided and fused with another landmass from the west to form present-day Sulawesi. At approximately the same time, the first small islands emerged from the sea where the Javan Plateau is situated today. Further tectonic movements caused more land to rise up on Java and Borneo. Since this time, few major apparent changes

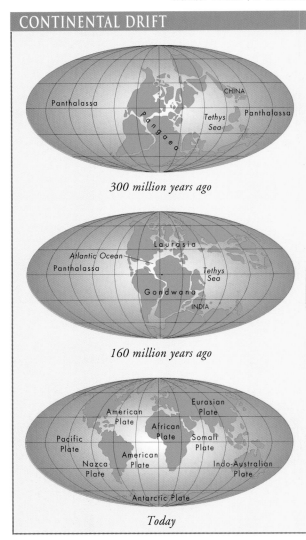

CONTINENTAL DRIFT

300 million years ago

160 million years ago

Today

have taken place within the overall pattern of land movement in the region. However, by no means is this process over. Volcanic activity, both on land and beneath the sea, is a continuing process in this region. Even today, the Australian landmass is still advancing on Indonesia and New Guinea; it may eventually collide. It is difficult to predict the outcome of this volcanic activity.

Earth movements and, more recently, volcanic activity have had a great influence on the physical development of Indonesia. An 'arc of fire' runs from the northern tip of Sumatra through Java and Nusa Tenggara out into the Banda Sea. About 100 volcanoes are still active in this region, reflecting continuous tectonic activity and exerting an ongoing influence on soils and vegetation by the periodic discharge of gas and solid matter. Yet, although volcanoes can cause high mortality and considerable destruction, in many ways they have been highly beneficial to people. The volcanic soils of Sumatra, Java and Sulawesi, for example, form some of the country's most fertile regions; a large proportion of the agricultural population congregate in these confined areas to cultivate the soils.

A LIVING LABORATORY
A small island in the Sunda Strait between Java and Sumatra was the scene of one of the most violent eruptions on Earth in recorded history. In August 1883, the volcanic island of Krakatau resumed activity after a period of dormancy. Clouds of smoke, together with large volumes of ash and huge blocks of lava were thrown out of its crater into the surrounding sea. As more and more materials were expelled, the framework of the island collapsed under the weight of the surrounding sea, which poured into the vast subterranean chamber and produced a massive explosion and a fountain of

*Left: Gunung Bromo
(1908).*

Below: Anak Krakatau.

*Bottom: map showing the
tectonic plates and activity
affecting the Indonesian
Archipelago.*

magma and ash which rose an estimated five kilometres into the air. When it fell back to earth, it produced huge tidal waves, *tsunamis*, which swept out from the island towards Java and Sumatra, eliminating entire villages and killing almost 40,000 people in the process. Furious winds swept out from the island and circled the globe seven times before finally becoming exhausted. As the smoke cleared all that remained of the former volcano was Rakata, an inactive mountain that marked the southern edge of Krakatau. In a brief space of time the centre of the island was transformed into an undersea crater some 270 metres deep and seven kilometres long.

All life on the island was presumably destroyed during these cataclysmic events; no organism is capable of withstanding the steam, smoke, poisonous gases and molten lava produced during such an event. Deep ash replaced the former island's forest cover. A barren landscape, totally devoid of wildlife, was all that remained. Yet amidst that destruction and desolation a research team visiting Rakata some nine months after the explosion, discovered one tiny spider living somehow amongst the steaming ash-ridden slopes, demonstrating the powers of dispersal and adaptability that many creatures possess. In time, other animals light enough to be 'rafted' across on floating vegetation, or carried on the wind – as well as seeds and other organisms carried by birds, bats and insects – also arrived to colonize the barren slopes of the island.

Scientists were presented with another living laboratory when, in 1930, a small island emerged from the sea along the northern rim of Old Krakatau's caldera. To begin with, Anak Krakatau, 'Child of Krakatau' as it is known, was as devoid of life as Rakata after the eruption in 1883; within a short period of time, however, animals and plants

began to colonize the barren slopes. Today, this smouldering island has many thickets of casuarina and wild sugar-cane growing on it, while nearby Rakata is once again covered in dense jungle, a mere century after being one of the most inhospitable places on Earth.

This is just one example of the very great power of Nature; many previous volcanic eruptions had been of far greater magnitude. In 1815 the island of Sumbawa in Nusa Tenggara underwent a major transformation: Mount (Gunung) Tambora erupted, expelling ten times more material than Krakatau, and killed over 90,000 people in the process. More than ten times as powerful again was the eruption of Mount Toba in northern Sumatra, 75,000 years ago. This eruption was followed by another one 45,000 years later. Few of the many people who visit this site, and sail across Southeast Asia's largest lake, realize that they are poised on the site of one of the greatest volcanic eruptions ever to have taken place on Earth.

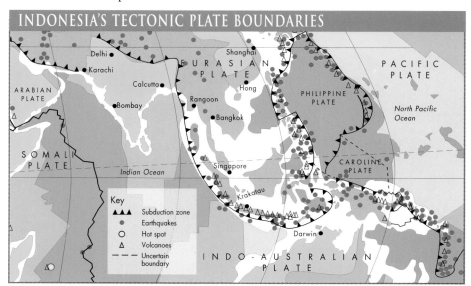

INDONESIA'S TECTONIC PLATE BOUNDARIES

Key

▲▲▲ Subduction zone
● Earthquakes
○ Hot spot
△ Volcanoes
– – – Uncertain boundary

The illustration shows a selection of species characteristoc of the various parts of the archipelago.

Sumatra

Thomas' leaf-monkey
Peacock pheasant
Greater racket-tailed drongo
Elephant
Sumatran rhinoceros
Tapir

Java and Bali

Javan gibbon
Warty pig (Java)
Bali starling
Banteng (Java)
Javan rhinoceros
Green jungle fowl

Kalimantan

Proboscis monkey
Rhinoceros hornbill
Rafflesia
Orang-utan
Argus pheasant
Bornean gibbon

Sulawesi

Spectral tarsier
Red-knobbed hornbill
Black macaque
Wallace's fruit bat
Maleo
Anoa

Nusa Tenggara

Orange-footed scrub fowl
Komodo dragon
Sandalwood tree
Lombok fruit bat
Timor python

Maluku

Chattering lory
Salmon-crested cockatoo
Nutmeg
Blue and white kingfisher
Goliath birdwing of Seram
Sail-fin lizard

Irian Jaya

Sugar glider
Tree kangaroo
Flame of Irian
Lesser bird of paradise
Cuscus
Two-wattled cassowary
Victoria crowned pigeon

LAND BRIDGES AND MOVEMENTS OF WILDLIFE

In keeping with its turbulent geological history, the Earth's climate has also undergone a number of periodic and occasionally dramatic changes. During the past 1.5 million years, the so-called Pleistocene period, the world's sea-level has undergone several major fluctuations. During particularly cold periods, many of the world's water reservoirs were frozen into massive ice blocks which covered vast regions of the Earth. Most of the water was locked up in the great frozen wastes of the North and South Poles. During these ice ages, when the sea-level was low and the shallow parts of the South China and Java seas were above water, this whole area, called the Sunda Shelf, or Sundaland, formed a continuous landmass. At times, Sumatra, Java, Bali and Borneo were physically joined to mainland Asia by a series of 'land bridges'. When the sea-level was at its lowest, it is even thought that one could have walked from Bali to Bangkok! In a similar fashion, in the east of the archipelago, Irian Jaya and the Kai and Aru islands were once connected to Australia. These connections allowed animals and plants to migrate along these land bridges. As the Earth's climate warmed again, water was released from the frozen ice masses. This caused the sea-level to rise, isolating many of the 'islands' once again, though not all connections were broken at the same time.

The periodic raising and lowering of sea-levels meant that connections between mainland Asia and the islands of the Sunda Shelf, as well as Australia and those of the Sahul Shelf, were periodically broken. During these periods of geographic isolation species of plants and animals, many of them new colonizing species, spread and quickly filled vacant niches. Successive waves of new species then had to contend with those already well-established, and each had to find a new niche if the preferred habitat was already occupied, or adapt to living under sub-optimal conditions.

This feature of repeated waves of colonization and specialization of plants and animals is now known from many regions, but nowhere is it displayed so vividly as in Indonesia. Early explorers and naturalists were puzzled by the extremely high and divergent levels of species found in the region. Among the first to document these important discoveries was the Victorian naturalist and voyager, Alfred Russel Wallace (a contemporary of Charles Darwin, the author of the controversial *The Origin of Species*). In Indonesia, Wallace noticed that in Lombok and islands to the east, for example, one could find cockatoos, parrots and marsupials – pouch bearing mammals – as well as thorny plants typical of more arid country. In contrast, on Bali and islands further west, monkeys, tigers, elephants and rhinoceros were encountered in the region's lush and varied tropical vegetation.

KALIMANTAN

SULAWESI

MALUKU

Wallace Line

JAVA

BALI

Weber Line

IRIAN JAYA

NUSA TENGGARA

Below: Dani hut, Baliem Valley, Irian Jaya.

Facing page: Jale, neighbours of the Dani, gathering dried timber.

Wallace postulated that such a clear-cut distinction had to be accounted for by some physical barrier which was no longer present: 'We have here a clue to the most radical contrast in the Archipelago, and by following it out in detail I have arrived at the conclusion that we can draw a line among the islands, which shall so divide them that one-half shall truly belong to Asia, while the other shall no less certainly be allied to Australia. I term these respectively the Indo-Malayan and the Austro-Malayan divisions of the Archipelago'. A study of the submarine topography of this region has revealed that two vast continental shelves lie beneath the ocean's surface, each covered by very shallow water, but separated from each other by deep waters. On the basis of his explorations and observations, Wallace proposed a faunal limit that divided Bali from Lombok and extended northwards through the Makassar Strait separating Borneo from Sulawesi and including The Philippines on the Asian side. Although certain revisions have since been made to this hypothesis, largely the exclusion of The Philippines (apart from the island of Palawan) from the Asian faunal area,

this important faunal boundary has since been dubbed 'Wallace's Line' in his honour. Even today, this artificial boundary remains an important feature for geographers and ecologists since it marks the dividing boundary between two continental regions, Asia and Australia, though plant species appear to pay less respect to it than animal species.

The Indonesian Archipelago is indeed inhabited by two distinct types of fauna, with species composition changing considerably from west to east. The flora, in contrast, is predominantly Malesian throughout the archipelago. Faunal distributions more closely reflect the ancient land connections, with placental mammals being found in the west and marsupials in the east. The islands of Sulawesi, Maluku and Nusa Tenggara lie in a major transition zone, 'Wallacea', which lies between the Indo-Malayan and Australian realms.

EARLY PEOPLES OF INDONESIA

The long presence of people in Asia has had a profound impact on the physical landscape of the region, as well as on the distribution and abundance of a large number of plant and animal species. In many instances close relationships developed between human civilizations and Nature, many of which still feature in some traditional beliefs and practices. Many native tribespeople of Borneo, for example, attach considerable impor-

tance to the sighting of certain birds, which are used to divine events such as planting and harvesting cycles. The presence of the scarlet-rumped trogon (*Harpactes duvaucelii*) is thought to indicate to prospecting hill farmers particularly fertile soils. The Asmat of southern Irian Jaya, and many indigenous people of the Mentawai Islands, also place considerable emphasis on the care and respect shown for certain species of tree and wildlife. In other cases the traditional respect for nature has broken down as population pressures grew and traditions changed and the process of environmental degradation – excessive hunting and clearance of forest cover – gradually set in.

Fossil evidence suggests that people have been present in Asia for a considerable time, possibly more than a million years. During the Pleistocene period, when much of the Eurasian landmass was covered in ice, Indonesia experienced a tropical climate. Low sea-levels enabled large land mammals to migrate towards the favourable living conditions of the Greater Sunda Islands. Early people became more attuned to hunting and their existence may have depended on following these animals – a constant source of food. One of the most successful of the earliest hunters, *Homo erectus*, an upright-walking human capable of using simple tools, is thought to have reached Java 750,000 years ago. During the remainder of the Pleistocene period *Homo erectus* continued to evolve. These primitive hunters probably lived in small, nomadic, self-sufficient groups and practised no form of agriculture. Such early hominids were possibly responsible for the extinction of certain slow-moving large mammals in Java, particularly tapirs, hippopotamus, giant pangolins and elephants, as well as some primates.

While this scenario was under way in Asia, a similar process of hominid evolution was taking place in Africa and Europe, as more developed forms explored distant horizons – always, to begin with, in pursuit of food. By the end of the Pleistocene period, as climatic conditions improved, waves of our own species, *Homo sapiens*, gradually spread throughout Asia, reaching many of Indonesia's islands by small canoe and raft. Like the successive waves of new colonizing plants and animals, *Homo erectus* gradually disappeared as the new Mesolithic culture took over. These tool-using people probably lived in caves or similar shelters, from where small nomadic groups practised a hunting and gathering economy. Fire was discovered and some groups began to create art and develop rites. By 3000 B.C., shifting cultivation was being practised. Crops cultivated probably included taro, yams, bananas, sago, wild millet and rice. Significant advances to agriculture in Indonesia – especially, the widespread cultivation of rice – came with the arrival of Mongoloid people from southern Asia around 2500 B.C., who introduced outrigger canoes, fine pottery and stone adzes.

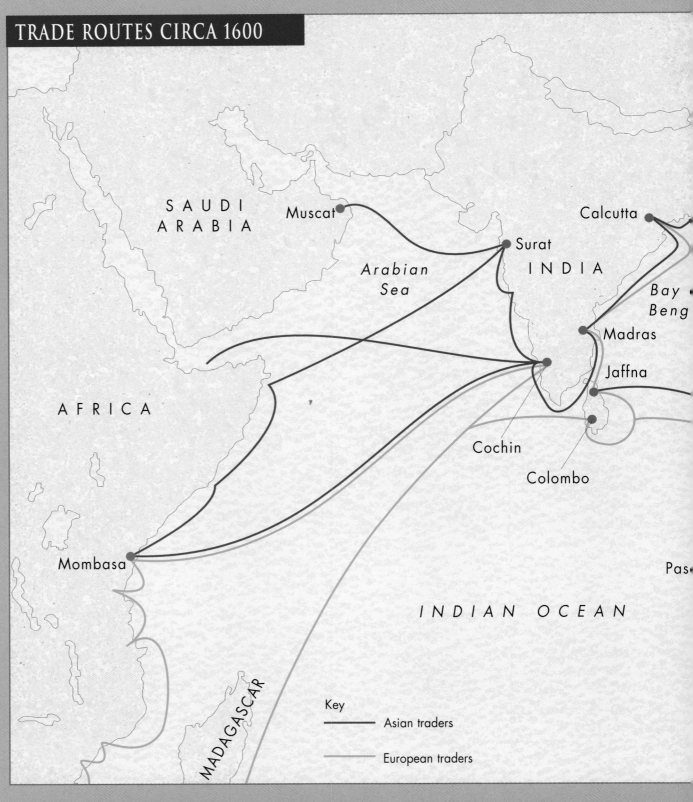

TRADE ROUTES CIRCA 1600

SAUDI
ARABIA

Muscat

*Arabian
Sea*

AFRICA

Surat

INDIA

Calcutta

*Bay
Beng*

Madras

Jaffna

Cochin

Colombo

Mombasa

Pas

INDIAN OCEAN

MADAGASCAR

Key

Asian traders

European traders

The islands making up the Indonesian Archipelago have long been at the heart of a strong and complex trading network. There is evidence indicating that the cinnamon routes shown opposite were operating in 200 A. D. and the sandalwood trade in 900 A. D. Today, oil and liquified natural gas trading is vital to the Indonesian economy.

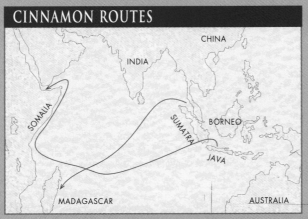

CINNAMON ROUTES

CHINA

INDIA

SOMALIA

SUMATRA

BORNEO

JAVA

MADAGASCAR

AUSTRALIA

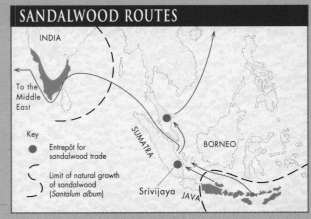

SANDALWOOD ROUTES

INDIA

To the
Middle
East

Key

Entrepôt for
sandalwood trade

Limit of natural growth
of sandalwood
(*Santalum album*)

SUMATRA

BORNEO

Srivijaya

JAVA

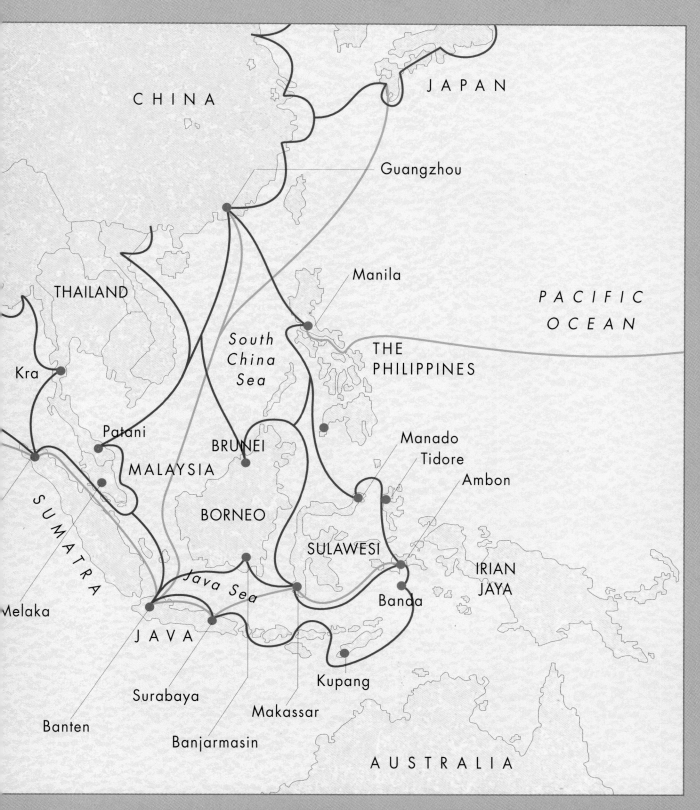

CHINA

JAPAN

Guangzhou

Manila

PACIFIC
OCEAN

THAILAND

Kra

South
China
Sea

THE
PHILIPPINES

Patani

Manado
Tidore

BRUNEI

Ambon

MALAYSIA

SUMATRA

BORNEO

SULAWESI

Melaka

Java Sea

IRIAN
JAYA

Banda

JAVA

Surabaya

Kupang

Banten

Makassar

Banjarmasin

AUSTRALIA

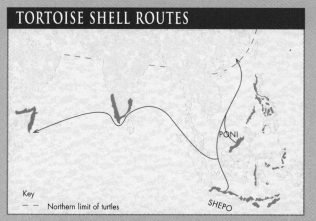

TORTOISE SHELL ROUTES

PONI

SHEPO

Key
– – Northern limit of turtles

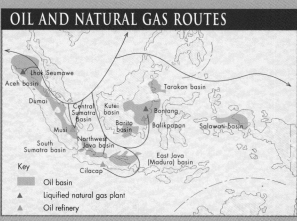

OIL AND NATURAL GAS ROUTES

Lhok Seumawe
Aceh basin
Dumai
Central
Sumatra
basin
Musi
South
Sumatra basin
Northwest
Java basin
Cilacap

Kutei
basin
Barito
basin
Bontang
Balikpapan

Tarakan basin

East Java
(Madura) basin

Salawati basin

Key
▨ Oil basin
▲ Liquified natural gas plant
▲ Oil refinery

I.van Ryne delin.   Publish'd according to Act of Parliment 1754

The City of BATAVIA in the Island of Java and Capital of all   La Ville de BATAVIA

the Dutch Factories & Settlements in the East Indies.   London Printed for Rob.t Sayer opposite Fetter Lane Fleet Street   Comple

CHANGING TIMES

Although exploration and internal trade played an important part in the development of civilizations in Southeast Asia, for many of the archipelago's people changes were heralded by the arrival of Indian, Chinese and Moslem seafarers in the first millenium. Chinese and Indian traders were regularly visiting the area by the first century A. D. Manufactured goods were exchanged for sandalwood, gold, spices, feathers, plant medicines and tortoise shells. With the traders came Buddhist priests and brahmins and new religious ideas, writing and systems of law were introduced. Linked to the fortunes of trade, often controlled by local rulers, kingdoms rose and fell. Srivijaya in Sumatra (7th to 14th centuries) derived its trade from control over shipping and trade in the Straits of Malacca, while Kediri (1050-1222) in Java flourished from the trading of spices between Maluku, China, India and the Middle East. However, by the 13th century the Hindu-Buddhist courts were in decline and merchants from Gujerat and Persia had brought Islam to Sumatra. Trading (*pasir*) states developed on Java's north coast and Islam took root, gradually spreading east. A little later came the European explorers and traders who realized that great profits could be made from exploiting the natural riches of the region. Increased demand for prized goods such as spices, fragrant timbers

and choice animal products, including the plumes of the birds of paradise, led to the early over-exploitation of some materials, and considerable changes to the landscape, as specialized growth of crops began. Rival groups of islanders and foreign powers vied for control of these lucrative products. One of the greatest changes to the landscape of Indonesia, however, came with the introduction of monoculture crops, particularly rubber and oil palm, but also tea, coffee, cinnamon and cloves, for which vast areas of lowland rain forest were cut down. Profitable though these crops may be, they cannot replace the natural beauty or wealth of the former forests. Interesting lessons can be learned from these developments, particularly regarding the economic risks associated with depending on a few, select exports. A growing realization of the value of forests, wetlands and coastal environments, in their natural state, has recently gained more support as people begin to appreciate the importance of maintaining the natural balance of the environment for the benefit of future generations.

Right: the port at Batavia (Jakarta) in 1754.

Below: Ambon in 1727.

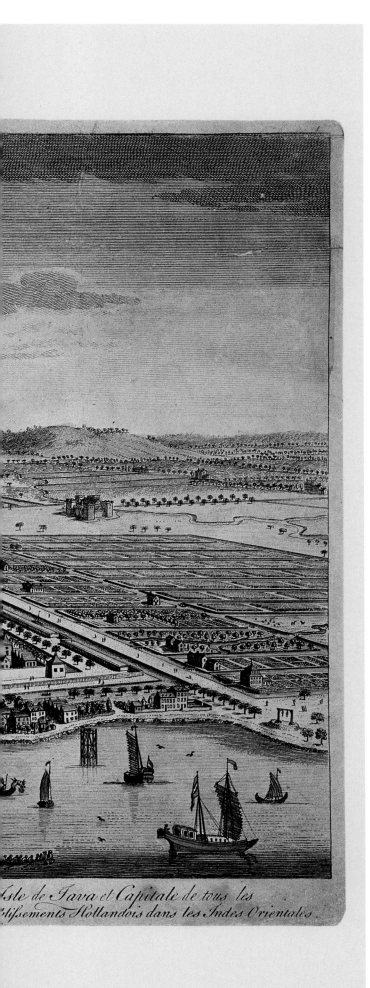

Isle de Java et Capitale de tous les ...tissements Hollandois dans les Indes Orientales.

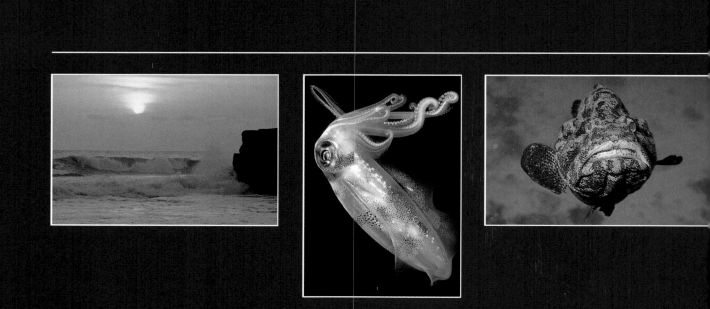

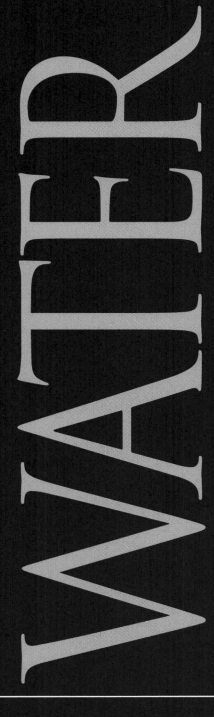

WATER

THE OCEAN REALM AND LIFE IN THE OCEAN

Preceding page: feathery stinging hydroids, and corals of several forms support a large population of fish.

Above: lizardfish.

Below: cave coral is particularly found in low light areas.

Right: chambered nautilus, Manado.

The oceans are a unique asset in our world. The Earth is the only planet in the solar system with water on its surface. The seas first formed as the Earth began to cool, shortly after its birth, and hot water vapour condensed on the rugged surface. Added to this slowly accumulating reservoir were the mineral rich outpourings from the volcanic vents deep inside the earth. In time, this soup-like cocktail received further materials from the eroding landmasses, mixing, combining and spreading to form the great oceans. The uniqueness of this ecosystem – the birthplace of all life on Earth – and its importance for the well-being of this planet cannot be overestimated.

The sea covers almost 70 per cent of the Earth's surface. Without the water that evaporates from it and falls again as rain, there would be little life on Earth. The waters of the oceans appear to be in constant turmoil. Even the scarred ocean floor and its margins are subject to continuous tectonic movement and change as the globe's oceanic and continental plates move.

The marine environment of Indonesia is dominated by two extensive shelf areas: the shallow Sunda Shelf to the west (the world's largest continental shelf), with a maximum depth of 200 metres at its edge; and the Sahul Shelf in the east. During the last Ice Age the Sunda Shelf was above water, forming a land-bridge with the rest of Asia. Today some areas are extremely shallow still – the sea between Kalimantan and Java ranges from 6 to 60 metres in depth. Between the two shelves a complex variety of environments can be found, including deep ocean trenches (some of which descend to more than 7000 metres) and basins that range from 2000-6000 metres, steep sided atolls and seamounts, submarine banks and volcanoes. Although people have long charted many of these submarine wonders, it has only been in recent decades, with improved marine technology, that we have been able to witness at first hand some of the fascinating life forms that have adapted to living at these depths.

The more visible coastal and marine ecosytems span a wide range of habitats, including the most extensive mangrove forests, seagrass beds and spectacular coral reefs in Asia. Mangroves are particularly extensive on the east coast of Sumatra, and the coasts of Kalimantan and Irian Jaya (which alone has 69 per cent of Indonesia's mangrove habitat). More popular are the country's colourful coral gardens and extensive reef systems in the deep clear seas off Sulawesi and Maluku – some of the world's richest ecosystems in terms of the corals, fishes and other reef organisms are found here. Other spectacular features include Taka Bone Rate in the Flores Sea, the third largest atoll in the world.

THE MOVING WATERS

The waters of the Earth are always going somewhere – a basic feature of oceans and rivers and the hydrological cycle that connects them. The reasons behind this are complex, resulting from a combination of the sun's heat and the motion of the Earth. Equatorial waters receive much of the sun's heat. As the surface waters of these oceans absorb the sun's energy, they expand and gradually spread outwards, flowing towards the North and South poles. The movement set up by these currents, in turn, causes colder water to flow in towards the Equator to replace that moving out. These warm surface currents and much colder, deeper ones are, in turn, affected by wind and the gradual rotation of the Earth which combine to create a series of swirling currents emanating from the Equator. These currents, which are a relatively stable feature, are responsible for maintaining the integrity of coastal and marine ecosystems as we know them.

Most of Indonesia lies south of the Equator, so its surface currents are influenced by the southeast (May to September) and northwest (November to March) monsoons. Surface currents reverse over most of the Indonesian seas in phase with these two monsoons. During the southeast monsoon, Pacific Ocean waters flow through the Halmahera and Seram seas into the Banda and Flores seas and through the Sulawesi Sea and Makassar Strait into the Java Sea. During the northwest monsoon, South China Sea waters flow south through the Karimata Strait into the Java Sea, reversing the flow which occurs during the southeast monsoon. There is little, if any, entry of surface Indian Ocean water into the enclosed confines of the Indonesian seas.

Man's interdependence with the sea, so strikingly observed in Indonesia, is an ancient affair; and since earliest times the rolling waves have fascinated, awed and inspired. Movement is a constant feature in all of the Earth's great seas. At times these movements are subtle, but their impact may also be felt several kilometres inland during particularly violent weather conditions. Such movement,

*Below: Uluwatu, Bali,
where the ocean swell from
Antarctica crashes into
limestone cliffs.*

*Right: Ujung Kulon, West
Java.*

The undersea world is a mysterious and, to many, a frightening realm which humans have only recently begun to penetrate. As explorations widen, a new world is gradually revealing itself and our understanding of how the oceans function is increasing. The submarine environment is not static; the ocean floor and its margins are constantly changing – new geological landscapes slowly emerging as a result of the internal forces deep in the Earth's core and the scouring effects of deep-sea currents. As on land, life in the ocean is dependent upon the availability of nutrients and minerals.

There is a never-ending flow of materials to the sea from the surrounding land. Each year the rivers of the world deposit 750 million tonnes of sediment into coastal waters; millions more are deposited as silt along the continental shelves of the great landmasses. Some of the essential minerals contained – nitrates, phosphates and carbonates – become dissolved in sea-water. Depending on the state of the currents and tides and on the nature of the materials, this mixture of

rocks, sand, silt and mud may become widely distributed across the continental shelf, or be concentrated at irregular intervals. This in turn may affect the occurrence, distribution, density and even variety of plant and animal life. In general, however, most of the incoming materials remain in the nearshore; little of the detritus carried down by rivers reaches the open depths, partially accounting for the much more limited range of life found there. Wherever these land-based materials enter the marine environment, some are immediately used by algae, molluscs and fish for growth and development, while others may be transported over considerable distances before being utilized by different organisms, or settling on the sea-bed.

Materials on the sea-bed vary considerably in content and texture; they may be solid rock or, more commonly, a collection of unconsolidated sediments of clay, silt, sand or gravel that has been washed off the land by rivers, or formed from countless billions of skeletons of planktonic and other animals. The underlying solid rock may itself be sedimentary, composed of sediments compacted under great pressure thousands of metres beneath the present sea floor, or igneous, formed from molten magma welling up from within the Earth. In Indonesian waters, particular concentrations of red clay are found in the Sulawesi and Banda seas and high concentrations of globigerina ooze, a calcareous sediment, have been recorded in the South

China Sea, northwest of Borneo, and the region of the Seram Sea.

The circulation of nutrients is essential for the growth and development of all marine organisms. The combined effects of gravity, tides, underwater currents and the wind are all vital in ensuring that these substances remain in motion. Despite this, some materials which become buried in the loose sediment or viscous ooze on the sea-bed are temporarily 'lost' to living organisms. Occasionally, deep water currents will rake through sediments, pushing these materials back into suspension and circulation by the current. On a smaller scale in terms of the immediate effect, but nonetheless an important factor given the number of organisms involved, are the constant burrowing actions of ground-dwelling species, both detritus and suspension feeders. These species agitate the sediments in search of food particles; churning up the materials that fall from the overhead waters, eating embedded food particles and stirring up and releasing particles for others to consume. Any nutrients ingested by these species will, in turn, work their way back into the nutrient cycle of the ocean as these animals die or are consumed.

While much nutrient material is washed far from the land, some is returned to shallow waters by currents called upwellings, which are initiated by the movement of water away from the shore. There is a constant movement of water to and from and around the coastal environment; changes in the Earth's rotation, wind patterns and the temperature fluctuations of surface waters are responsible for moving the surface waters away from the land. To replace these outflowing waters, cool water flows in from the deep offshore regions, stirring up the sediment and bringing a rich and regular source of minerals and organic nutrients, capable of supporting rich fisheries and associated wildlife.

Most of the plant and animal life of the oceans is concentrated on and around the continental shelves. In Indonesia the extensive areas of continental shelf are shallow platforms with some localised undulations. Nowhere else in the ocean are sunlight and nutrients, the basic elements of life, brought together in such profusion as the continental shelves. Like their terrestrial counterparts, marine plants (algae and phytoplankton) manufacture useful foods through the process of photosynthesis. At the outer edge of the continental shelf, the land plunges away, sometimes in an unbroken fall of several kilometres, before gradually spreading out to form a broad, gently sloping area beyond which lies the ocean floor. The continental slope often contains remarkable, deep gorges, called trenches. The submarine landscape around Indonesia is particularly dramatic, enhanced by the countless tiny islands and the intense underwater volcanic activity along the 'ring of fire'. Much of this region still awaits detailed exploration.

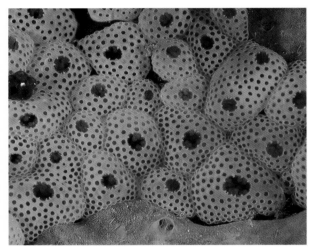

however, is essential to the thousands of living creatures that have evolved to live in the sea, many of which show remarkable adaptations for surviving under what are frequently hostile conditions.

Along coastlines, tides are the most obvious changes in sea-level. The rhythmic rise and fall of the sea and the regular change of offshore currents are familiar to people living on the coast. Tides are generated by the forces of gravity between the Earth and other celestial bodies, chiefly the moon and the sun. The moon, being close to Earth, exerts a great pull and produces two bulges in the seas, one facing the moon and the other on the opposite side of the globe. Because the Earth rotates, many coasts experience two such bulges every 24 hours and so have two high tides daily. In Indonesia, because of its complex mix of islands and straits, tidal flows are more complicated.

The effects of the sun are usually concealed by those of the moon but, about twice a month when the Earth, moon and sun are in a direct line, the combined gravitational forces of the sun and moon are exerted upon Earth, producing exceptionally high 'spring' tides. On two other occasions, the three bodies form a right angle and the influence of the sun partially cancels the effect of the moon, resulting in a weaker pull and lower 'neap' tides.

Most of the motion we see is in the form of waves, lolling quietly along a sheltered seashore or crashing with impatient fury on an exposed

headland. These features are the work of wind driving against the water. The height of a wave depends on three factors: the strength of the wind, how long it blows and the extent of open water across which a wind can blow. The greatest waves are recorded on the oceans, where the wind has an uninterrupted passage for thousands of kilometres. Waves do not move the water any considerable distance, but they do ensure that the upper surface is thoroughly mixed, an important feature in circulating oxygen and nutrients.

The combined effects of the ocean's currents, tides and waves have vital implications for life in the marine setting; for they are responsible for the circulation and transportation of nutrients, as well as for the dispersal of fish larvae and plankton. The stability of the ocean environment has importance for all life within it as well as for animals and plants which live around its fringes. Many species synchronise not only their feeding activities but also their reproductive cycles with the patterns of the tides.

BIOLOGICAL DIVERSITY OF THE OPEN OCEANS

Beyond the shallow continental shelf lies the vastness of the open ocean. This least explored domain is the last frontier on Earth. Here life can be found not only in the upper surface waters but also in the very deepest reaches of the ocean, up to

15 kilometres below the surface, even in the darkest layers of mud and detritus on the floor of the ocean.

Unlike the waters of the shallow coastal zone, those of the open ocean contain relatively low concentrations of nutrients essential for plant growth. Without this plant growth, few animals can survive, and the level of biological diversity is low. Despite its low fertility, the open ocean provides a more stable and less demanding environment than, for example, the seashore. Sudden or severe fluctuations in temperature or salinity and dryness do not occur. Even the most violent of storms rarely has an effect that is noticeable at any great depth. Circulation of oxygen and nutrients at these limits is dependent on the elaborate network of currents.

Inhabitants of the clear, well lit surface waters face a threat to survival that does not confront most coastal-dwelling animals; a total lack of places to hide. Animals of the ocean cannot dive into a rock crevice or conceal themselves in the sandy bottom. There are no coral citadels amongst which to lose predators. Yet the open ocean inhabitants are hardly defenceless: many of the large, drifting animals such as jellyfish are armed with batteries of stinging cells, similar to those of coral polyps. Others rely on different tactics. Flying fish, for example, take to the air, breaking through the waves, 'flying' for up to 15 metres before plunging back into the water in the hope of losing their pursuers. Yet other species find safety by clubbing together to form large shoals that twist and gyrate through the water, confusing and dazzling potential predators. An alternative to finding a hiding place is to rely on camouflage. Many open sea swimmers, such as sharks and whales, have distinct colouring, particularly silvery white undersides and a much darker back. Planktonic creatures such as copepods, combs, jellies and larval fishes are almost transparent and often manage to avoid being detected.

GETTING ABOUT – DRIFTERS AND HITCHHIKERS

Getting around and controlling movement in such a vast open space can be a problem for some species. Most of the smaller species rely on the ocean's currents for dispersal and movement; some have developed specialized features that assist with ocean travel. Among the many elaborate drifting species are the large jellyfish. The tissues of a jellyfish are almost 95 per cent water, which reduces its

tendency either to rise or sink in the water column. Its umbrella-shaped bell is a thin sac filled with a gelatinous substance. In the centre of the bell is a digestive cavity, hanging from which, like a tattered curtain, is the animal's funnel-like mouth. Simple sense organs responding to light or gravity help to orientate the animal in an upright position. Rhythmic contractions of the bell give the jellyfish a slight upward push to keep it from sinking. Trailing beneath the bell are long tentacles, studded with nematocysts or stinging cells, which paralyse small animals they touch. Paralysed prey is then hoisted into the mouth and digested.

Another energy-saving way of getting about involves hitching a lift by attaching onto another, more mobile, species. Barnacles are probably among the world's greatest travellers as they fasten on to driftwood, ship's hulls, large fish, turtles and even the biggest of the whales. Parasitic sea lice, too, are common hitchhikers. At times the concentration of lice becomes so great that they become an irritation to the hosts, who rely on a special relationship with cleaner fish and crustaceans to rid themselves of these annoying companions. Floating clumps of weed also provide anchorage for many species; in this way some mobile species such as crabs, molluscs, tubeworms, shrimps and even fish are transported to other regions. Fish such as the remoras have developed special suction cups, which allow them to cling firmly even to some of the fastest swimming species such as sharks.

All plants and animals living near the surface must somehow avoid sinking into the abyss. In order to photosynthesise, plants must remain within the upper section of the water column – where light penetrates. Many animals, in turn, must remain in this section near the tiny drifting plants that form the first link in the ocean's food chain. Unless these organisms possess special features to keep them afloat, they will sink because their body tissues are heavier than water. Most fish species have a special gas-filled organ called a swim bladder

Below: hundreds of young barracuda school together in fantastic formations in the upper waters. As the fish grow older they tend to adopt more solitary habits.

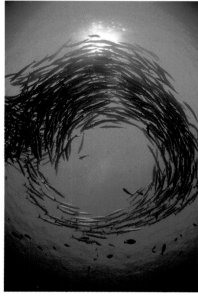

SPECIES OF WATER COLUMN

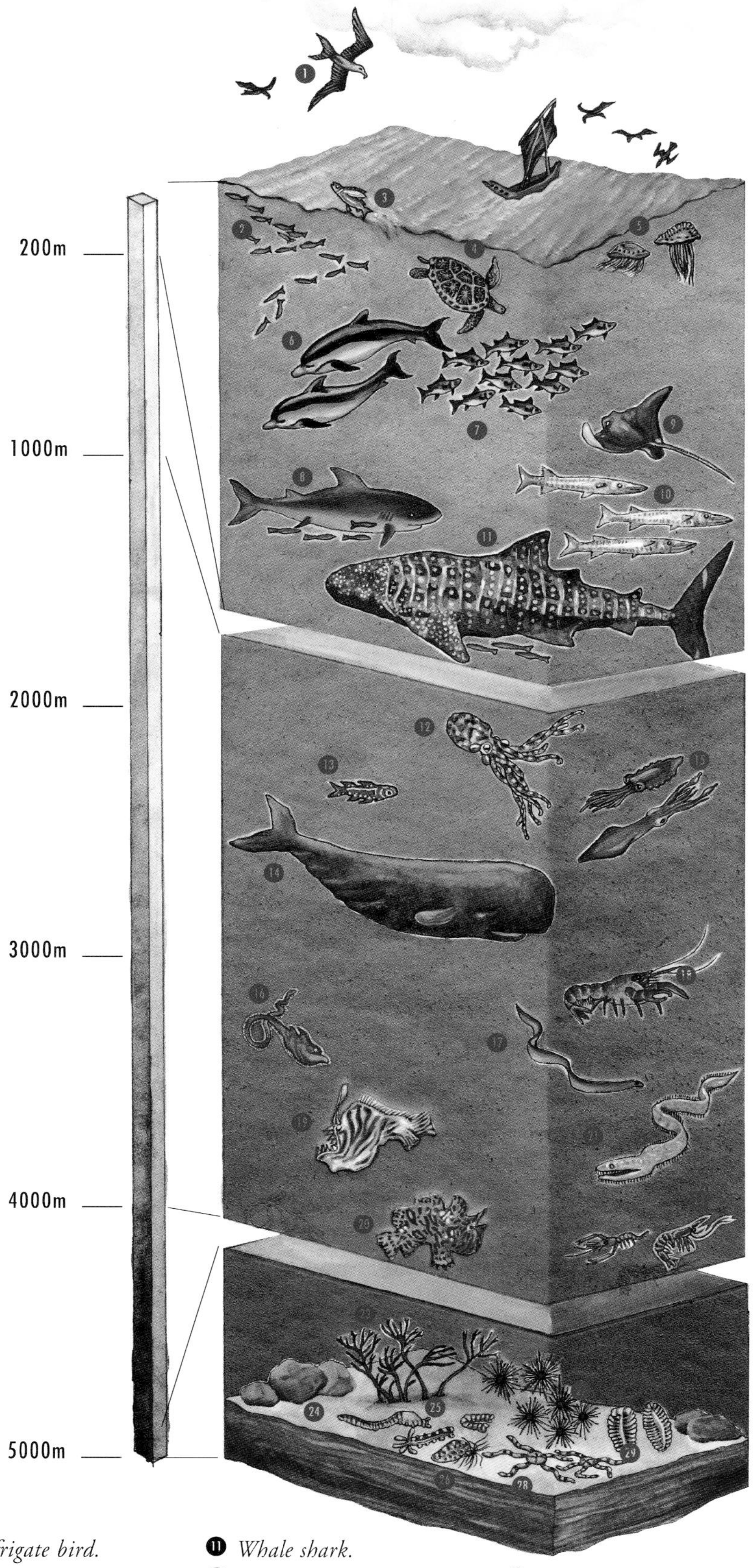

200m

1000m

2000m

3000m

4000m

5000m

❶ Lesser frigate bird.
❷ Mackerel.
❸ Flying fish.
❹ Green turtle.
❺ Jellyfish.
❻ Dolphin.
❼ Tuna.
❽ Shark with remoras.
❾ Manta ray.
❿ Barracuda.

⓫ Whale shark.
⓬ Octopus.
⓭ Lanternfish.
⓮ Sperm whale.
⓯ Squid.
⓰ Chimaera.
⓱ Deep sea eel.
⓲ Blind lobster.
⓳ Shaggy anglerfish.
⓴ Striped anglerfish.

㉑ Gulper eel.
㉒ Deep sea shrimp.
㉓ Featherstar.
㉔ Sea cucumber.
㉕ Sea cucumber.
㉖ Crab.
㉗ Sea urchin.
㉘ Brittlestar.
㉙ Sea pen.

inside their bodies, but some species, such as tuna and swordfish have to swim continuously to maintain bouyancy. The amount of gas in a swim bladder can be adjusted to compensate for different depths and pressures, enabling the fish to remain motionless in the water at a preferred depth. Gas chambers are also used by a range of specially adapted floating organisms such as nautilus and the Portuguese man-of-war.

THE OCEAN DEPTHS
Descending to the depths of the ocean is like entering another world; a twilight zone that finally gives way to one of total darkness. No plants survive at such depths. Even in the clearest water, there is insufficient light for photosynthesis at depths greater than 130 metres. The sun's warming rays too, are quickly absorbed by surface waters, leaving a cold, inhospitable world. All deep-sea animals are cold-blooded and have body temperatures close to the low temperature of the water. As a result, most probably grow more slowly and reproduce later and less frequently than warm water species. Animals living in these seemingly desolate and hostile conditions have to find food and mates in complete darkness. At such depths, pressure is also a problem: at about 1000 metres the pressure is almost 100 times greater than at the surface. This apparently has no effect on the animals provided that there are no air or gas chambers in their bodies. The tissues of organisms living at such depths are full of fluids which are at the same pressure as the surrounding water. The pressure imposed on bodily organs is therefore matched by the internal pressure of body fluids, so maintaining a pressure balance and preventing the animals from exploding or deflating.

Unwelcoming as these conditions might appear, what they do have to offer is a stable environment. As a result, during the course of evolution, Nature's wonders have even reached into these blackest and coldest of conditions, and mechanisms for survival have been engineered. The adaptations that these creatures have developed to cope with such conditions are among the most bizarre of any in the animal kingdom, particularly as to the way in which they obtain food. Food is scarce at these depths and survival here is dependent on dead organisms and waste products drifting down from the surface waters in what has been described as 'faecal rain'. While the greater part of these materials is consumed as it drifts slowly downwards, enough reaches the sea-bed to provide essential nutrients for the small communities of burrowing or sedentary animals, the basis of the food chain for this ecosystem. They make up a surprisingly active biological community on the sea floor. Many fish of the ocean depths are little more that tooth-filled mouths attached to expandable stomachs. Gulpers, for example, have trapdoor jaws

Left: whale shark.

Cuttlefish.

Sea pen.

Below: long legged Oliva shrimp.

and elastic, sac-like stomachs that can expand to several times their normal size to accommodate prey larger than themselves. Gulpers are one of a wide range of species that use light to attract prey to within striking distance. Although the use of light seems inappropriate for animals living in total darkness, many species have developed sophisticated luminous organs that enable them to recognize like species, as well as to attract prey and deter predators. Some species possess their own light-producing cells, while others, such as luminous fish, rely on the presence of luminescent bacteria. As they swim, the aptly named anglerfish and lanternfish produce flashes of light. In the case of the anglerfish, the light source is positioned at the end of a long filament that is dangled over or in front of the mouth. As other species move closer to investigate the source of light – possibly a luminescent shrimp or worm – the fish strikes, snapping its jaws shut, impaling the prey with its vicious curved teeth.

Not all of the animals of these crypt-like conditions rely on such elaborate feeding mechanisms. Many of the smaller fish, as well as shrimps and prawns, undergo daily vertical migrations to the the surface. When they hatch, the larvae remain in the surface waters for some time, feeding off the rich plankton before descending to their rightful homes in the gloomy depths.

Above: spiny catfish.

Below: blue-eyed cardinal-fish.

Orange-lined tail cardinal-fish.

WHERE LAND AND SEA MEET

The range of marine ecosystems in Indonesia is enormously varied. Especially varied are the coastal ecosystems, as might be expected from an archipelago. From the estuaries where fresh and salt water meet, to coasts with rocky and sandy habitats, rich mudflats and mangrove forests, to coral reefs teeming with life, a vast range of habitats supports an astounding collection of species. Few ecosystems illustrate the range of challenges faced by, and opportunities provided to, different species as clearly as those existing at the interface between the land and the sea. Each specific habitat supports quite different animals and plants, which interact to form complex communities. The many life-supporting systems represented in marine ecosystems are easily disturbed and degraded by human interference; careful management of these resources is necessary.

GATEWAY TO THE SEA

The area where water from the mountains, forests and valley plains finally enters the ocean realm is one of the greatest mixing bowls on Earth. Nutrients and sediment swirl about in the strong currents and swells, as fresh water from the turbulent rivers passes over the heavier salt water before the two finally mix. Sediment loads collected from the uplands and valleys are eventually shed as the current slows down against the mass of the ocean water. The great river systems of Irian Jaya, Java, Sumatra and Kalimantan drain vast hinterlands. The Kampar River in Central Sumatra, with its headwaters in the mountains near the west coast, winds its way across country finally delivering its load through a wide estuary. The Kayan and Mentarang rivers in northeast Kalimantan end in broad fan-shaped deltas. Other rivers lack deltas or estuaries, and meet the sea more abruptly.

The daily cycle of the tides, the oscillating levels of salinity, fluctuating temperatures, and the frequently cloudy, murky waters character-

istic of estuaries and tidal flats, make these difficult places in which to live. Clearly any organism that lives in such a place must be able to withstand a wide range of physical and chemical conditions. But for those species which can, the rewards are considerable, as the amount of nutrients entering this system each day is far greater than those contained in either pure fresh or salt water.

Living conditions in the brackish waters of estuaries can be hazardous. It is very important that plants and animals living in water maintain a specific, balanced concentration of dissolved salts within their body tissues. For if an organism is placed in water with a lower salt concentration

than is contained in its body fluids, water may enter its body and cause it to swell. Conversely, if the external salt level is greater than that within the body, water flows out of its tissues and it may shrivel. Many aquatic species have limited tolerances for such salinity changes, and perish if they are exceeded.

Changes in salinity levels, as well as in other features, are usually fairly gradual along the course of an estuary. But sharp breaks can be created at times of heavy tidal flow, when heavier salt water passes upstream beneath the downstream flow of fresh water. This creates the phenomenon known as a 'salt wedge'. In association with this gradation of conditions, different species of plants and animals have adapted to these zones, where conditions vary with the tide, and have developed particular thresholds of tolerance. At the upper limit of the estuary, freshwater fish dominate the water column, giving way downstream to different species, such as catfish, halfbeaks, larval shrimps and oysters; the gradual change signifying a steadily increasing level of salt water. In stretches where the waters still mix, schools of mullet join sea perch to forage for algae and other smaller fish, while at the edge of the estuary, as the waters fan out through the upper sea levels, typical coastal species occur, such as pufferfish and cardinalfish.

Working a seine net, Tangkoko Bay, North Sulawesi.

Above: sea urchin on a ship-wreck off Flores.

Right: minute crab larvae.

The brightly coloured reef crab.

The hard rocks of Peucang Island, Ujung Kulon are resistant to the erosive forces of the sea.

Following page: lontar palms and giant milkweed on the sand dunes of Madura Island.

ROCKY SHORES

A wide range of coastal habitats can be found throughout the archipelago. Rocky shores are common; their hard, exposed surfaces are frequently subjected to the strong forces of the sea which include high winds and crashing waves. Erosion of the rock face is a constant feature of these shorelines. Sometimes eroded material may accumulate at the base of the rock face as shingle beach but, more frequently, the offshore currents are so strong that all eroded material is immediately washed out to sea. Rocky shores vary considerably in their appearance and vegetation cover. Some consist of tall, vertical cliffs which offer few opportunities for colonizing plants and animals. but which may provide important nesting sites for large colonies of ocean-faring birds. Others may form a tiered structure, offering sheltered platforms, crevices and cliffs of various sizes.

What at first appearance might seem to be an inhospitable, harsh place to live is, in fact, one of the most interesting and biologically diverse sections of the marine and coastal environment. Animals and plants living in such exposed environments need to resist being swept away from their home by the pull of the waves. In addition they must face the problem of frequent changes in temperature and light intensity, as well as avoiding dessication and being continuously submerged. An animal in moderately warm water at high tide may be left stranded at low tide in a small rock pool where the temperature can soar under the influence of the sun. Species have responded to this challenge by using many clever adaptations. Some, like the seaweeds, have developed tough, root-like holdfasts which become encrusted on the substrate. Instead of resisting the waves, their flexible stems and leaves wave backwards and forwards in the turbulent waters; special bouyant air bladders keep the fronds near the surface where they can photo-synthesise, but offer little resistance to the currents. Barnacles adopt a different strategy, and remain securely fixed on a position. To resist the pull of the waves they secrete a powerful cement to attach their six-sided shells permanently to hard surfaces. Others, like the starfish and limpet, remain mobile but can cling firmly to surfaces through the use of hydraulically operated tube-feet which act as suction cups. Life on the shoreline is therefore extremely varied, with no two shores being the same in terms of structure or species abundance and distribution.

The variety of means by which the different animals and plants survive on the shoreline is best viewed at low tide. Different layers of life become apparent: the backshore is typified by the presence of colourful lichens, blue-green algae and snails and primitive-shaped arthropods which feed on these species. Lower down, on the foreshore, or intertidal zone, desiccated-looking barnacles form dense clusters between the low and high tide-marks, often resembling a carpet of tiny pyramids. Plants and animals in this zone need periodic immersion in seawater to breathe, feed and replenish moisture, but can withstand hours of exposure to air and sun. Others, however, can only tolerate a certain amount of exposure to waves and air. At low tide, barnacles withdraw their long, feathered feeding tentacles and firmly close their shells, sealing in enough water to survive. Species such as starfish, sea urchins, crabs and molluscs search for refuge among the damp fronds of seaweed or in rock pools. Most life is concentrated in the lower part of the foreshore, where animals and plants only risk being exposed at the lowest of tides. Abundant seaweeds offer shelter and protection to a wide range of crus-taceans, molluscs and small fish. Representatives of many offshore fish species also visit this nearshore area to feed or breed.

Although distinct zones are apparent at low tide, there is constant movement between them when the tide is fully in: snails, large and small, scale the cliff face to graze o algae; crabs stalk fish; small crustaceans go about their daily routines, and larger fish come inshore to feed or lay their eggs on the seaweeds.

PROFILE OF A ROCKY SHORE

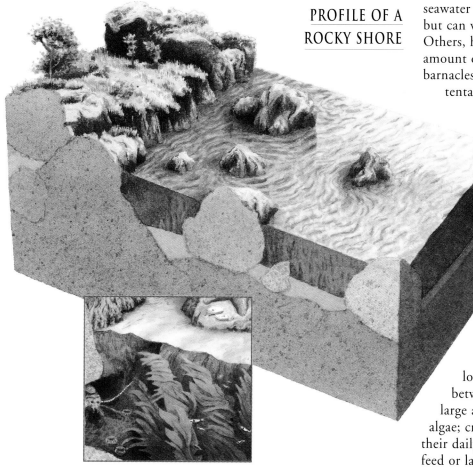

SANDY BEACHES

Among Indonesia's major attractions are its splendid beaches – dazzling white sands fringed with turquoise water; or black volcanic sands that soak up the sun's energy. Less obvious than the beaches themselves, but no less attractive, is the rich assemblage of wildlife they contain.

The structured organization of life on rocky shorelines is not replicated on a sandy beach. Few plants grow on such beaches, largely because the surface is constantly shifting, offering no firm base for roots. Although beaches may at first appear to be largely devoid of wildlife, this is not the case. Apart from a sometimes spectacular array of shore-birds which feed and roost on sandy beaches, the most obvious animals are ghost crabs, often intent on digging a new burrow or scurrying around the surface scavenging for morsels. Most of the life in this ecosystem, however, takes place below the surface, within the sand.

With few exceptions, burrowing is the common way of life on intertidal beaches. Beach-dwelling animals rarely expose themselves; even when the sand is covered with water, only part of their body will protrude above the surface, usually to feed or breathe, the remainder being firmly anchored in the burrow. Most sand-dwelling animals are long and thin, well-adapted to wriggling easily between the sand grains. Many, like the polychaete worms, are soft-bodied; while others such as the molluscs have tough outer shells for protection.

Being buried in the sand offers some security for these species, but it also leads to difficulties when it comes to feeding or finding a mate. Even breathing in the tiny spaces between the sand grains is a problem which species have had to overcome. Many worms construct deep U-shaped tubes, in which they live, both ends being firmly plugged with sand at low tide. As the waters return, hundreds of cilia (feather-like structures), on the side of the worm begin to beat in a rhythmic manner. This serves to draw water down into the tube, allowing the worm to breathe and feed off the tiny plankton it filters from the water. The water then passes out through the other end of the burrow, taking with it any body wastes. Using a different technique, molluscs have tube-like siphons that draw water deep into the sand, extracting oxygen and trapping tiny organisms on the sticky mucus of their gill filaments. Burrowing animals play an important role in aerating and depositing nutrients in the sediment, making it possible for other species to live there.

The turning of the tides is a frenzied period on the beach; as the tide recedes, sand-dwelling species get ready to rest after feeding. Shorebirds, attracted by the potentially rich pickings – several thousand worms can find shelter within one square metre of sand – flock to the water-line and probe the sands for a juicy meal. Different species of wading birds have different feeding techniques, specially adapted to a particular niche, such as deep water, or for a preferred prey item. Curlews, for example, have long, downward curving beaks that probe deeply into the sand for large polychaete worms. Sanderlings and sandpipers, in contrast, are much smaller birds with short, pointed beaks designed for stabbing tiny, fast-moving prey such as small shrimps and other crustaceans. In addition to supporting a resident population of shorebirds, the beaches and shorelines of Indonesia are of great importance as resting and feeding grounds for the many species which migrate from the north to southern temperate regions each year. Without coastal resources to sustain them on their way, many would certainly perish.

But it is not only the birds which take advantage of the rich pickings on offer on the sandy beach. The economic value, and the impor-tance of the hidden life of sandy beaches to other ecosystems, are often not fully appreciated. In Indonesia, the collection of shellfish, crabs and other fish on the foreshore is a vital source of food and income for many coastal communities. Each day, thousands of people across the archipelago wade in the shallow waters, casting and retrieving small filament nets which trap small fish and a wide range of crustaceans; while others probe the soft sediment at the water's margins, digging for clams and other molluscs.

Left: cattle egret foraging for small fish and crustaceans.

A tern scanning the waters for fish.

A heron alighting on a deserted beach. It is expert at catching fish: spearing them with its long, pointed beak.

Above: the lesser frigate bird is an oceanic species; it is able to snatch fish from the surface of the waters without landing.

PROFILE OF A SANDY SHORE

Right: the mudskipper is one of the few species of fish capable of surviving for periods out of water. It 'walks' over the mud using its pectoral fins as crutches. Feeding and courtship occur out of the water.

At low tide crabs emerge from their burrows to forage for food. The brightly coloured front claws are often used to attract mates.

Above: tapering breathing roots of a Sonneratia mangrove tree. A single Bakau seedling (Rhizophora sp.) has established itself.

Facing page: the tangled mass of aerial roots of this established mangrove forest (Rhizophora sp.) at Baluran, East Java, serves to trap sediment and reduces the impact of the waves on the shoreline. The raised bumps on the roots are specialized breathing pores.

MANGROVES

At low tide, a mangrove forest is not a particularly inviting place with its deep mud, dense network of protruding roots and its dark decaying atmosphere. Yet this junction and mixing site of three major ecosystems – land, salt water from the ocean and, often, fresh water from the rivers – plays a significant role in maintaining the well-being of the coastal and wider marine environment. A variety of unique adaptations are displayed by species living within this ecosystem.

Characteristic of muddy estuarine shores of sheltered coastlines in the tropics and subtropics, the mangroves' tangled, arched and intertwined roots combine with the soft sediment to guarantee that any passage will be a difficult one. The dark, closed canopy adds further to the almost sinister appearance of this environment. Despite first impressions, however, these habitats are teeming with life. Half concealed in their burrows, small crabs lie in ambush for a passing snack; others scurry busily about the surface of the mud and the mass of tangled tree roots, scavenging dead fish and other flotsam left behind by the ebbing tide. Snails graze contentedly on the green films of algae covering the mud and exposed mangrove roots. Mudskippers jump and slither between the small pools of water in the pock-marked sediment, while shoals of tiny fish and prawns drift back and forward in isolated pools of warm water. Wading birds of all shapes and sizes strut along the shoreline, probing the soft mud in search of a tasty morsel. At the turn of the tide the whole ecosystem undergoes an almost magical transformation. The waders retreat to the crowns of the mangroves to rest and preen, the crabs withdraw to their burrows, sealing themselves in firmly against the incoming tide, and a new set of animals – shellfish, worms and other invertebrates – emerge from the mud to feed under cover and protection of the steadily rising waters.

Mangrove ecosystems are highly productive in terms of energy storage and transfer. Dead and half-eaten leaves that fall into the tidal waters, together with the waste products of animals and roosting birds, are the basis of a food web which supports a rich and varied ecosystem. Bacteria and fungi – as well as crabs, worms, snails and other species – rapidly digest and absorb the nutrients from these materials. In turn, these organisms die or are consumed by larger predators, including fish. At high-tide the tangled roots of mangroves form a sheltered environment and an important feeding zone which provides a nursery for the young of many marine species, including a large proportion of commercially important species that are caught in the open oceans.

Mangroves grow on inhospitable substrates which lack oxygen and have a high sulphur content. Little oxygen penetrates the salt-laden mud; even one centimetre beneath the surface the only living organisms in the black, foul-smelling sediment (containing iron sulphide) are anaerobic bacteria. Most plants could not survive under such conditions but some mangroves, such as those of the genera *Avicennia* and *Sonneratia*, have overcome this problem by having special 'breathing' roots, called pneumatophores, which grow upwards through the mud – in contrast with other plants. These pointed roots are covered with breathing pores which allow the plants to absorb additional oxygen from the air, which is especially important in helping to eliminate salt from the water which the roots absorb. Other species have similar structures on their aerial roots.

Most mangroves have shallow rooting systems on account of the nutrient-deficient and toxic substrate. Living in a zone where plants are exposed to regular tides and currents, as well as violent storms, structural support is obviously a vital factor for survival. To compensate for their shallow roots, mangroves of the genus *Rhizophora* have developed extensive stilt-like roots which provide strength at the base of the tree.

Living on the edge of the waves, another obstacle mangroves have had to overcome is that of seed dispersal. To help ensure that most seeds are not washed out to sea, they remain attached to the parent tree until mature. At this stage the propagules, as they are known, develop a long tap root.

tannins for cloth and leather preservation (especially for leather sails); and a range of food (fruit, sugar, tea substitutes, cooking oils), medicines and fuel. The rich fisheries resources, particularly prawns, are heavily exploited: the stilt-like roots of many mangroves offer suitable anchorage sites for shellfish, including mussels and oysters. Prawn fisheries – an important source of income and subsistence for many people – in particular depend upon these calm, sheltered, nutrient-rich waters for breeding and growth of young larvae.

Much of the Java coast is dotted with *tambak*; brackish water ponds in which prawns, shrimps and milkfish are cultivated. A traditional practice for many centuries, with the increased demand for prawns worldwide, it has in recent years been expanded and intensified, resulting in mangrove destruction on a large scale. Poor management and limited understanding of the ecosystem have meant that these ventures have not always been successful and much land has been degraded in the process. Removal of mangrove forests for fuelwood or woodchips, and drainage and reclamation of mangroves for building land, have also had a marked impact on the Indonesian coastline. Coastal erosion is especially noticeable following removal of mangroves, as is a decline in larger fish catches. Today, in some places, mangroves are being replanted in an effort to repair some of the damage. However, it is extremely expensive, time consuming and difficult to restore or match the valuable role which these natural ecosystems provide.

Facing page: on Madura Island mangrove seedlings have been planted as an anti-erosion measure.

Left: the archerfish ejects a jet of water to knock an insect into the water where it can be quickly captured.

Above: a fiddler crab, which takes its name from the male's enlarged pincer, which is waved to and fro to attract a mate.

When the propagule finally falls off the tree the spiked end helps it to stick upright in the mud. Poised in this way, the seedling can produce leafy foliage above the mud and at the same time develop a network of supporting roots lower down; these provide additional strength at the base.

The largest expanses of mangroves in Indonesia are found in Irian Jaya (17,500 square kilometres), Kalimantan (11,500 square kilometres) and Sumatra (10,010 square kilometres); together they account for more than 90 per cent of the country's total mangrove coverage. The immense deltas of the Kayan, Mentarang and Mahakam rivers in eastern Kalimantan, like much of the southern coast of Irian Jaya, contain vast unbroken stretches of mangroves.

One of the most important functions mangroves serve is the protection they offer to the coast from storms, by acting as natural wind- and wave-breaks and by stabilising shifting shorelines; when they disappear their protective role is eliminated and the land is exposed to the forces of the sea. Mangroves also trap silt and filter pollution from the water column – two hazards which can seriously affect seagrass beds and coral reefs.

Among the many products which people extract from mangroves are: wooden poles and planks for construction purposes; tree trunks for charcoal and fuelwood, and as a source of paper; leaves for animal fodder and compost; synthetic dyes and

PROFILE OF A MANGROVE

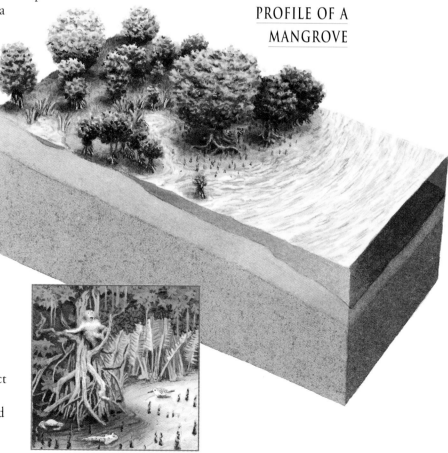

Above: seagrass meadows, near Manado.

Below: although green turtles spend most of their life at sea, females must return to land to lay eggs – often to the beach where they hatched.

The dugong is one of Indonesia's rarest and most endangered species.

Facing page: a giant clam.

Following page: gliding through the water, a pair of green turtles mate. Remora fish hitch a lift.

SEAGRASS

A little further out to sea, often in the coral flats, protected by fringing coral reefs, in the warm sparkling shallow waters the waving meadows of seagrass are the antithesis to the dank, closed ranks of the mangrove forest. Completely different in structure to the mangroves, seagrasses serve a similar role in trapping fine sediment from the water column, their roots acting much like those of the giant forest trees to bind the fine particles together on the seabed. Without such plants, the constant scouring action of the currents and waves would wash these particles far out to sea. Seagrass beds provide an important feeding ground for some of the rarer animals in the region, particularly dugong and marine turtles. They also offer refuge to a wide range of fish species, quite different from those which seek the sanctuary of the tangled mangrove roots. Seagrass meadows are particularly vulnerable to dredging, pollution and deposition of industrial waste in the coastal zone.

Seagrass beds are less well defined in distribution than mangroves; they are scattered in the shallow waters off Sulawesi, Nusa Tenggara, the myriad of islands that comprise Maluku and in sheltered zones off the coasts of Irian Jaya.

FOCUS ON THREATENED SPECIES

Perhaps the most endangered group of animals in the world's oceans today are the marine turtles, six of the seven living species having already been severely depleted. The unusual life-style of these archaic species – a life in the ocean, with females returning to land to lay their eggs – exposes these animals to a wide range of human-related hazards, including over-exploitation for their eggs, meat and valuable shells, accidental capture in fishing nets, pollution, and coastal development. Five species of marine turtle frequent the seas round Indonesia, the largest being the leatherback turtle (*Dermochelys coriacea*) which may weigh up to 850 kilograms. This endangered species feeds primarily on jellyfish, squid, crustaceans and molluscs and is known to undertake lengthy migrations to and from nesting beaches. Three of the remaining species of turtle are poorly represented in Indonesian waters: hawksbill turtles (*Eretomochelys imbricata*) occur throughout the archipelago, while the olive ridley turtle (*Lepidochelys olivacea*) occurs only in the western islands and the loggerhead turtle (*Caretta caretta*) is restricted to the north. The only species which is not considered endangered in Indonesia – one of the few places in the world with viable populations – is the green turtle (*Chelonia mydas*).

One of the most unusual members of Indonesia's marine fauna is the lethargic dugong, a large herbivorous mammal that superficially resembles a seal. Dugongs are long-lived animals, up to 50 years, but have a very low rate of reproduction. Females do not give birth until they are between the ages of nine and fifteen years and only produce further offspring at intervals of three to seven years. Living in small family groups, these specialized animals occupy a diminishing habitat. Dugongs feed primarily on seagrass beds, sculling their way through the warm waters, grazing on leaves and foraging beneath the sediment for carbohydrate-rich rhizomes. Dugongs have very inefficient digestive systems; each animal must consume at least five per cent of its body weight (an adult may weigh up to 900 kilograms) each day. They are not common animals; in Indonesia they are found mainly in the shallow waters of Maluku and parts of Sulawesi. Although dugongs have no natural predators their population may be declining. Their slow movements make them easy prey to hunters; despite legal protection, dugongs are hunted for their meat, body oils and tusks. In addition, many are caught in fishing nets and either drown or are killed by fishermen. Increasing pollution and boat traffic in the shallow coastal regions is also thought to affect the distribution of this sluggish species. Loss of habitat through increased sedimentation – often the result of forest clearance from upland areas – further threatens these unique animals.

One of the monsters of the shallows is the giant clam (*Tridacna gigas*). However, it is a monster in size only: its reputation for trapping divers is certainly unfounded. The impressive fluted, scalloped shell of the clam may grow to more than one metre in diameter and weigh almost 50 kilograms; the clam itself may weigh no more than three kilograms. Different colour shells are found – blue, green, purple or brown – the result of pigments from the symbiotic algae which live around the huge, convoluted edge of the mouth. Giant clams feed by passing vast quantities of water through their gills, filtering out plankton. They are long-lived animals – some living up to 100 years of age. Once settled on the coral or sea-bed, the clam never moves, apart from opening and closing its shell when feeding. Giant clams are restricted to certain areas of the Indo-Pacific region. In many places their populations are now greatly reduced as a result of over-exploitation for their decorative shells and meat.

IMPORTANCE OF THE COASTAL ZONE

The coastal waters of Indonesia are a feeding haven to large groups of marine mammals, reptiles, fish and, of course, hundreds of different species of bird, resident and migratory. Care and management of these areas are vitally important to the well-being of these species, as well as for the immediate and long-term benefit of people. Increasing pollution, both from domestic and industrial sources, is a major concern in Indonesia. Waterways and lagoons are still widely treated as disposal grounds for liquid and solid waste material. Unnatural enrichment of shallow waters, such as that caused by the introduction of organic material, promotes the growth of high densities of tiny algae. The resulting 'algal blooms' are not only unsightly, but also reduce the level of free oxygen in the water, depriving fish and plant life of this essential resource. Many fish may therefore die as a result. Another problem with the build up of algae is that many species contain minute levels of harmful toxins. Filter feeding fish and molluscs eating large quantites of these algae progessively accumulate the toxins in their own tissues. Humans eating such fish risk paralysis, or even death, from such ciguatera poisoning.

The coastal zone provides many important services, especially for people living in coastal settlements, and not only for the rich supplies of fish and other species they provide. The shallow coastal regions with offshore reefs and inshore mangrove forests protect the coastline from the adverse effects of high tides and storms, eliminating the need for expensive artificial breakwaters. Removal, or destruction, of the reef ecosystems, such as through dynamite fishing and extraction of corals for building material, takes these services away, resulting in flooding and storm damage. Increasingly the coastal zone is being developed as a source of leisure and recreation. If controlled, ecotourism, diving and boating activities can provide an important economic benefit to local communities and regional authorities. It is becoming more widely appreciated that the preservation of coastal resources intact has a great deal of merit – far more than the short-term gains extracted from ill-considered activities.

Facing page: as dawn breaks a group of fishermen come together, Sunda Strait.

Above: the morning collection of milkfish fry, Madura Island; they will be transferred to tambak ponds and, once grown, gathered for sale.

Below: as the sun sets over Labuan Bajo Bay, small fishing boats anchor for the evening.

LIFE AT THE EDGE

Above: a large table coral captures maximum sunlight, while shading out some of the smaller branching corals beneath.

Facing page: octocoral polyps with their eight tentacles.

A cluster of soft coral polyps, their feeding tentacles withdrawn during the day.

Teeming with life, this densely packed coral garden off Manado, North Sulawesi, is mostly comprised of staghorn and cabbage coral.

THE LIVING REEF

A visitor's first experience of a coral reef in Indonesia is an unforgettable event. No secondhand acquaintance can prepare one for the breathtaking beauty which unfolds within the turquoise waters surrounding the coral reefs. Extensive coral gardens beckon the diver to take a closer look. A dazzling selection of shimmering colours assaults the eyes, an infinity of shapes and sizes crowds the senses. There is colour and movement everywhere: curious fish rise from the coral wall, darting to and fro, and glittering shoals of small fish approach one another on a collision course, only to dart off in another direction at the final moment before impact. Everywhere, thousands of species await discovery and enjoyment.

Coral reefs are the work of living organisms which build up in a painstakingly slow fashion over many centuries. The most important building block of every coral reef is a tiny form known as a polyp. It seems unbelievable that such small organisms – they range in size from one to fifty millimetres in diameter – could be responsible for such elaborate constructions. Corals are among the greatest architects in the animal kingdom. In some ways a coral reef resembles a large building site – frenzied motion taking place everywhere you look, the reef growing in some places while being eroded at others; day and night different organisms are at work somewhere along the reef. Corals grow slowly – a reef 500 metres deep may take from 1000 to 8000 years to form, with new coral growing on the foundation of older, dead coral. One of the fastest growing corals is staghorn, a branching type of coral. Under favourable conditions, such as those at the outer edge of a reef where constant wave action provides abundant nutrients and dissolved oxygen, it may grow up to 20 centimetres a year. The growth rate of other species, however, may be as little as five millimetres a year.

There are two basic types of coral – hard and soft. Polyps of hard corals are made up of two sections: an inner, soft, jelly-like mass that is the living polyp, surrounded by a tough limestone skeleton which is secreted by the outer cells of the polyp to form a hard, often intricately patterned case. Soft corals have a similar body plan, but lack the outer limestone skeleton. Both types form colonies. The living tissues of a coral formation are therefore found only on the outer surface. Below the surface, more and more lime is deposited and in this way the entire structure gradually grows, both upwards and sideways.

Finding space on which to grow is sometimes a problem on a reef. To colonize new sites, corals reproduce, producing eggs and sperm. Eggs may either be held within the body cavity and fertilized by sperm borne in on the water current, or both eggs and sperm may be released to the water column by different polyps, with fertilization taking place externally. Fertilized eggs develop into tiny, pear-shaped animals which are propelled by minute hair-like cilia. Able to survive for several weeks, these microscopic larvae are carried great distances by the ocean currents. When they finally settle, larvae seek to become attached to solid surfaces – sometimes the larvaes' own ancestors – and if conditions are favourable, once anchored, the outer skin begins to form a calcium deposit and the head of the tiny polyp develops a set of tentacles with which it feeds.

In most corals, as the polyps grow, they divide in two to form a parent and daughter polyp. The older polyp is eventually cut off from its offspring by the formation of a limestone partition between the two, though a connection of living tissue remains. In turn, each polyp will divide again and again, constantly expanding and adding to the growing reef structure, forming colonies of thousands, even millions, of little animals. The colony as a whole therefore consists of a thin living skin on top of multiple layers of empty limestone chambers.

Within the living tissues of all reef-building corals are millions of tiny, single-celled plants (dinoflagellates) called *zooxanthallae*, without which the corals cannot live. Safely protected within the tissues of the polyp these yellow-brown organisms use the sun's energy to convert carbon dioxide and water into carbohydrates (a source of usable foods) and oxygen. The relationship is mutually beneficial: while the *zooxanthallae* gain from having a safe home, and a supply of carbon dioxide and waste from the animal, the polyp benefits not only from the regular supply of oxygen in its tissues for respiration but also from a transfer of some of the stored carbohydrates produced by the plants.

Closely related to the familiar sea anemone, each coral polyp has a mouth, surrounded by a ring of tentacles, which leads to a hollow, cup-shaped body. Each of the tentacles is armed with a battery of microscopic stinging darts called nematocysts. These are used to defend the animal from potential predators and also to capture prey. Polyps feed on tiny plankton, as well as small shrimps, larvae and worms. The tentacles can move by contracting; and, on making contact with its prey, poison from the nematocysts is injected into the animal which either paralyses or kills it.

(1) Dolphin.
(2) Barracuda.
(3) Spotted eagle ray.
(4) Plate coral.
(5) Porcupinefish.
(6) Cave coral.
(7) Barrel sponge.
(8) Banded pygmy angelfish.
(9) Razorfish.
(10) Blue triggerfish.
(11) Whip coral.
(12) Brain coral.
(13) Lionfish.
(14) Bubble coral.
(15) Candy-striped cleaner shrimp.
(16) Cup coral.
(17) Two-coloured dottyback.
(18) Blue-spotted stingray.
(19) Reef crab.
(20) Green turtle.
(21) Shark.
(22) Moray eel.
(23) Fan-shaped gorgonian coral.
(24) Butterflyfish.
(25) Emperor angelfish.
(26) Giant clam.
(27) Anemonefish.
(28) Sea anemone.

A small creature unlucky enough to brush against a tentacle is quickly paralysed and passed through the mouth into the polyp's digestive tract. Some corals have short tentacles lined with cilia that help bring food to the mouth. Beating rhythmically, these cilia set up water currents strong enough to waft small prey inward along the tentacles. When the polyp is not feeding, the cilia beat in the reverse direction sweeping away silt and other debris.

CONDITIONS FOR GROWTH

Corals are demanding creatures that can only grow under very specific conditions. Essential for all species is shallow, clear water which allows sunlight to penetrate to where corals live, for the benefit of their associated *zooxanthallae*. Corals are therefore unable to grow in deep water or shaded areas. Sea water temperatures need to lie within the range 16-36°C, but most active reef growth takes place between 23-25°C. Corals are also very intolerant of fresh water and silt. They cannot survive where rivers empty into the sea, as the waters are turbulent and cloudy, and the sediment load interferes with the animal's feeding and breathing systems. Such stringent living conditions mean that most corals can only grow in clear tropical waters. Apart from the Caribbean, the Atlantic Ocean holds no corals, largely because of the depth of its seas. Optimal conditions for growth exist throughout the Indian Ocean and the Indo-Pacific region. The greatest concentrations of corals occur within a wide arc that reaches from northern Australia north through Sumatra to include Borneo and The Philippines and east to include New Guinea, ending again in Australia around the Great Barrier Reef. As many as 3000 species of sea creature have been recorded from a single reef in this region.

When corals build reefs they do not follow a standard blueprint. Instead, these structures develop in a wide range of shapes and sizes, largely dependent on the terrain of the region. Three main types of reef are recognized: fringing reefs, barrier reefs and atolls. Fringing reefs develop around rocky shorelines and islands and are the first stage in the development of many reefs. Barrier reefs usually lie parallel to the shoreline and are separated from the coast by a shallow lagoon. On the seaward side, however, the terrain drops steeply to depths of thousands of metres. One of the most common forms of reef in the Indo-Pacific region is the atoll; they are ring-shaped reefs mostly found in mid-ocean. The lagoons enclosed within the rings are generally shallow, but the water around the outside of the atoll may be several kilometres deep. It was Charles Darwin who first suggested how atolls formed around sunken volcanic islands. As the island began to sink into the sea, existing fringing reefs kept pace with the rate of depression and managed to remain near the surface. As the island continued to sink, sedimentation built up the sea-bed around the reefs, providing additional support to the structure.

Below: a group of large barrel sponges, decorated with multi-coloured featherstars, Manado.

Facing page: a green hawkfish hovers alongside a deep red gorgonian fan coral.

The maze-like, convoluted patterns on this ridge coral are produced by asexual subdivision of the coral polyps, without the formation of dividing walls.

No two reefs are the same. The structure and species composition varies considerably between reefs – even those within the same region. Corals themselves come in all shapes, sizes and colours. The domed, convoluted patterns of brain corals such as *Leptoria phrygia* contrast with the colourful, branching fan corals and the long tendrils of the whip corals. Others, such as *Turbinaria mesenterina*, are able to alter their shapes to suit local conditions. In shallow water where the sunlight is intense that coral takes on a convoluted shape, while in deep water conditions it develops broad, plate-like formations which take advantage of the reduced light.

As the reef is a living ecosystem it needs nutrients and minerals to keep it going. Nutrients are generally scarce in the waters that bathe a reef, but copious quantities are locked away in the living tissues of the reef and the numerous forms of life it supports. These are passed on from one species to another through the complex food web of the reef, as crustaceans consume smaller prey such as worms, as small fish eat the shrimps and as larger fish in turn feed off smaller fish. When the largest of predators die, their flesh will be eaten by a range of other species, particularly micro-organisms. In this way none of the valuable nutrients are wasted. Coral reefs operate a tight and efficient system of nutrient recycling.

BIOLOGICAL DIVERSITY OF REEFS

The most striking aspect of any coral reef is the abundance of life compared with that of the surrounding sea. Like other major ecosystems, such as tropical rain forests or vast savannas, the coral reef is made up of a number of distinct communities, each containing a complex assemblage of plants and animals which may have evolved by altering their structure or behaviour over the millennia to exploit the many different, and constantly changing, conditions in which they live.

Coral polyps provide the foundations of every reef; more than 500 species have been identified worldwide. Corals, however, are not the only group of animals represented in this ecosystem. Coralline

red algae, which encrust themselves in lime, cement the actual reef together. Packed in, around and between the various corals, are coralline algae, sponges, sea fans, anemones, sea cucumbers, sea squirts, clams and a diverse assemblage of shellfish, crustaceans and, of course, fish. There has been much debate over the question whether

coral reefs contain more species than tropical forests. Nobody is quite sure how many species live in either and so the contest cannot be resolved.

Beneath the bright blue seas of Flores and northern Sulawesi lie underwater gardens of unimaginable splendour – the patterns of colours, shapes and textures presented always unique. Huge vermilion barrel sponges stand out from the reef floor pumping large volumes of water through their pores each day, filtering out the tiny plankton which sustain much of the life on these reefs. Magenta organ pipes and a kaleidoscope of coloured coral formations dance in the currents. Delicate sea fans seem about to snap at any minute, remaining rigid even in a swell. Thousands of colourful fish swarm and bustle around the reef, scattering at the approach of a larger predator, seeking refuge among the corals or in the crevices of the reef's face. Occasionally a school of tuna or barracuda pass by, as may a solitary white-tipped shark. Giant rays and migrating marine turtles glide silently through the upper waters. This is an everyday scene on any of Indonesia's many spectacular coral reefs.

Most corals are active only at night. During the day the polyps withdraw their tentacles to within their body cavities. As darkness falls, an almost magical transformation comes over the reef as millions of thread-like tentacles unfurl from the coral polyps to trap the rich clouds of rising plankton. Feather-armed crinoids (featherstars) unleash their long, curling stalks to drift idly with the currents, trapping tiny plankton on their delicate tendrils. Nudibranchs – shell-less sea slugs whose striking colours have earned them the title 'butterflies of the sea' – which have spent the daylight hours hiding in the coral rubble at the base of the reef, emerge to feed on sponges, temporarily safe under the shadow of night. Reef lobsters emerge from rock crevices to feed on carrion, worms and even small fish. Even the much-feared moray eel may leave its lair to pursue some tasty morsel. A pair of special 'nostrils' on its snout helps it follow the odour trails of other species as it wanders through dark reef tunnels.

Among the reef's most beautiful plankton gatherers is the delicate featherstar. Forming a lacy bowl with its branching, cilia-lined arms, the featherstar emerges at night to take up a suitable position on the tip of a coral branch. Its dainty arms may either be arranged like a fan and held perpendicular to the current, or they may form a barrel shape, wafting tiny prey into a central mouth. Lacking the symbiotic algae of their hard coral relatives, these echinoderms are not restricted to living in sunlight and may occur on overhangs, wherever water currents can provide them with a reliable supply of plankton. These beautiful, multicoloured species reveal their true glory only at night, safe from the predatory habits of coral-eating fish.

1. *Featherstar (crinoid).*
2. *Gorgonian fan.*
3. *Sea squirts (tunicates).*
4. *Featherstar in fan coral.*
5. *Featherstar.*
6. *Sea slugs (nudibranchs).*
7. *Featherstar.*
8. *Whip coral.*
9. *Sea slugs (nudibranchs).*

Facing page: soldierfish, which sometimes collect in a tightly packed shoal under a coral overhang.

Below: a dusky parrotfish finds shelter in a cluster of corals. These fish, which change colour throughout their life cycle, are grazers; feeding by scraping algae from the coral surface and by crushing chunks of coral with their sharp beaks. The finely crushed coral is excreted as a milky cloud – a major source of coral sand.

Among the many fascinating fish which patrol the reefs at night are the flashlight fishes; two species occur in Indonesian waters *Anomalops kataptron* and *Photoblepharon palpebratus*. These small grey-black fish have special organs under their eyes which contain millions of light-producing bacteria. Hunting in shoals, flashlight fish turn these 'lights' on and off, by means of a shutter which covers the continually lit-up light organ, to attract zooplankton on which they feed. The intermittent flashes of light are also thought to help the fish stay together in a single shoal and probably help to confuse would-be predators.

Many reef fish change colour at night, choosing muted shades which help camouflage them from potential predators. Other species employ different tactics. The parrotfish, for example, seeks refuge among the many crevices on the reef wall. To help prevent detection by larger predators, some fish even secrete a mucous envelope around their bodies – which not only tends to break up the fish's body outline, but may also help disguise its smell. Tiny damselfish seek refuge amongst the branches of stinging corals.

Of the coral-eating fish, the parrotfish is undeniably the most destructive. These fish have specialized sharp beak-like teeth at the front, with which they nip off pieces of coral, and round ones at the back to grind up the gritty mouthfuls and extract the nutritious polyps. Other species have more refined ways of plundering the coral. The crown-of-thorns starfish, for example, applies itself closely to a coral head and ejects its digestive fluid directly into the coral, which it then extracts as a soup.

The solid foundation of the reef provides a convenient hiding place for many species. Among the extraordinary reef-burrowing species are the *nyale* worms, known in the South Pacific as Palolo worms. During the day, these animals rest in excavated tubes within the reef, emerging partially from their homes at night to feed. Their breeding behaviour is synchronised with the phases of the moon. As the spawning season approaches the hind section of each worm's body swells with eggs or sperm. Shortly after the full moon the worms reverse partially out of their burrows and the hind section breaks off in the current and floats to the surface. There the thin walls of the body sac break and the eggs and sperm are released. Within a few hours, the fertilized eggs hatch into free-living larvae; these drop to the bottom after three days and immediately adopt the burrowing habit of their parents – who have remained in their tunnels.

Facing page: white mouthed moray eel.

The venomous spines and extravagant colouration of the lionfish are sufficient deterrents to most predators.

Grouper.

Left: the peppered moray eel, concealed within the crevices of the oral, has 'nostrils' which are used not for breathing, but for detecting odour trails in the dark reef tunnels.

The large eyes of this mantis shrimp suggest that it is a nocturnal species.

Below: a tiny bicoloured shrimp is perfectly camouflaged against the spines of a sea urchin.

THE MANY FACES OF THE REEF – A NICHE AND A NEIGHBOUR

The wrinkled face of a reef wall is not always the solid structure it first appears. Frequently riddled with caves, tunnels and crevices it offers the possibility of sanctuary to a range of species, providing essential resting and sleeping quarters for some species and an anchorage for others.

While the tiny, innumerable plankton are the base of the food chain providing nourishment for the coral polyps and many other associated species, they do not necessarily satisfy the needs of all the other reef-dwelling or reef-associated species. Many species are skilled and active hunters. The small, transparent skeleton shrimp, for example, has two pairs of hooked, grasping appendages which are held aloft as the animal stalks the reef in search of a potential meal. The aggressive behaviour of these and other predators is seen in the way they often approach and tackle much larger prey. The starfish is another key predator which specializes in feeding on sessile prey such as shellfish and corals. When feeding on molluscs, its sucker-like arms attach firmly to the shell and then gradually prise the two halves apart until it is able to reach the animal's soft flesh.

In addition to the more aggressive, predatory reef fish, there are other larger adversaries to contend with, particularly those that appear out of the gloom of the ocean depths specially to feed off the reef's riches. Species such as jacks, barracuda and shark frequently venture into the reef environment to feed, withdrawing again to the depths when satiated. Even renowned predators like the octopus are not immune to the attacks of moray eels which, at times, appear to act as the reef's own watchdogs.

Proper grooming is important for fish since they are commonly plagued by skin fungi and parasites such as fish lice. On coral reefs there are special places that are recognized by fish as communal cleaning stations. Large groupers and butterflyfish are among the many species to take advantage of the services of the cleaner wrasse, tiny blue and white fish that meticulously pick off lice, dead scales, and other debris from their patient clients. The risks to these cleaner wrasse appear considerable since they frequently venture into the cavernous mouths of much larger fish and risk becoming a meal in themselves, as they pick morsels of food from the teeth of these predators. Yet they are never eaten, since the role they play in ridding other fish of their parasite burden is too important.

Many shrimps also serve as personal hygienists to a wide range of fish. Others, such as the blind pistol shrimp, have developed an equally elaborate system of mutual trust and dependence. This species excavates a short burrow on the sand at the base of the reef or in a sandy hollow in the reef. But it will not be the sole occupant of this home. During the day, small gobies will rest outside the entrance to the burrow. The shrimps will stay beside the fish, remaining in contact with them using their long antennae. At the first warning of danger from the goby, both shrimp and fish hurriedly withdraw to the safety of the burrow, only to emerge when the goby signals the all clear. In this way, the goby is provided with a safe home and the shrimp with a private alarm system.

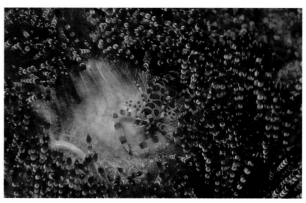

❶ *Tiny golden damselfish hover near a large gorgonian fan.*
❷ *Cuttlefish have ten tentacles and very efficient eyes which are highly developed compared with most invertebrates.*
❸ *A well-concealed eye is the only clue distinguishing this greater blue-ringed octopus from its coral background.*
❹ *A small goby rests in a sheltered part of the reef.*
❺ *The red-spotted blenny. Blennies rarely expose more than their head.*

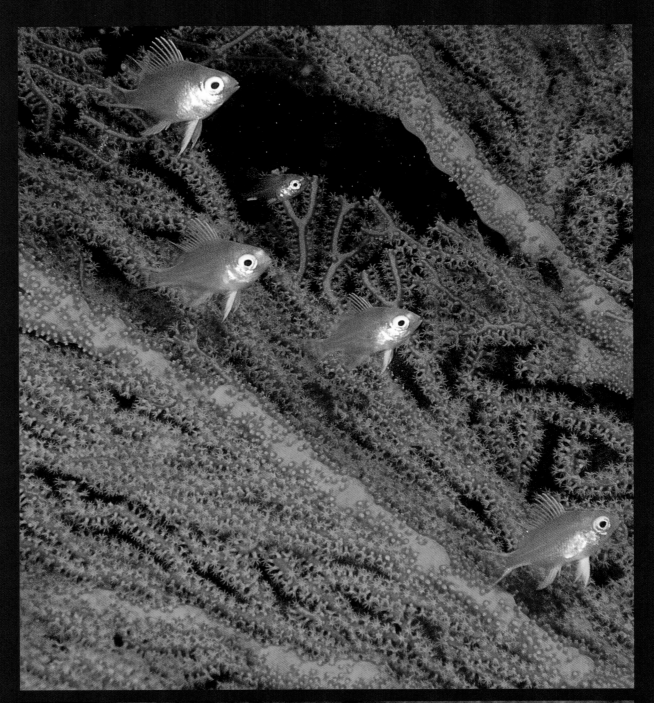

Above: rounded porcupine-fish.

Below: scorpionfish.

Like gigantic, multi-storey apartment blocks, coral reefs are some of the busiest and most densely populated living spaces anywhere on Earth. Finding a home on the reef, however, is not as easy as moving into a new apartment. With so many organisms dependent on securing a position in full sunlight, free space on shallow underwater ledges is usually at a premium. Even when an organism has managed to obtain a foothold on the reef, like the other inhabitants, it too faces a continuous struggle to protect and maintain its homestead and in obtaining sufficient food for survival. As a result of this variety of factors, many species have developed a range of intricate relationships which enable them to survive in these enchanted underwater gardens.

The teeming array of life, making up the dynamic environment of the coral reef, contains many creatures which in some way are interconnected and often mutually dependent upon one another. The basic food producing organisms including the microscopic plankton in the upper water column and the coloured algal *zooxanthallae* in the coralline tissue, provide the first stage of the food web. Many fish and marine invertebrates feed on the coral by grazing, while tiny fish, filter feeding bivalve molluscs and sponges filter the planktonic soup and provide a further link in the reef's food web as prey for yet other species. These in turn are preyed upon by larger species, many of which venture into the shallow reef seas from the open ocean. In this way, nutrients and energy that are first produced by the tiny plankton move through the food chain before finally ending up in the top tier of predators such as groupers and barracudas. The nutrient flow on the reef is almost a closed system; whenever an animal or plant dies or is eaten, its nutrients and minerals are quickly absorbed; thus little is wasted from the system or lost to the community.

STRATEGIES FOR SURVIVAL
LOOKS AREN'T EVERYTHING

Species have developed many responses to ensure their survival. One of the most striking features of Indonesia's coral reefs is the dazzling array of shapes and colours, both of corals and fish. Many of the corals are coloured green or brown by the presence of tiny photosynthetic algae (*zooxanthallae*) living within their outer living tissue. The startling colours and loud patterns of many reef fishes serve a variety of purposes, and sometimes indicate that the species is poisonous or, at the very least, highly distasteful to other species. The extraordinary lionfish and scorpionfish are particularly obvious on account of their bold colours and elongated spines. Few predators would risk injury by attacking such unappetizing fare. By mimicking these poisonous species to avoid predation, essentially through bluffing, several other species (which are highly edible) have developed similar body colours and patterns. This strategy may be carried further, as in the case of the sabre-toothed blenny (*Aspidontus taeniatus*), a tiny fish which resembles a cleaner wrasse. Blenny frequent the same cleaner stations as the wrasse which remove parasites and dead skin from large fish but, instead of cleaning these fish, the blenny, which otherwise behave in a manner similar to the wrasse, actually bite chunks out of the fins of the much larger fish.

The gaudy colours of many fish may also serve as effective camouflage: contrary to first impressions, species such as the bright red cardinalfish are perfectly camouflaged, resting in crevices during the day and emerging at night to feed on larvae and tiny fish. At night they are largely invisible, since red wavelengths of light do not penetrate deep into the water, making these fish appear black. Other species, such as trumpetfish and octopus are great artists, sartorially speaking, changing their appearance to blend with their immediate surroundings. In the case of the octopus, such changes can be made very quickly. This adaptation allows it to excel at avoiding detection and at lying in ambush for unsuspecting prey. It is also used for communication; one example of this is its use in courtship behaviour.

SAFE HAVENS

Apart from the highly obvious shoals of fish, some of the most abundant and attractively coloured animals on the reef are the segmented worms, many of which rest on, or within, the coral, constructing a calcareous tube around their soft bodies for protection. Safe within this tube, the worm periodically exposes a glorious crown of delicate feather-like structures called radioles which trap minute particles of food. Among the most spectacular of these animals are the Christmas tree worms (*Spirobranchus giganteus*) – also known as bottle brush tube worms on account of the dense arrangement of their radioles. Tube worms are extremely sensitive to disturbance. Their delicate radioles are a major temptation to many reef fish and molluscs, so at the slightest touch or in response to sudden movement they are rapidly withdrawn inside the tube. This quick reaction is due to a well-developed network of muscles linked to a highly responsive nervous system served by light- and pressure-sensitive cells in the radioles.

While many reef-dwelling animals hide away in the nooks and crannies of the reef wall, others secrete a tough outer mantle or shell for protection, the most striking examples of this being found amongst the crustaceans and molluscs, particularly the giant clams and large tritons. Yet even such armour plating is often insufficient to deter large predators; nurse sharks easily crunch open molluscs, while some tiny crabs have engineered a way of opening up even the largest of them. Some molluscs even drill holes through the shells of other species to reach the flesh of their prey.

A number of other creatures use the shells of dead animals for protection. Unlike their relative, the coconut crab of Eastern Indonesia, hermit crabs are soft-bodied and rely on finding discarded shells into which to crawl. As the crab grows, it will exchange its 'home' for another larger shell. To reduce the risk of detection even further, some hermit crabs allow sea anemones to attach themselves to their home. Both species appear to benefit from this arrangement: the crab gains from better camouflage, and the anemone is provided with a mobile home and may receive a share of the scraps of the crab's meal. The importance of this relationship is seen when the crab exchanges its shell and physically transfers the anemone from the old shell to its new home.

Many of the smaller reef fish, such as the shrimpfish, cardinalfish and anemonefish, rely on the protection offered by the long thin spines of sea urchins, or the drifting, deadly tentacles of the sea anemone. In return for such personalised security services, the anemone or sea urchin receives occasional titbits of food from the fish who also ensure that the animal's spines do not become clogged with weeds, or other settling plants or tiny animals – many of which may be parasitic.

INTIMATE ASSOCIATIONS

In contrast to those species which seek shelter in crevices and abandoned shells, others actually take refuge within living species. A sea cucumber, for example, is often host to other species, most commonly a tiny pearl fish, which burrows through its host's intestine lining to feed on the sea cucumber's food reservoir. Occasionally the fish may leave the host, but it always returns to its niche.

RECONNAISSANCE AND DEFENCE

Competition for food and living space is not confined to the mobile inhabitants of the reef. A continuous silent battle is waged on every single reef between the millions of coral polyps that make up the fabric of the reef. Corals regularly monitor their immeditate surroundings with special elongated 'sweeper tentacles', which may be 20 times the length of their normal tentacles, and which are used to keep the immediate vicinity clear of competitors. Poisonous barbs on the tips of these tentacles deter weaker corals from invading the space. Other corals secrete poisonous compounds, known as 'terpenes', which leach out from the coral to kill nearby organisms. These behaviours help reduce competition and the risk of being overgrown by other settling coral polyps.

A coral reef is a world of intense struggle. Competition for space is fierce where growth conditions are optimal; there is rarely a site which has not been occupied. The residents of the reef have adopted a wide range of responses to these problems. Some flee, hide, inflate themselves to great proportions, or threaten their adversaries with poison or sharp barbs. Sooner or later, however, most individuals succumb to the pressure of predation from a larger or stronger species. To cope with this pressure, various species have devised a range of reproductive features which augment other defensive strategies. Many species produce copious numbers of offspring, while others are more selective and invest more energy in producing fewer offspring. Those which do survive, however, together with the behavioural and anatomical modifications the species may have developed, could contribute to the long-term evolution and hence survival of the species.

Above: Christmas tree worms.

Below: sea cucumber.

Ghost pipefish.

77

One of the best known associations on the reef is probably that between the aptly named anemone-fish and the sea anemones. These brightly coloured fish shelter and live within the anemone's tentacles; they have never been seen living apart from anemones. Although known to possess powerful stinging cells, and capable of paralysing other fish of similar size, the anemone does not sting its clownfish. This close association seems possible because the fish disguise their odour and taste by covering their scales with a layer of mucus, some of which is obtained from the anemone. This hides the true nature of the fish and effectively tricks the anemone into thinking that the fish is part of its own body, which it will, of course, not attack. The anemone may benefit a little from food caught by the fish, or from other small prey that the fish might lure towards the anemone, but the main benefit seems to be for the fish, which also lay their eggs on the surface of the anemone, safe from predators.

Not all reef species react in such a benevolent manner to neighbours. As corals are dependent on sunlight filtering through the water, there is constant search for space on the exposed reef walls. The stinging cells of some corals are used aggressively to keep others away. Some species develop extra-long tentacles with which they are able to monitor the wider area for competitors. As with ordinary nematocysts, these tentacles can kill other polyps they encounter. Yet other corals engaged in the battle for space produce lethal chemicals which slowly kill potential competitors in the vicinity.

One of the most destructive animals of the reef ecosystem is the crown-of-thorns starfish, *Acanthaster plancii*. This species grazes exclusively on coral polyps, methodically working its way across a patch of reef. Occasionally near-plague proportions are reached, bringing destruction of an entire coral community. Some branching corals, however, have devised a natural solution to this problem by hosting small numbers of crabs among their fronds. If a crown-of-thorns starfish climbs on to the corals, the crab nips its tube-like feet with its pincers, repelling the predator. In return for this service, the crab benefits from the protection offered by the coral's stinging tentacles.

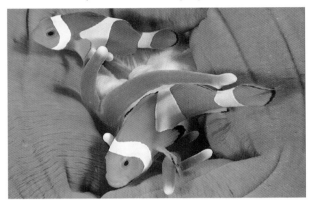

Above: the brightly coloured mantle of the thorny oyster is the only feature which reveals the presence of this animal on the reef. A range of organisms have colonized the upper shell of the oyster, providing effective camouflage against starfish and other predators.

Left: the crowded living conditions on a reef are highlighted by the abundance of multi-tentacled zoanthids, colonial ascidians and a range of hydroids on this slender projection. Different feeding styles are adopted by different species, some producing long-stalked feeding arms to reach above the crowded conditions on the lower level.

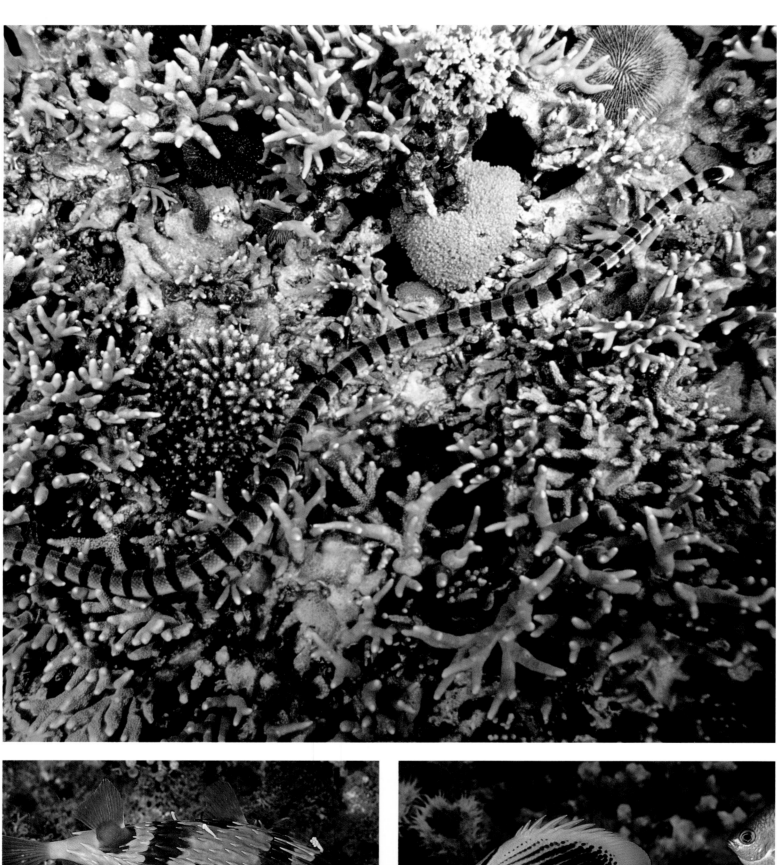

Staying alive is as great a problem for the many reef fish, and other organisms which seek food and shelter in this habitat. To avoid being eaten by something else many animals have gone to great lengths to develop elaborate defence mechanisms. More than two-thirds of all reef organisms contain toxic substances, making them unpleasant to eat. Hiding is an obvious choice, but safe hiding places are limited on the reef and are themselves often frequented by predatory species such as moray eels. Camouflage is another frequently adopted tactic which has been perfected by species such as butterflyfish which use a clever combination of colours and patterns to break up the body outline. Yet other species have a 'false eye' on their tail or dorsal fin, which draws a predator's attention to the wrong end of the fish, often enabling it to flee without being caught. The solitary, slow-moving pufferfish, for example *Arothron nigropunctatus,* inflate their bodies with water when threatened, making it impossible for most predators to swallow them. Still other intriguing techniques that some species have developed to help ensure their survival are illustrated by the scorpionfish (*Scorpaenopsis* sp.) lionfish (*Pterois* sp.) and porcupinefish (*Diodon hystrix*) each of which has developed prominent, poisonous spines on the head and body.

THE VALUE OF REEFS

Coral reefs are not just colourful playgrounds for the multitudes of fish and other exotic life forms that they support. Their calm, warm waters act as an important nursery area for many crustaceans and fish. Reefs have traditionally been an essential source of food for coastal-dwelling communities, a tradition which, if carried out in a sustainable manner, is of considerable economic value to the country. Many of the fish species trawled from deep, offshore waters also rely on the nearshore breeding grounds around coral reefs. Disruption of the reef ecosystem can have wide implications for people and nature.

Indonesia's reefs are attracting more and more visitors each year. The financial gains for local communities through provision of accommodation, guides, boats and equipment can be considerable: sometimes enough to convince local residents that protection of the reef ecosystem in its natural splendour is a far more lucrative activity than exploiting it for its fish stocks or shells. Some marine reserves such as Bunaken Marine Park, North Sulawesi, are now well equipped to deal with these influxes. But despite the recognized importance of these reefs, and the potential for using these resources in a non-destructive way, the corals of the Indonesian seas are still threatened.

The previous analogy of a coral reef to a building site seems now sadly ironic. Large areas of Indonesia's once beautiful coral reefs have been destroyed to extract the limestone deposits that the tiny coral polyps have amassed over the centuries. Blocks of coral are broken up to provide material for the foundations and walls of houses, are crushed to produce lime, or are used as building blocks for piers and for breakwaters designed to reduce the impact of storms onshore. In their natural life, however, corals serve this purpose much more effectively.

The state of the world's coral reefs has never been so perilous. These precious resources are increasingly threatened, largely as a result of the short-sighted activities of human beings. Among these are water pollution, siltation, dynamite fishing, removal of coral for construction purposes, uncontrolled tourism and collecting of ornamental fauna for the aquarium trade. Increased exposure to ultra-violet light due to the depletion of the ozone layer and more frequent and intense storms as a result of warming seas could combine to make this situation even more critical. The cost of artificially replacing many of the services which reefs provide is unimaginably high; the complexity of the wildlife that these structures support could never be replicated. Greater attention must be given to ensuring the long-term protection of these resources. Indonesia, which hosts a large proportion of the world's coral reefs, including some of the most diverse and spectacular of all reef ecosystems, has an important role to play in protecting its own natural heritage for the future benefit and enjoyment of her people.

Facing page: a black and white banded sea snake glides through the masses of coral in search of fish and crustaceans.

The poisonous spines of the freckled porcupinefish can be raised to enhance the fish's appearance when threatened.

The beautiful spot-tailed butterflyfish has a long, thin mouth which is an adaptation for plucking small animals from the cracks and crevices of the reef.

Below: the predatory long-nosed hawkfish has an elongated beak which enables it to pluck the exposed tentacles from feeding coral polyps, such as on this young gorgonian coral.

PEOPLE AND THE SEA

PEOPLE OF THE SEA

Western images of Indonesia have often centred on the beauty, natural riches and sheer expanse of the region's seas. Many Indonesian people, however, have a mixed reaction to the sea. Traditionally it has been feared by a large proportion of the population; being perceived as a wild environment, beyond the confines of human civilization. For inland-dwelling people, such as the Balinese who revere the mountains and volcanoes as the homes of gods, the sea represents a realm of sickness, death and calamity. In addition, pirates and raiders roamed these seas, their attacks and lawlessness causing some communities great distress over the generations. In many areas including Java, Bali, Sumba and parts of Timor people still fear the sea. Many of the people of Toraja, Sulawesi, still view the sea as a natural adversary.

However, it is not surprising, for this nation of islands, that seafaring is deeply rooted in the culture of certain other groups of Indonesia's population. The Bugis and the Makassarese are widely recognized as being the most skilful boat builders and sailors in Indonesia. For centuries the most important shipbuilding centre was the Bira Peninsula, southern Sulawesi, where *prahu* are still crafted entirely from timber. Unlike European construction of boats, it is still common for the traditional technique of building the shell first, held together with wooden dowel-pins, which are later incorporated into the final structure. Although now being replaced by much larger ocean-going cargo vessels, colourful Bugis schooners, *pinisi*, still form an important part of the inter-island shipping network, carrying timber and other commodities around the archipelago.

Another group of people who have enjoyed a long relationship with the sea are the Bajau. These highly skilled mariners have even made the sea their permanent home, living a life almost exclusively in coastal waters. Although many Bajau have now forsaken their traditional lifestyles for more settled situations, a large number continue to reject the pull of the land. They derive their living from catching fish and collecting and trading a range of other products such as shells and *tripang* or dried sea cucumber. Increased demand for *tripang* from markets in China and Japan has led to over-exploitation of many coral reefs.

Above: one of the many products harvested from the sea in Indonesia, seaweeds are widely collected at low tides and brought ashore for drying and sale.

Above: a master craftsman plies his trade following traditional ways and skills handed down over the generations; these elegant prahus are still constructed entirely from wood.

Right: A series of hand-built prahu line a beach of the Bira Peninsula, southern Sulawesi, nearing completion.

THE WHALE HUNTERS OF LAMALERA

The whale hunters of Indonesia are another traditional but poorly known group of seafarers. The deep seas of Eastern Indonesia and the various straits between Flores and Lombok are an important migration corridor for whales moving between the Pacific and Indian oceans. Subsistence hunting of whales is an old practice in parts of Indonesia, with records dating back more than 200 years; long before modern day whaling began in these waters. Today, this tradition is only continued at two villages: Lamalera on Pulau Lembata and Lamakera on nearby Pulau Solor, east of Flores. Using hand-crafted *prahu,* a small force of seamen sets out in search of the large sperm whale, the preferred species. When one is sighted, the crew frantically races after the whale, evaluating its size. If it is too large, or the boat is too far out from shore, the chase may be called off. If not, however, the *prahu* crew close in on their quarry and, standing in the prow of the boat, the harpooner hurls himself into the water in pursuit, plunging a simple harpoon deep into the animal's body. Sharks, particularly the large whale shark, manta rays and other large fish such as marlin are also captured in much the same manner. Every part of the prize is used, from teeth to flesh. It is carefully divided up, according to custom, between the members of the crew of the day and those of the corporation responsible for the building and maintenance of the boat.

Fishing in this way is by no means a full-time occupation for the islanders, who rely on growing crops as their mainstay. Small scale, inshore fishing is also widely practised; but a large catch, such as a sperm whale, can provide a major boost to the status and income of these people. In addition to the important subsistence nature of these catches – much of the flesh is traded for other materials, including food – strong cultural traditions have developed around this practice. Whales and whaling figure in the origin myths of some groups. One Lamalera clan, Olé Ona, claims to have been brought to the village on the back of a whale. For coastal communities on the islands of the Keis and Pagai, as well as Lembata, marine animals such as fish, turtles and crocodiles are thought to represent the forms adopted by lost souls trying to get back to the land, and many local taboos have been instated to prevent or restrict hunting of these creatures. Islanders are still so impressed by the tremendous bulk of the blue whale (*Balaenoptera musculus*) that traditional restrictions which prevent any hunting of this species are still honoured.

FORTUNES FROM THE SEA

In addition to fishing, many people, particularly those on small islands, frequently supplement their livelihoods by collecting and trading goods from the sea. Although its importance has now declined, the catching of large turtles once played a major part of many ceremonial systems, such as the *punen* system in Sumatra. While men were away fishing, women and children had to remain in their homes, their lives ruled by strict taboos, so as not to jeopardize the mission by upsetting certain spirits. In recent years, marine turtles have been heavily exploited for their valuable shells which are carved and polished to provide a range of ornaments – and meat, most of which is exported to Japan. Giant clams have suffered a similar fate. In terms of financial rewards, however, the jewel of the sea is the pearl oyster. The actual pearl consists of layers of calcium carbonate which are secreted around tiny invading particles, such as sand grains which slip inside the shell as the animal is feeding. While this process happens accidentally in the ocean, today pearl farming has become big business and nothing is left to chance. In the carefully controlled market of pearl trading, even the ways in which pearls are actually seeded in the host shellfish remain a closely guarded secret. The clean, nutrient-rich waters around Lombok and Flores offer ideal conditions for oyster aquaculture. The pearl oysters are still collected by teams of divers in what is a hazardous and increasingly more difficult task as oysters become scarce and divers are forced to spend more time under water.

Above: whale oil is used to provide lighting, Lamalera.

Facing page: catching squid, Manado.

Drying fish, Komodo.

Shark hunting, Lamalera.

Below: the traditional whaling boats of Lamalera with their tripod masts and lug sails.

Above: Torosaije village, a Bajau coastal settlement in northern Sulawesi.

PEOPLE OF THE SEA: THEIR HISTORY AND CULTURE

Sea nomads, of which the Bajau are one group, have lived for centuries on the open seas. Their origins remain unclear but they are widely spread in Southeast Asia. It is commonly held that they orginated from the southern part of Peninsular Malaysia and from there spread to Thailand, Burma, The Philippines, and many parts of Indonesia such as Sumatra, Kalimantan, Sulawesi, Maluku and Flores. Some historians have suggested it was the Bajau who initiated trading relations between southern China and northern Kalimantan. The Bugis, originating from Sulawesi, also have great seafaring and trading skills and were responsible for opening up trade routes with China. However, it was said that a Bugis ship would always have Bajau sailors, whose knowledge of the seas was paramount. The Bajau and Bugis have a common bond, forged by their dependence on the sea. According to legend, the princess of the Gowa Kingdom was lost at sea. She was found by the Bajau, and in gratitude the king gave a concession to the Bajau allowing them to live in Sulawesi and the surrounding waters. The Bajau's maritime skills were used between the eighth and twelfth centuries by rulers of the Srivijayan kingdom to extend their area of influence; and they were employed by the Sultan of Melaka in the fifteenth century to defend his shores. Over the centuries the Bajau have played a key role in helping to unite the archipelago. This they have done through their common language (Malay), which is spoken wherever they live in the archipelago. Also they do not perceive the sea as a barrier; rather a link between the islands.

At one time all Bajau families lived in boats – a *bido* or *soppe*. Today, smaller versions of these boats, *lepa*, are used. They were nomadic, moving in groups of 20 to 30 *bido* to different locations, selected primarily for their fishing potential. The Bajau still living in this way catch a variety of coral fish, which is dried and salted. The other main trade and barter goods are pearls and sea cucumbers (*tripang*). The Bajau tend to concentrate their fishing activities near coral reefs, around mangroves and in estuaries. When the weather permits they also catch fish in the deep, offshore waters. Today, most Bajau live in coastal villages but there are some who still live in their *lepa* (dug-out canoes), moving within relatively confined geographic areas.

The Bajau of the Gulf of Tomini, northern Sulawesi, represent one of the last groups living almost completely on their *lepa*. *Lepa* are hand carved from *meranti* wood and usually measure about seven metres. Outrigger boards are added, and a roof thatched with nipa palm leaves provides some shelter. Located about three hours by boat from Torosiaje, a small fishing village on the gulf, the Bajau live and work as they have for centuries: on the sea. They live entirely on their boats; from birth to marriage to death. Families as large as eight live together with all their possessions – simple fishing implements, cooking utensils, clothes and even chickens. These conditions may seem crowded, but the Bajau are comfortable. One Bajau elder, when asked if he would prefer to live on land, said, 'No, why would we want to do that? We are people of the sea. We could not endure to be in a place without movement and change.' The Bajau language shows how this love of the open sea influences their sense of community. For these people the sea is their meeting ground. The Bajau call themselves *orang sama* (the same people) and those who do not speak their language, *orang bagai* (all other kinds of people).

Every aspect of their lives is based on a close relationship with Nature; with the open sea and the mangrove and coral reef ecosystems which serve as breeding and fishing grounds for many of the marine species they catch. Their livelihoods, beliefs, folktales and names are all connected with their environment. Most Bajau names describe the natural surroundings at the time of birth. One woman's name literally translates as, 'bird which sits on top of the palm tree which has fallen into the water', another, 'three black clouds in the sky'. The Bajau survive through their deep understanding and appreciation of the sea. The close feelings they have for their surroundings are instilled from an early age; before children are four years old they are paddling their own boats and by seven they are actively fishing.

A DAY IN THE LIFE OF A BAJAU COMMUNITY

An average day begins just before dawn by looking for fish. Some families collect fish caught in their nets the previous night, others set up new nets. The Bajau protect their nets by rubbing them with a solution made from mangrove tree bark. They use a variety of fishing techniques: fishing in coral areas, setting bamboo traps if the water is calm and diving up to 15 metres deep to spear large fish. Women and children search for *tripang*, often catching them by hand or with a spear. If the waters are rough the men employ a form of kite fishing to catch garfish (*julung-julung*). The men also dive for large oysters. Many of these men can hold their breath for up to five minutes. They use only wooden goggles made from *palapi* wood and discarded glass. Around mid-morning most families will gather again to eat – mostly freshly caught fish, fried with chillies, and rice or sago. While they dry and

smoke *tripang* and oysters; and salt fish, for market, the Bajau themselves prefer to eat fresh fish. Cured fish is reserved for land dwellers. The afternoon is spent preparing fish for sale. Women usually take this produce, the Bajau's prime source of income, to nearby village markets in the early morning. Essentials such as rice and cooking oil are bought with the proceeds. In the afternoon some families go to neighbouring islands to collect fresh water and firewood in the form of dead mangrove roots. At the end of the day a trumpet made from a shell is blown to recall any boats still at sea. It calls for the wind, asking it to take the weary fishermen home to dinner and family. The *lepa*, scattered during the day, group together in the late afternoon in a protected cove.

The clustered *lepa* form a small floating village. As the sun sets, women prepare the

The garfish feeds on small flying fish. The Bajau, fishing from their boats, attach a leaf, nylon thread and bait to a bamboo pole. As the leaf flies up and down in the wind like a kite, so does the bait, attracting the fish. When the leaf dips, that indicates that a fish has been caught. This is called layang-layang or kite fishing and the technique is used for fishing over shallow reefs.

evening's food and children play in *sampans* (small canoes). An elderly woman sings while she cooks. She sings of a man, alone on the sea, looking up at the stars and thinking of his loved ones. A neighbour joins in and then another. Across the boats stories and conversations are shared – a village without walls.

If the weather is good and the sea is calm the Bajau may continue their fishing into the night. The Bajau move about to avoid over-exploiting resources. By placing their oars in the water they are able to detect subtle differences in tides and currents and indicators of sheltered, calm waters where fishing might be lucrative. Once they have found the coral, they have found the fish. The stars and currents guide them home. Older Bajau estimate distance from land just by paddling into the current and 'feeling' the distance. Their close affinity with nature allows them to tell the time and seasons as well as to predict favourable fishing conditions and locations. By examining budding seagrass, for example, they know the day of the month: these buds open to release their seeds on the third day of the month, then until the tenth day they remain inactive when they again open, remaining in this state till the fifteenth. They remain inactive until the third day of the next month, when the cycle stars all over again. The Bajau know that when the north star is above the south star, the weather will be good and the sea will be calm. When the *tiga bintang,* or three stars, are in the western part of the sky they know the wind will blow from the west. When these stars are in the eastern part of the sky the wind will come from the east. When the *bintang timur* or east star rises it is near 4.00 am. By reading such natual clocks and calendars, these skilful fishermen and seafarers can avoid storms and easily find fish.

The sea is their home. They know its rhythms and mysteries. Its riches fill their lives. A Bajau lullaby captures this spirit: a child cries for his father to return home, the mother sings, 'Don't ask why he doesn't come home, he is a child of the sea. And for the child of the sea, the sea is his home.'

THE FUTURE

Living a life on the sea is not easy. Some Bajau have abandoned their traditional life-style and have settled in coastal villages. Many, however, have found it difficult to adjust to settlement in villages, where society is often geared to an agricultural way of life. Some villages have even been abandoned. National fishing regulations, often geared to big business, as well as pollution, and destruction of mangroves, have also had a great impact on their traditional ways. The future for the Bajau depends upon the realization that their knowledge and traditional practices should be encouraged and that they have much to contribute in safeguarding Indonesia's extensive coastal environment.

Left: market at Banjarmasin, South Kalimantan. Here the Bajau sell their tripang and salted fish in exchange for rice and fish and other commodities.

THE SPICE TRADE

The 'Realm of the Thousand Islands' – Maluku – is a tranquil, unassuming and largely unspoilt fragment of the Indonesian Archipelago. It is difficult to imagine that this sleepy backwater was once at the hub of some of the greatest trading routes the world has ever known. Several centuries ago, a handful of these tiny islands, rarely figuring on contemporary maps, were at the centre of an international power game and savage warfare, as Indonesian and European powers grappled for control of the lucrative spice trade. Reports of the region's fabled spices instigated some of the most daring voyages of discovery ever undertaken.

Long before the first Europeans set foot in the Maluku islands, however, an elaborate trading system based on spices operated as a lifeline for many communities. Early inter-island trade in spices was linked to the main staple of the islands, sago. Sago palms cannot grow on all of the islands of Maluku because of their aridity, so early entrepreneurs traded some of the islands' natural riches for this vital food source. Chinese seafarers and merchants were also dealing in these precious commodities for more than 1000 years before the Europeans entered the arena. The earliest records of the use of Indonesian spices outside Maluku can be traced back to the Early Han Dynasty (260B.C.-A.D.200) in China. Pliny the Elder also described the passage of cinnamon

Facing page: a coastal village in the Aru Islands, Maluku.

Below: early Portuguese maps of the fabled Spice Islands.

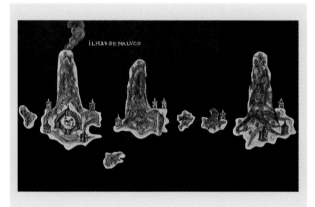

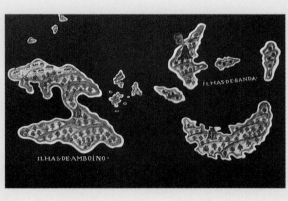

and other spices from Indonesia to Madagascar and East Africa and from there to Rome. Stories of great wealth derived from tiny aromatic spices gradually filtered through to Europe, but it was not until the fourteenth and fifteenth centuries that Portuguese and Spanish navigators deliberately set out in search of these islands and their exotic commodities, with the promise of great wealth they were expected to produce.

The praises of the 'Spice Islands' and value of their harvests had been sung in the West for centuries, and from the sixteenth century onwards these tiny islands became the subject of wars and treaties to secure control over the trade and production. Explorers such as Ferdinand Magellan and Sir Francis Drake all witnessed and savoured the secrets of these islands. At the heart of these mis-

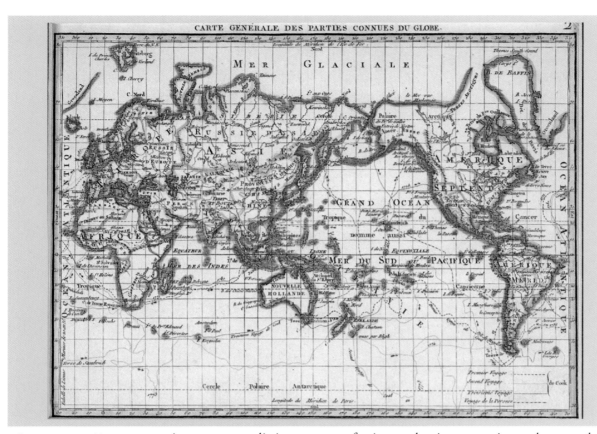

CARTE GENERALE DES PARTIES CONNUES DU GLOBE.

Above: James Cook's voyages at the end of the eighteenth century took him and his crew through parts of the archipelago.

Below: pepper and cloves – two of Indonesia's most important spices.

exchanging Chinese porcelain, cloth, food and other materials for spices. On a smaller scale, Bandanese seafarers conducted much of their own trade using oar-propelled *kora-kora* outrigger canoes. However, this changed in the seventeenth century with Dutch enforcement of monopolistic trading whereby the entire nutmeg and mace crops were sold to the Dutch at a fixed price. The local growers and traders gained little other than unwanted imported goods in return.

Of lesser fame than the seductively named Spice Islands, but of equal importance in the spice trade, were the islands of Java and Sumatra; the source of high quality pepper, perfumed resins and crystals of camphor. Pepper was first introduced from India in the seventh century A.D. and vigorously traded during the time of the Srivijaya Empire, for 500 years from the eighth century onwards. Strong trading links were developed with India and, in particular, China. For the Portuguese, and later the Dutch, pepper was the most lucrative of all the spices traded.

sions were two distinct centres of spice production. One was a group of small islands in North Maluku, a mini archipelago in its own right, which was devoted to the clove trade. Cloves were native to only five islands: the rival Sultanates of Ternate and Tidore, as well as Motir, Mokian and Batjan (now Bacan). The other site of spice production was the remote Banda Islands further south, which produced the much coveted nutmeg and mace. These prized possessions were jealously guarded by local rulers for many centuries. Warships powered by hundreds of sailors prowled the seas under the auspices of the sultans of Tidore and Ternate, yet these islands had no trading boats of their own, relying instead on the large vessels of Javanese, Malayan and Arab traders. Bugis seafarers, as well as being the sea nomads of Indonesia, were among the most successful inter-island traders of those days,

The turbulent times of ensuing warfare, and domination by foreign powers over the spice trade, eventually led to the collapse of the market. Today all that remains of those heady days are fading vestiges of forts and plantation houses, built to protect the rights of colonial interests on the most important islands. Fort Victoria still stares out to sea over the Bay of Ambon while Fort Duurstede plays a similar role on Saparua, to the east. Dwarfed by the nearby Gunung Api, the now restored Fort Belgica on Neira Island, together with other crumbling monuments, are witness to similar occupations in the beautiful Banda Islands during the heyday of the spice trade.

Spices are still widely grown on many of the islands of Maluku, but they no longer form a major part of the national economy. Mace and nutmeg continue to be an important part of the local economy, but most of Indonesia's production now comes from North Sulawesi. Falling world prices and continued rivalry for ownership of nutmeg plantations has led to a reduction in quality and of the number of trees maintained. Today Indonesia is no longer self-sufficient in cloves, a major component of the local *kretek*

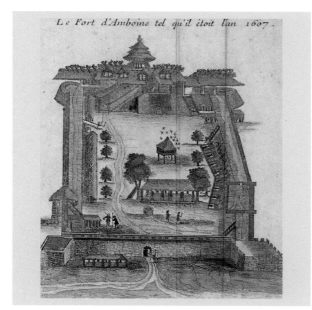

Le Fort d'Amboine tel qu'il étoit l'an 1607.

cigarettes. Although the archipelago is the world's principal producer of cloves it is also the largest importer, and now looks to the tiny islands of Zanzibar and Pemba, off the coast of East Africa, for most of its imports.

While spices were clearly the leading commodity influential in determining early trade patterns, as new routes and hungry markets opened up to the increasing number of European traders, many other products from the islands were included in the cargoes. The feathers of birds of paradise from Aru and Irian Jaya were particularly sought after in Parisian fashion houses, and aromatic timber, such as sandalwood, from Timor and Sumatra, mother-of-pearl from many of the islands, and damar and other resins from the country's rain forests were all eagerly sought and traded.

THE CULTURAL IMPORTANCE OF THE SEA

Superstition is widespread amongst seafarers, and festivals are a common feature of the coastal communities in Indonesia. Ceremonies are held to celebrate the beginning of the new season's estuarine fishing in eastern Sumatra and coastal fishing in eastern Java, and to acknowledge a good catch in Irian Jaya. Rituals are commonly applied where marine resources are being exploited; people visiting Enu in the Aru Islands to collect turtle eggs observe special rites which limit the harvest. Strict taboos also surround the taking of turtles in other areas such as the Mentawai Islands, while in Irian Jaya, and again in the Mentawai, the skulls of dugong and turtles are hung in sacred places to placate the spirits. Magic rituals are also important to the coastal fisherman of Aceh and Java.

In the Sangihe Islands, an area habitually fished by a native islander used to become a reserve for a period following his death. Anyone caught fishing in such areas was subject to heavy fines and even enslavement by the family of the deceased. Beliefs have also resulted in the creation of special reserves,

such as one on the southern coast of Java, which surrounds the shrine of the Goddess of the Southern Seas, Kangjeng Ratu Kidul, a patron of the rulers of Mataram (the region around Yogyakarta). Chronicled as having communed with members of this ruling house, she is still believed to reign from her watery palace and to favour pale green; walkers from the shore, unwise enough to be wearing this colour, are drawn into her undersea realm.

An important festival that is respected and eagerly awaited in Indonesia each year, surrounds the breeding behaviour of the segmented palolo worm (*Eunice viridis*). Once a year, shortly after a full moon, the festival, known as *bau nyale*, takes place. When they mature, the ends of these small worms break off and cloud the waters with millions of tiny packages containing eggs or sperm. As these drift towards the surface they burst, releasing their contents, which mingle in the surface waters to produce fertilized eggs that eventually develop into small wriggling *nyale* worms. Although stories vary, according to one local legend the *nyale* represent the beautiful daughter of the King of the Moon who, wanting to relieve the people's hardship, gave herself to the powers of the sea so that there might be a continuous supply of food for her people. The sight of the *nyale* worms coming back to the land is therefore interpreted as the princess returning each year. Highly esteemed as special food, the worms are usually prepared by being wrapped in coconut leaves and are then steamed. This important fertility cycle is deeply embodied in the rituals of many island groups, particularly on Lombok and Sumba where special ceremonies are held at which harvest cycles for the coming year are forecast.

Left: Ambon Fort (1607).

Below: Nyale festival, Waikabubak, Sumba Island.

Following page: seascape at dawn.

CONSERVING THE GREAT RESOURCE

Below: egrets gather where nets are hauled in, Sunda Strait.

Offshore jack-up rig in the Java Sea.

THE VALUE OF COASTAL RESOURCES

The bountiful oceans of this planet are commonly viewed as being an endless resource. For centuries the waters have been harvested for their abundant and valuable fish stocks as well as the more limited, but precious, resources obtained from other species such as the large whales and fur seals. The same oceans that provide such important economic benefits have also been widely treated as convenient dumping grounds for a range of solid and waste materials, some of them highly toxic to the environment. Improved technology has also enabled humans to explore the depths of the ocean and extract the considerable mineral riches – oil, gas and ores – that lie buried beneath the sea-bed. The state of the world's oceans has deteriorated considerably in recent decades, largely as a result of misconceptions regarding the limits of their natural resources and abuse and over-exploitation.

With a total coastal length of more than 81,000 kilometres, comprising 14 per cent of the Earth's shorelines, Indonesia has the world's longest coastline. Almost 80 per cent of Indonesia is composed of sea. An estimated 87 per cent of its waters are sheltered; the remainder face the open ocean. The coastal areas of Indonesia contain some of the most biologically productive resources found anywhere in the region. This productivity is the result of a number of factors, including the input of minerals and nutrients washed down from highland regions, as well as from the constant weathering and erosion of coastal features such as cliffs and beaches. Indonesia's marine and coastal ecosystems are thought to be more diverse, complex, extensive and productive than those of any other nation of comparable size. Extensive mangroves and coastal swamps, together with thousands of coral reefs and shallow, unpolluted seas, are among the most productive habitats in the region, supporting a large fishing industry and protecting adjacent coastal lowlands.

The coastal zone in Indonesia supports the highest concentrations of human population in the country. The marine and coastal waters and adjacent land areas support a variety of important economic sectoral activities including shipping and ports, oil and gas development, fisheries, aquaculture, coastal agriculture, coastal forestry, mining of tin, iron sands, coral and sand, industry, tourism, transportation and communications, and coastal community services.

Marine fisheries supply much of the protein consumed in Indonesia. About 40 per cent of the country's oil and tin is produced offshore, while coastal areas in the lower reaches of large rivers include some of the most fertile agricultural land in the country. Coastal tourism activities are an important and growing source of foreign exchange for Indonesia. In 1987, the total product of marine and coastal activities was estimated at 36.6 trillion Rupiah ($US22.3 billion), just under 22 per cent of the Gross Domestic Product. Their combined growth rate is at least twice that of traditional land-based activities, suggesting that their role in the sustainable economic development of Indonesia can only become more prominent. If managed properly, the country's coastal and ocean resources are capable of sustaining a high level of productivity. As our appreciation of the hidden benefits of a healthy marine environment becomes clearer, conscious efforts are being made to protect the environment. In particular, the sustainable use of these resources, as against unsustainable exploitation, has become a major objective of integrated coastal zone management programmes which are now being designed for many parts of the archipelago, such as Cendrawasih Bay, Irian Jaya.

Of major importance for the Indonesian economy are its offshore mineral reserves: particularly of oil and gas, which together have played a crucial role in providing resources to fund development programmes. Most recent estimates suggest that while the proved recoverable petroleum reserves amount to some 1,142,000 tonnes, the final amount is likely to be much greater, since only 34 of the country's known oilfields have been explored to date. In addition to petroleum, Indonesia also has substantial reserves of natural gas, estimated at 2068 billion cubic metres. More than half of these reserves are located offshore, particularly in the South China Sea near the Natuna Islands. Apart from these valuable resources, tin mining is also an important activity in some parts of the coastal zone. Indonesia is one of the world's leading exporters of tin, with reserves estimated at 1.6 million tonnes – 43 per cent of which are located offshore.

FISHING – A WAY OF LIFE

Catching fish must rank among one of the oldest ways of exploiting the sea. As Indonesia is a nation of islands it is not surprising that so many people are attracted to live on, or near, the coast – the sea's natural riches act as a great magnet. At present there are an estimated 7100 coastal communities in Indonesia, many of which rely on traditional ways of fishing in nearshore waters. These include a range of simple techniques that include individuals probing the sediments in search of burrowing marine invertebrates, sailing boats scooping up small numbers of nearshore fish and crustacea in nets, and large, deep sea fishing vessels which trawl the ocean floor in search of large shoals of commercially valuable fish species. Of these, traditional fishing practices are especially important for communities within easy reach of the country's many coral reefs, while commercial fisheries provide considerable national revenue.

Despite the fact that an extremely wide range of edible marine fish occur, just a few species support the really large commercial fisheries. In Indonesia the most commonly exploited pelagic resources include tuna, mackerel, sardine, anchovy (*ikan bilis*) and others such as members of the Carangidae (*kuwe*) and scad (*layang*) families; while demersal species harvested include snapper (*kakap*), grouper (*kerapu*), shrimp, lobster and shellfish. An estimated 68 per cent of the country's fish harvest

is taken from within its territorial waters. Indonesia's seas provide an estimated 60 per cent of the protein in the diet of the population, almost 80 per cent of which lives near the coast. In the province of West Java alone, marine fishery production comprises 47 per cent of total fish and shrimp production in the province.

Uncontrolled fishing activities have already had a major impact on the Indonesian marine environment. Overfishing from national and foreign vessels has led to reduced stocks of many offshore species. Widespread collection of delicate corals, pretty sea shells and sea turtles has led to their disappearance in certain parts of the country. Giant clams, also, have been heavily over-exploited, for their massive decorative shells and for their meat – which is a delicacy in East Asian countries. Many former breeding sites of the giant clam are now completely devoid of these molluscs.

Fish bombing and dynamite fishing are among the most destructive fishing practices in Indonesia. Unfortunately, both activities are still relatively widespread, despite efforts to curb and eliminate them. Using home-made devices and a range of locally available materials – a former ammunition dump was the source of much of the explosives used around Biak and in Cenderawasih Bay, Irian Jaya – fishermen toss these bombs into shallow reef waters. The resulting explosions kill all life within the immediate area causing the fish to float to the

Above: a liquified natural gas (LNG) tanker loading at Bontang, Kalimantan.

surface where they can be easily gathered. The technique is extremely wasteful as it is not selective – all living organisms are stunned and many smaller species needlessly killed – and damaging because it destroys the coral polyps, removing the basic fabric and food base of the reef.

Southeast Asia is thought to have been the centre of origin of mariculture – the practice of farming fish, prawns, molluscs and plants, such as seaweeds, in brackish water. Today a wide range of species is grown in ponds, including milkfish, banana prawn, tilapia, tiger prawns, mullet, barramundi and mangrove crabs. While mariculture has considerable potential for boosting local income, now more intensive forms are often conducted in a manner which results in localised environmental problems which, in the long-term, reduce or negate any potential benefit which the system offers. One of the most serious problems arising from mariculture in Indonesia has been the conversion of mangrove swamps to ponds for raising fish and prawns. Valuable, sheltered natural nursery and breeding grounds for inshore and deep sea fish species have been destroyed as mangroves have been cleared. Removal of mangroves also results in less sediment and nutrients remaining in the nearshore zone, since these are washed out to sea. Another problem relates to the collection and overharvesting of eggs or fry of selected species from the coastal waters. This can upset the natural food chain of the nearshore ecosystem. Milkfish fry, for example, are heavily collected in the shallow waters around Java and transferred to warm, brackish water ponds known as *tambak*. As the fish grow, they are transferred to larger and deeper *tambak* until such time as they are ready for harvesting. Natural recruitment of juveniles to the wild fish population is therefore seriously reduced, resulting in fewer eggs laid in subsequent years and, eventually, reduced catches. The addition of fertilizers to the waters of these ponds in order to boost algal growth for fish food, and the release of nutrient- and detritus-rich waters from the ponds have resulted in localised pollution in the coastal zones of many parts of the archipelago, particularly around Java.

The economic potential for the sustainable use of many different types of fisheries – offshore, coral reef and inshore ecosystems – is considerable in Indonesia, yet these resources are not currently being used or managed at anywhere near their maximum potential. Improved methods of mariculture need to be introduced which would result in less damage to local environments and would also reduce the quantities of wild fish fry and crustacea being taken from the wild. Management of coastal, particularly reef, fisheries is essential since these ecosystems not only play an important role in the lives of millions of people, but they also act as a basis for potentially important economic development in the form of ecotourism – an activity which, if properly managed, could bring much greater economic rewards to local communities than fishing alone.

HEALTH OF THE OCEANS

The marine and coastal environments of the Indonesian Archipelago have been considerably altered in the past few centuries. Many activities have had a negative, though often localised effect, on these ecosystems; resulting in a loss of biological resources and a steady worsening of the overall health of the seas. Almost every section of this environment is now affected by human activities. Tidal flats, for example, are threatened by a number of developments, including conversion to fish ponds and salt production ponds, reclamation, disturbance and netting of shorebirds, encroachment by villages, disposal of domestic and industrial waste and accumulation of toxic compounds. The most serious of these activities – given the high human population living within the coastal zones – relate to an alteration to the coastal habitat or an increase in domestic sewage which can lead to sudden bursts of algal growth ('algal blooms') which may asphyxiate all fish life in the shallow waters and represent a major health risk for humans living in the region.

Intertidal habitats – mangroves, seagrass meadows, mudflats and reefs – and species which frequent the land-sea interface (oysters, dugong, crabs, turtles, waders and

seabirds) are especially vulnerable to fouling, poisoning and death as a result of oil spills. The shipping lanes along which oil is transported – particularly those of the narrow Malacca, Sunda and Makassar straits – are studded with reefs and islands. These natural phenomena pose a constant threat of shipwreck and oil spillage to ships. Accidental oil spills or well blow-outs clearly threaten adjacent coastal environments, and those areas to which they are linked by currents. These may include areas of tourist development, important wetland nurseries for commercial fisheries species, seabird colonies and turtle nesting beaches.

Pollution problems are accentuated by the relatively enclosed nature of Indonesia's seas, which increases the residence time and concentration of noxious chemicals. Offshore drilling is a constant threat to the marine environment, as is the passage of more than 80,000 oil tankers through the Straits of Malacca each year – one of the world's busiest shipping lanes. Of particular concern is the extraction of oil resources. Apart from providing an important component of Indonesia's exports, oil is the main commercial energy source in the country.

Below: one of the Kepulauan Seribu (Thousand Islands) which stretch north of Jakarta. It is surrounded by coral flats.

Facing page: development with minimum aesthetic damage: the Kupu-Kupu (Butterfly) Hotel on the Ayung River, Ubud, Bali.

Following page: coral flats on the Aru Islands, Maluku. When the ground is too stony or sandy, or the waves are too strong, mangroves like these Rhizophora trees survive with difficulty.

MODERN PRESSURES AND THE FUTURE OF INDONESIA'S SEAS

Indonesia's coastal and marine environment is steadily attracting more and more attention from developers and planners. It is also being increasingly tapped to provide additional food for a steadily growing population. As these pressures continue to mount, there is a serious risk that further uncoordinated and inappropriate development will take place both in and around the coastal environment which, in the long-term, could lead to a gradual loss of natural resources and a worsening of social and environmental conditions for communities living in these regions.

Environmental- and social-related problems of the coastal zone are not uniformly distributed throughout the archipelago. Problems of pollution are, for example, much more severe around the port of Jakarta than on any of the Maluku islands, while ill-planned developments on the hinterlands of Java, Sumatra and Bali will also have greater consequences on the local environment than those of less-densely populated regions. Regardless of the location, however, every effort should be made to correct existing problems such as pollution from sewage or industrial outfalls, waste dumping at sea, inappropriate fishing practices and ill-sited developments. In addition, every effort should be made to ensure that the environmental impact of ongoing or planned developments is kept to a minimum in order to preserve the integrity and beauty of these abundant, valuable and often irreplaceable resources.

The wide distribution of marine and coastal resources throughout the country offers an exceptional opportunity, through careful development, to bring improvements in social welfare and food security and to provide a greater diversity of income-earning opportunities to less advantaged regions and coastal communities. Resources on the main islands are coming under growing pressure as the populations swell and demands for a better standard of living become more urgent.

Wise conservation of Indonesia's natural resources offers one practical solution to many of the problems currently facing this region. This includes the establishment, protection and management of additional protected areas in the coastal and marine environment, better management of fisheries, with strict regulations on catch size and fishing techniques, enforcement of stringent controls over mineral exploitation and extraction techniques, tighter controls on coastal developments, particularly in areas with exceptional levels of biological diversity such as near coral reefs, and the control of shipping and pollution. With these considerations in mind the Government of Indonesia plans to establish a marine protected area totalling some 200,000 square kilometres by the year 2000.

The oceans are the last great resource on Earth. The future of Indonesia's seas is very much the responsibility of her people and government. By the year 2000, Indonesia's population is expected to reach 215 million. There is increasing pressure on land-based resources that have traditionally been relied upon to support the quality of life of the Indonesian people. The productivity of these resources is now approaching its upper limit; to increase it further would require additional losses of natural forest to provide fertile soils for shifting cultivation, together with heavier application of artificial fertilizers to boost crop production, and of herbicides and pesticides to control pest attacks which are frequent and which often devastate large areas of crops. Neither of these developments is environmentally sound and can cause habitat degradation, loss of species and of natural resources such as clear, permanent water supplies. Experience of similar situations elsewhere in the world has shown that this should be avoided at all costs.

Given this scenario it is therefore most likely that more Indonesian people will begin to look to the resources of their country's coastal areas and open seas for enhanced economic development and employment opportunities. At present, Indonesia has a rich natural endowment in these areas which is sufficient to accommodate a growing population. However, urgent steps need to be taken to improve the coordination of marine and coastal resource development if their potential is to be realized fully. Indonesia has already taken positive steps towards developing a more representative system of protected areas, which should help preserve some of the most valuable biological and scenic sites from destruction. However, regardless of such efforts, the marine environment remains a changing, integrated one and it is not sufficient to concentrate on simply protecting a few selected sites and hope that the remainder of the ecosystem will look after itself. There has never been a greater need for coordination in the management of the region's marine and coastal resources; mounting pressures from economic and social desires to exploit and develop these ecosystems must be matched by a strong environmental component. This will ensure that these fragile environments are not abused in a wasteful or otherwise inappropriate manner; rather that they are carefully and willingly managed for the long-term health of the environment. In its natural state, a healthy environment brings innumerable benefits and pleasures to the people of Indonesia and the many visitors who come to share, enjoy and appreciate the country's rich culture and natural beauty.

LAND

TROPICAL FORESTS

Images of steaming, decaying jungle, marauding tigers, crocodiles, mosquitoes, bloated leeches, savage tribesmen and worse horrors lurking behind giant trees were once popular images of tropical forests.

Today, thoughts are more commonly focused on issues relating to conservation, tropical timber, indigenous people and, of course, wildlife.

The sinister nature of the jungle seems to have been overshadowed for the moment, and more benign and virtuous aspects of this exceptional environment – now usually referred to as tropical rain forest – and its vulnerability, are highlighted in its place.

A more realistic appreciation of a tropical forest lies somewhere between these two extremes. This appreciation encompasses the excitement of witnessing the spectacular wildlife the forests support, the fascination of understanding the ways in which the animals and plants have evolved to live together and off one another, and an increasing awareness of the need to protect the remaining vestiges of these majestic forests, for the benefit both of people and wildlife.

When humans first appeared on Earth, about half of the world's land surface was covered with trees. Today less than one-third remains forested. Over 4000 square kilometres of forest are cleared or degraded every week; an area almost equal in size to Lombok. Indonesia's forests currently cover about two-thirds of the land area and are probably, along with the oceans, one of the nation's most valuable natural resources.

MAGNIFICENT BUT FRAGILE

What are tropical forests? Straddling the Equator, tropical forests are one of Nature's greatest living manifestations. In no other environment on Earth has such a profusion of life, animal and plant, evolved to such levels of biological diversity and complexity. The stable climatic conditions near the Equator – the amount of sunshine and the day's

length change only marginally throughout the year, combined with the effect of copious light, warmth and moisture providing a hot-house atmosphere – encourage lush, prolific growth of plants of great variety within a rain forest. This growth, in turn, supports a wealth of insect and animal life which feeds on the plants as well as on each other in a complex web of survival. Living together, in the humid tropical forest, they create and maintain what is probably the most ecologically diverse ecosystem on the planet.

No two tropical forests are the same: some occur in relatively dry tropical regions, where temperatures and rainfall vary according to the season; while others occur in some of the wettest areas on Earth, where rainfall and temperature remain fairly constant throughout the year. Both of these broad forest categories, as well as the various intermediate types, are extremely diverse in terms of the range of wildlife each supports. Different trees and plants have adapted to specific niches within these habitats. In one hectare of tropical rain forest it is common to find well over a hundred different kinds of tall tree. This is almost as many as the complete native tree flora of Europe.

Tropical rain forests – the most widespread forests in Indonesia – are very wet places. Rainfall is not constant, but tends to fall in concentrated downpours that send even the animals scurrying for shelter. The combination of warmth and water makes the trapped air beneath the forest canopy very humid; often saturated with water. But water brings life to the rain forest – in great abundance.

Tropical forests have long been misunderstood. They are commonly viewed as a source of quickly exploitable resources. The land can be cleared and used for commercially viable activities such as agriculture. It is not usually recognized that tropical forests grow under some of the most vulnerable conditions on Earth – on some of the poorest soils, under the hottest conditions and in areas which receive some of the highest levels of rainfall in the world – sometimes up to 6000 millimetres a year. These areas have often been referred to as 'green deserts'. Strip away the forest and the fragile soils are exposed to torrential rainfall which leaches out the nutrients; eventually, the soil itself is washed away, leaving a barren landscape capable of supporting only greatly degraded vegetation. Plants and animals that have taken millions of years to evolve vanish with the forest. Fortunately this is not the whole story: there are extensive areas of Java and Bali which were once forested and today remain verdant; and, in Sumatra, 2.5 million hectares support rubber forest smallholdings.

FOREST STRUCTURE

The structure of the rain forest is dictated by sunlight. Indonesia's forests resemble a kaleidoscope of plants, each acting as a sophisticated chemical factory. All green plants use solar energy to manufacture simple sugars from water and carbon dioxide absorbed from the atmosphere, in a process known as photosynthesis. These sugars can be used immediately to fuel growth or for respiration, or may be stored in the plant's tissues.

Height is of considerable importance. If a light-demanding plant does not grow, it risks being over-shadowed by its neighbours and condemned to shade where, starved of light, it cannot flourish and may die. (Some trees die if exposed to full sunlight.) Forests are not the random collection of odd-shaped and -sized trees and bushes they first appear to be. A cross-section of the forest reveals a structure; firstly, emergent trees with broad crowns which protrude from the main canopy. Below this lies a second layer of large trees with wide spreading crowns which make up the main canopy. Lower down are yet more trees still growing towards the canopy in search of light. Finally, depending on the type of forest, a series of subsidiary layers occurs with smaller trees, bushes, herbs and flowering plants. These live in a twilight world; less than three per cent of the light falling on the canopy filters to the ground. Here some species, specially adapted to living in the shade, are found.

Contrary to popular opinion, fostered by the lushness of the tropical forest, the soils of tropical forests are not especially rich in minerals or nutrients. A relatively small proportion of the nutrients in a tropical forest lies in the soil; most of them are stored in trunks and larger branches, as well as roots of plants. A wide range of organisms such as bacteria, fungi, soil animals and, of course, the roots of millions of plants compete for whatever minerals are available. These essential growth products are often therefore limited resources. In their quest for survival many trees have developed a close association with certain fungi which assist with the capture and uptake of some of these vital nutrients. These mycorrhizal fungi, as they are known, penetrate the plant's roots and live off the carbohydrates in the root system. In return, they extract precious nutrients from the soil through delicate thread-like extensions (fungal hyphae), and channel these back into the plants. Many species of plant cannot grow without the assistance of these tiny fungi, and on nutrient-poor soils the proportion of species with a mycorrhiza increases.

Tropical forests contain two crucial interfaces – the ground and the canopy layer. At the lower end, a continuous process is under way, breaking down and recycling materials that fall from the canopy, such as leaves, fruit, branches and even dead animals. Living within the forest soil are large armies of termites which play an essential role in breaking down dead organic matter, chiefly leaves and decaying timber, liberating these to the plants as recycled nutrients. Beneath the scant litter layer of fallen leaves, hundreds of species of ant perform similar functions.

At the upper interface of the forest, similar activities are taking place as insects, birds and even mammals such as monkeys and squirrels pollinate the day- and night-blossoms of the many tree species, helping to ensure a successful fruit crop. The seeds of some species are eaten by these animals and scattered around the forests as they range, widening the distribution of these plants.

Such intricate patterns of living are commonplace in the tropical forest. Most nutrients are not wasted (barring occurences like material falling into rivers); this would be a major loss of valuable and limited nutrients. Left to its own devices the rain

Facing page: looking up at the forest canopy reveals some of the organized structure of the rain forest; some sunlight filters through to the ground layer while the vast majority is absorbed by the broad, spreading crowns. It is noticeable that the branches of neighbouring trees do not touch. Scientists estimate that as much as half of the Earth's animal life may live within the canopy layer.

Rhinoceros beetle.

Stag beetle.

Below: bees are one of the many pollinating agents for palm flowers. With their bulk and coarse bristles they collect large amounts of pollen from the male flowers which are later deposited on other palm flowers.

HOW PLANTS GET AROUND

Reproduction is crucial to survival. Being rooted in one place can be a major hinderance to this process, particularly in the crowded accommodation of the tropical rain forest. To overcome this disadvantage many plants have developed close relationships with a range of animals.

The first stage of reproduction is pollination – the transfer of pollen from the male part of the flower to the female part. Many plants rely on the light pollen grains being borne on the wind to other flowers of the same species. A more reliable technique involves attracting an insect or bird to the flower with the offer of rich nectar, pollen being transferred to the animal which then flies on to deposit it on another flower of the same species. Bees, butterflies and sunbirds fulfil this role by day, while many night-flowering plants rely on moths and bats to perform a similar service.

Once the flowers have been successfully pollinated, seeds are produced. Many trees and flowering plants encase these seeds in a nutritious fruit coating. Encouraged to eat these fruits, animals ingest large amounts of seeds, most of which pass through the gut without being damaged. In some species, passage through the gut of an animal is essential to stimulate germination. Far ranging species such as primates, hornbills and elephant ensure that the seeds are transported and deposited over a wide area, far away from the parent plant. Without these mediators, many seeds would remain on the ground surrounding the parent plants – struggling in their shade.

Facing page: proboscis monkey.

Left: spotted cuscus.

Below: tree shrew.

play a vital role in controlling the world's climate and in regulating water cycles. In recent times they have also provided us with useful food plants – many of which have since been cultivated successfully – as well as important medicinal plants and others that have proved vital for the growth and development of industry. We have by no means exhausted the supply of valuable items which can be 'borrowed' from forests. The protection of the Indonesia's natural forests is therefore of the utmost importance to Indonesia and the rest of the world.

LIFE UNDER THE ROOF

Looking down on the forest from above, the vista is of a sea of rippling leaves with occasional dark chasms between trees. This garden in the air forms one of the main concentrations of life in the forest. The backbone of Indonesia's forests is clearly its large trees, many of which rise straight up from the ground for 45 metres or more before halting as a thick canopy of lofty, swaying, green crowns. Incredible as it may seem, some trees grow even taller, rising another 20-25 metres above this platform, their equally large crowns perched on stout trunks resembling the massive columns of a cathedral. These 'emergent' trees, as they are termed, are frequently dipterocarp species, abundant in Sumatra and Borneo. Dipterocarps are of considerable ecological and commercial importance. Dipterocarps obtain additional anchorage from broad, fin-like buttress structures around the base. These specialized support systems are found at the

forest is a balanced, self-sufficient system which depends on rapid recycling for its very existence.

A first time visitor to an Asian tropical forest is always bewildered by the paucity of wildlife on show. Where is the seething mass of wildlife that they have read about and seen on television? Unlike the vast, unbroken vistas of the African savannas, tropical forests do not provide easy views of the resident wildlife and the great dipterocarp forests are relatively poor in food supplies, thus sustaining only moderate animal populations. Yet tropical forests are one of the richest ecosystems in the world in terms of the diversity of wildlife. The animals and plants are there – it's largely a question of patience and knowing where to look. With a little experience, one can soon begin to appreciate some of the natural wonders that are only found in these rich but shrinking habitats. A privileged glimpse of an orang-utan swinging from a vine, the inquisitive and playful antics of a tree shrew, a 'leaf' that becomes a butterfly when you pass by, a beautiful orchid that blooms for just a few hours before withering, even the footprints of a rhinoceros or tiger – two of the most endangered species in Indonesia's forests – can provide an unforgettable experience.

The vast majority of the forest's inhabitants do, however, avoid the detection of most visitors, but this is not entirely deliberate. Most of the larger animals and almost all of the birds and insects live in a part of the forest that few people get to see at close quarters: the canopy of leaves, towering some 40-50 metres above the ground. Nowhere else in the forest is there such profusion of life. Rather than being a separate, isolated level, however, there is a constant passage of animal life between the canopy and the ground layers: at peak hours, trees and climbing plants act as major highways of activity for ants, squirrels, lizards and other species.

Tropical forests are crucial to life on Earth. Together with the forests of the colder temperate regions, they are the powerhouses of the planet and

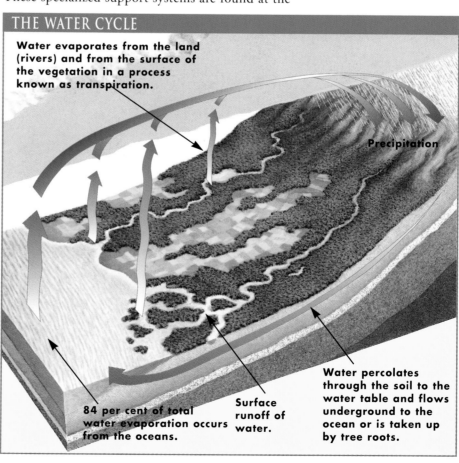

THE WATER CYCLE

Water evaporates from the land (rivers) and from the surface of the vegetation in a process known as transpiration.

Precipitation

84 per cent of total water evaporation occurs from the oceans.

Surface runoff of water.

Water percolates through the soil to the water table and flows underground to the ocean or is taken up by tree roots.

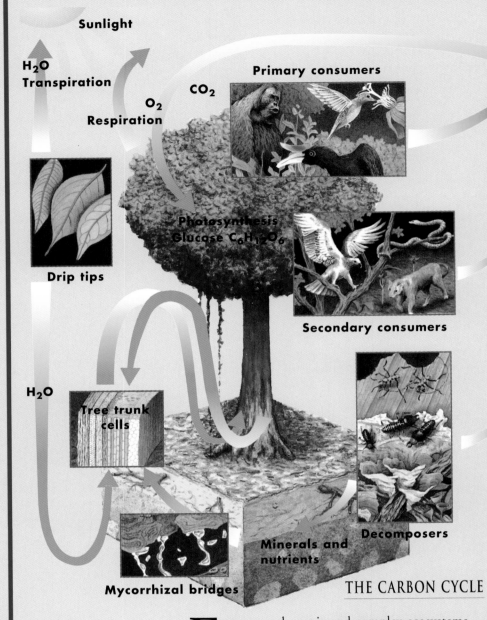

Sunlight

H₂O
Transpiration

O₂
Respiration

CO₂

Primary consumers

Photosynthesis
Glucose C₆H₁₂O₆

Drip tips

Secondary consumers

CO₂

H₂O

Tree trunk cells

Minerals and nutrients

Decomposers

Mycorrhizal bridges

THE CARBON CYCLE

Forests are dynamic and complex ecosystems. A forest is not merely a stand of trees. It is an assemblage of trees, the substrate on which they depend for support, nutrients and moisture, the others plants with which they interact, the animals that feed on them, a wide range of micro-organisms, and the soil and atmospheric conditions that influence the distribution and abundance of all organisms in the forest. Forests are largely self-sustaining; they require only water and sunlight. All other requirements, particularly nutrients, are obtained and secured by an effective method of recycling. Forest ecosystems are always changing and are resilient; they possess the ability to restore themselves if external disturbances are not too drastic. This ability to adapt and yet sustain themselves is a remarkable feature, particularly evident in tropical forest ecosystems.

THE FLOW OF ENERGY
The study of forest ecology is concerned with the movement of energy and nutrients between and within the biotic and abiotic components. The energy source for every ecosystem is sunlight which is required by all green plants for their growth. Carbon dioxide, nitrogen gas and water hold vital carbon, nitrogen, and hydrogen atoms. Through photosynthesis, plants capture and lock up about one per cent of the sun's energy which reaches Earth. Green plants and some types of bacteria use either solar or chemical energy to convert simple inorganic molecules, such as carbon dioxide and water, into complex organic compounds, such as glucose and other compounds necessary for life. These organisms are termed 'producers'. Producer plants contain chlorophyll (a green pigment) and other pigments which absorb different wavelengths of solar energy.

Organisms feeding either directly or indirectly on producers are called 'consumers', since they cannot themselves manufacture the organic nutrients they need to stay alive. An organism that consumes producers is called a 'primary consumer' or 'herbivore' (plant-eater). Herbivores in turn are consumed by 'secondary consumers' or 'carnivores' (meat-eaters). Most of the dead organic matter in a forest ecosystem consists of dead plant material, animal corpses, animal wastes and dead micro-organisms. Of these, plant litter – dead leaves, fallen trees, decaying branches and rotting fruit – is the most important. Organisms which obtain nutrients through the breakdown of these waste products of living organisms into simpler substances are called 'decomposers'. In wet tropical environments, the decomposition process is rapid and constant. Within many tropical rain forest ecosystems the majority of the nutrient reserve is held in the plants and the litter layer of the forest floor. Decomposition of litter and the subsequent release of nutrients is, therefore, a vital part of the nutrient recycling process.

NUTRIENT RECYCLING
The flow of nutrients in forest ecosystems forms a complex pattern. Some elements move predominantly between the living organisms and the atmosphere, whereas others generally move between the organisms and the soil. Some elements follow both pathways. There is also an internal cycle within plants and animals which acts to conserve nutrients within individual organisms. Based on these differences, the cyclic movement of elements in ecosystems can be assigned to one or more of three major types: geochemical cycles (exchanges of chemicals between ecosystems), biogeochemical cycles (exchange of chemicals within ecosystems) and biochemical cycles (redistribution of chemicals within individual organisms). Of all of these, the biogeo-

chemical cycle is the most important for forest ecosystems. Inorganic elements are obtained from the atmosphere or soils. Chemical elements present in organic foods are absorbed by animals and microbes and are returned to the atmosphere and soils through respiration and decomposition. A number of key elements are recycled.

The carbon cycle (opposite) illustrates how carbon dioxide is converted into organic matter via photosynthesis. In turn, it is released by living organisms into the atmosphere through respiration. Nutrients, other than carbon, are obtained by terrestrial plants mainly from soils. The nitrogen cycle relies on nitrogen stored in the soil, mainly in the form of nitrate and ammonium ions. Some bacteria found in soils are capable of 'fixing' nitrogen as are some specialized blue-green algae.

Mineral elements that constitute vital nutrients are derived mainly from the breakdown of organic matter in the soil. Nutrient uptake from the soil occurs via the fine root hairs of plants. The uptake is often assisted by the presence of mycorrhizae: fungal filaments act as a bridge between the root and mineral solutions in the soil or decomposing matter, facilitating the speedy uptake of nutrients such as phosphorus. Physical breakdown of rocks and sub-soils, through weathering caused by rain and wind erosion, also results in the release of nutrients into the soil, as does chemical weathering of rocks which is very rapid in the tropics.

THE FABRIC OF FOREST ECOSYSTEMS

An ecological niche is the place where a particular species – plant or animal – lives and where all the physical, chemical and biological factors that it needs to survive and reproduce are available. It is a reflection of how individual species fit into the ecosystem – how they transform matter and energy and how they respond to and modify their physical and biotic environment. The ecological niche should not be confused with an organism's habitat, which is its physical location or locations. A common analogy is that an organism's habitat refers to its 'address' in an ecosystem and its ecological niche to its 'occupation' or 'lifestyle'. For example, the habitat of the Kuhl's sunbird, *Aethopyga eximia*, includes the edge of montane forests and plantations. Its ecological niche includes trees for nesting, its food and the pollen it disperses through its habit of feeding on nectar. According to the competitive exclusion principle, 'no two species in the same ecosystem can occupy exactly the same ecological niche indefinitely'. The more similar the niches of two species, the more they will compete for the same food, shelter, space and other resources. Different species, however, can occupy similar ecological niches in different ecosystems. The niche concept helps explain why the population size of the various species in a stable ecosystem remains fairly constant in the long run regardless of the

number of offspring a species can have. The carrying capacity, or maximum number of individuals of each species that can live in a particular ecosystem indefinitely, is set by the number of niche spaces available for the species.

LIVING TOGETHER

Populations of different species living in the same biological community can interact in a number of ways, mainly through competition, predation or symbiosis. These phenomena can affect both the structure and function of forest ecosystems by changing population sizes and by altering energy flows through food webs.

As long as commonly-used resources are abundant, they can be shared by different species. However, when two or more species in the same ecosystem attempt to use the same scarce resources, there is competition. For example, if one tree species can multiply and grow faster than others, it can create a dense overhead canopy that prevents other shade-iintolerant species from flourishing.

The most obvious form of species interaction is predation. Predation results in the death of the organism. Although usually thought of in terms of animal-animal interactions, it can also involve plant-animal interactions and even plant-plant interactions. A beetle boring into a seed is a predator, as are carnivorous plants, like pitcher plants (*Nepenthes*), which catch and digest insects.

An interaction in which two or more species benefit from living together, is called symbiosis. There are three major types of symbiosis: mutualism, commensalism, and parasitism. Mutualism is a symbiotic relationship between two different species in which both parties benefit. For example, butterflies and bees depend on flowers for food in the form of pollen and nectar. In turn, the flowering plants depend on pollinating insects to carry the male reproductive cells contained in their pollen grains to the female flowering parts of other flowers of the same species. Among commensal species one benefits from the association while the other is apparently neither helped nor harmed. Epiphytes, for example, use host trees to gain access to sunlight. They also use their own leaves and cupped petals to collect water and minerals that drip down from the tops of trees. The tree neither gains nor loses from this relationship. Parasitism, on the other hand, is when one species benefits to the detriment of another. The parasite usually obtains most of its nourishment from the host. Examples of parasites include leeches, ticks and some fungi and some vines.

Above: the black sunbird is a specialist nectar feeder, its long, curved beak can reach down the narrow collars of many flowers to the nutritious food which the plant provides to attract pollinators.

Above: two of Indonesia's many species of orchid.

Right: a slice through an epiphytic Myrmecodia plant reveals an inner mosaic of tunnels and chambers, some of which are used to hold ant eggs and larvae, as well as insect carcasses scavenged from the forest floor.

Facing page: strangling figs start life as epiphytes, whose aerial roots reach the ground and take root. They may hasten the death of the host tree by depriving its crown of sunlight. As the host tree dies and decays, the hollow framework of lattice-like roots of the fig tree provides an important refuge for many small mammals, lizards and birds.

base of many tall trees of lowland forests, providing added strength at the weakest point of the tree, particularly in shallow or wet soils where roots do not penetrate and where the substrate affords little anchorage.

Beneath the canopy are medium-sized trees which rely on whatever light penetrates. Further down, others take what advantage they can of very heavily filtered, dappled lighting. Where virtually no sunlight filters through the canopy the forest floor supports relatively little plant life. Apart from the raised, intricate network of tree roots and a thin layer of leaf litter and occasional fallen branches, there may be a scattering of slow-growing seedlings and herbs. Whenever a large gap in the canopy does occur, such as that following the demise of one of the forest giants, a landslide or a fire, certain shade-demanding species may die but there is also a terrific surge of growth as other species of tree, flowers and climbers boost their growth rate in a mad scramble towards the precious light and a means of securing and dominating that space. Vigorous light-tolerant species are the first to prosper, creating favourable conditions for seeds of shade-tolerant species to germinate and for the seedlings to grow and eventually supersede the initial gap fillers. This process, known as succession, is a daily occurrence in the battle for sunlight in the forest.

Climbing plants are an important component of tropical forests, especially lowland rain forests in Southeast Asia. Some climbers, like rattans and pitcher plants, start life as lowly rosette plants and then suddenly put out a long, slender stem which has some means of climbing. Some species have evolved special features to help them reach the sunlight: rattan, for example, has leaves tipped by flexible two metre long whips each armed with clusters of hooks which latch on to nearby trees, allowing them to reach the canopy roof. Others contend by

coiling themselves around their chosen host shortly after germinating, and growing with the plant. When they reach the canopy, climbing plants produce a profusion of leaves, competing with trees for sunlight.

Not all climbers grow from the ground up: so called 'strangling' figs, for example, do the opposite. Figs are a favourite food of many birds and mammals. The fig seeds pass through the gut and may be deposited in the tree tops where the animals feed. When one of these seeds germinates, a small bush develops, from which a long thin root emerges and grows downwards. Additional side roots also begin to form and gradually encircle the host tree, forming a lattice network of stout stem-like roots around it. The roots continue to grow until they reach the ground, where they tap into the soil as a normal root would do. Within a few years, deprived of sunlight in the canopy and nutrients at the soil level, the supporting tree will probably die before the younger fig tree. In time the tree decays to leave the now hollow, free-standing network of fig roots.

Another typical feature of primary rain forests is cauliflory, whereby flowers and fruit appear directly from the trunk of the tree rather than from the tips of branches. Two of the largest fruit, the durian (*Durio zibethinus*) and jackfruit (*Artocarpus heterophyllus*) are produced by this method. Some species of fig (*Ficus* spp.) also employ this technique of fruiting. Apparent advantages of this adaptation are that large fruit can be produced on account of the firm support provided by the trunk and that the fruit are within reach of some of the larger mammals of the forest, particularly elephants.

Little space is wasted in the forest. Thick, knotted woody climbers, with their crowns in the sky, reach up to the canopy from the soil where they obtain water and nutrients. Epiphytes, plants which have no connection with the ground, but grow

AN ANT AND A PLANT

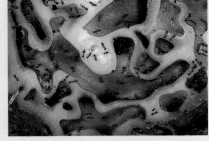

Two of the most common living organisms in a rain forest are ants and plants. Many epiphytes growing on nutrient-deficient soils have developed special relationships with ants. The heath forests, *kerangas*, of Kalimantan, provide one such example. Here the *Hydnophytum* epiphytic plant offers a safe home to a colony of ants in a swollen, tumour-like protruberance on the stem. Housed in this structure the ants gain the additional benefit of protection from predators such as pangolins and are able to raise their young in relative safety. The plant also gains from the relationship as the presence of ants deters leaf-eating animals and some of the food and faeces deposited by the ants in the cavities they occupy are absorbed by the plant.

Many types of ant-plant associations have developed in the rain forest, some plants even encourage ants to settle by producing sweet, sugary liquids. Many epiphytes also benefit from such associations, particularly plants of the genus *Myrmecodia*, as well as a range of ferns. Other plants, especially fast-growing species, ecourage ants to live in their hollow stems. In return for this accommodation, ants keep the tree free from potential attackers such as caterpillars and clinging vines.

TYPES OF FOREST IN INDONESIA

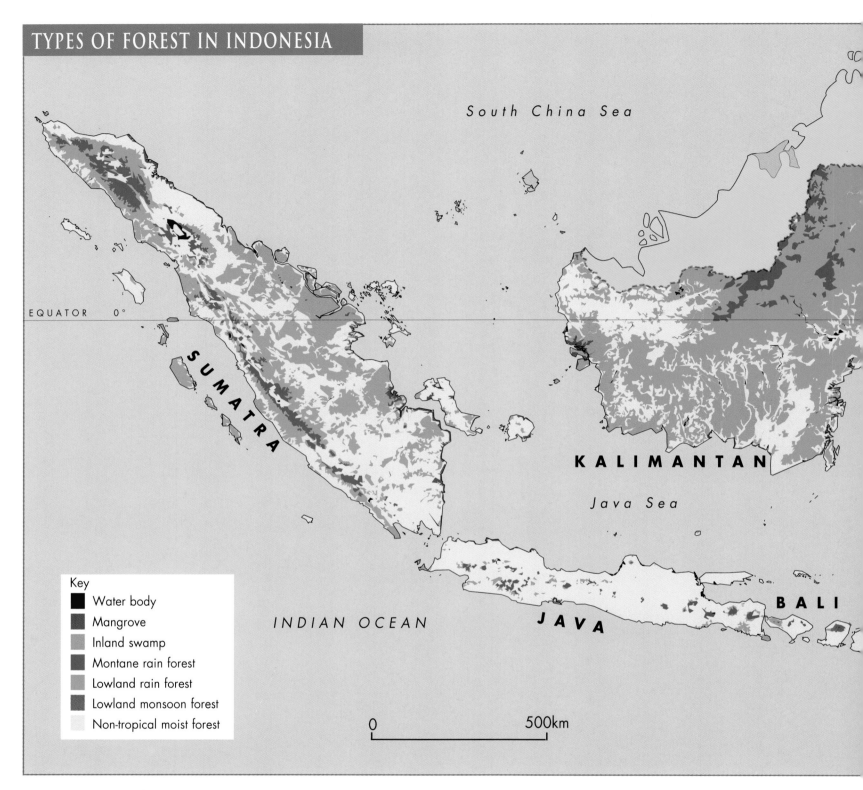

Key
- ■ Water body
- Mangrove
- Inland swamp
- Montane rain forest
- Lowland rain forest
- Lowland monsoon forest
- Non-tropical moist forest

South China Sea

EQUATOR 0°

SUMATRA

INDIAN OCEAN

JAVA

KALIMANTAN

Java Sea

BALI

0   500km

poised on other plants in the upper reaches of the canopy, are common features of tropical forests, often festooning the branches with leafy plants and colourful flowers. Some of these species are specially adapted to living only in the moist, shady parts of the canopy, while others, including exquisite orchids such as *Vanda tricolor,* are sun-loving species and occur high in the canopy. Most Indonesian orchids are epiphytes.

As different plants have evolved to suit the different niches of the forest layers, so too have the insects and animals. In some instances, close associations have formed between two or more species, each providing a benefit to the other.

FORESTS OF INDONESIA

The Indonesian Archipelago lies within a biogeographic region often referred to as Malesia – defining the geography and plant life of this part of the world. Malesia consists of ten distinct sub-regions: Sumatra, Java, Nusa Tenggara, Borneo, Sulawesi, Maluku, New Guinea, Peninsular Malaysia, The Philippines and the Solomon Islands. In such a vast area, with so many different soil and climatic conditions, it is not surprising that a wide range of forests is represented.

The forests of Sundaland alone are characterized by an enormously rich tropical flora. Java, with a mere 4600 species of native flowering plants, is one

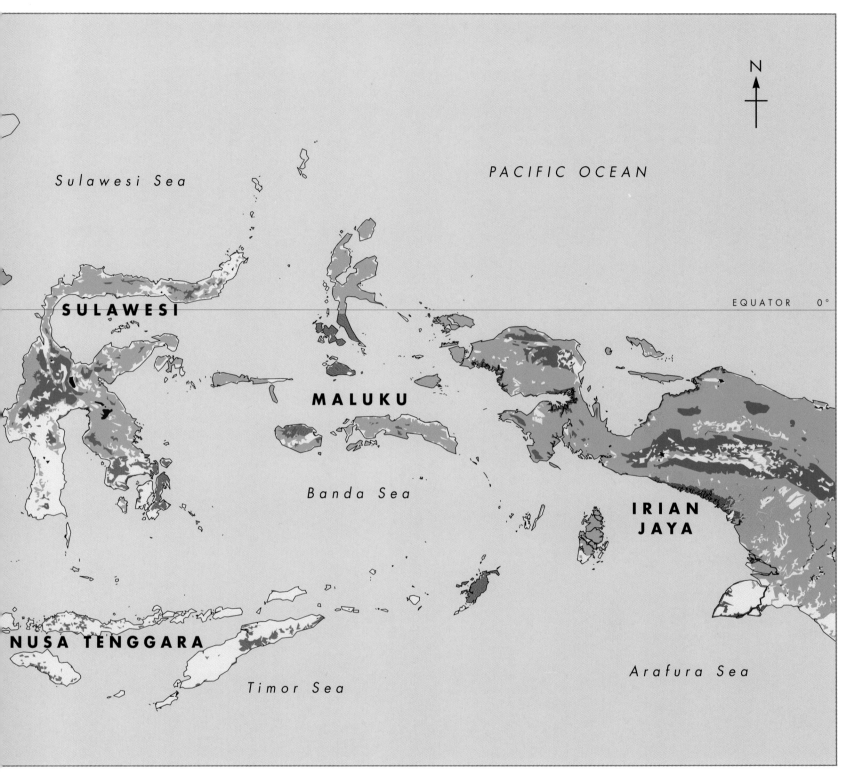

N

of the poorer islands in terms of floral diversity. Ancient and more recent volcanic eruptions, together with greater aridity and the actions of man, are responsible for the relatively low level of plants represented. Other regions such as Irian Jaya, the western part of New Guinea, have approximately 9000 species of flowering plants, of which some 90 per cent are endemic.

The main forest types encountered in Indonesia range from evergreen lowland dipterocarp forests in Sumatra and Kalimantan, to seasonal monsoon forests and savanna grasslands in Nusa Tenggara, and non-dipterocarp lowland forests and alpine ecosystems in Irian Jaya. Other major habitat types

that occur are peat swamps and freshwater swamps (both of which are particularly extensive in Sumatra, Kalimantan and Irian Jaya), heath forests (Kalimantan supports the largest area of this vegetation type in Southeast Asia), forests on limestone and ultrabasic rocks (Sulawesi has the most ultrabasic habitats on Earth), lower and upper montane forests and alpine meadows such as those on the highest mountains of Irian Jaya, Sumatra and Java.

Of these, by far the most extensive, with an estimated area of 780,000 square kilometres (41 per cent of the total land area) is lowland rain forest. Tropical lowland forests are characterised by prolific growth and the high levels of biomass they

Above: the distribution of major forest types in Indonesia, from information supplied by the World Conservation Monitoring Centre, Cambridge, UK.

contain, by the conspicuous presence of large, woody climbing plants, large buttressed trees and the prevalence of trees with tall, smooth-barked trunks. Other adaptations by which plants have evolved include leaves with unserrated edges and 'drip tips', designed to let water run off easily. In contrast to northern temperate forests that grow on soils with high levels of organic matter, lowland forests, such as those of Sumatra, hold most of

their organic matter in the crowns (about 60 per cent), while less than 40 per cent is in the soil and just one per cent in the leaf litter. Brightly-coloured flowers are scarce in lowland rain forests; splashes of colour often signify the presence of fungi rather than flowers.

Monsoon forests and savannas – areas with true deciduous plant growth – cover much of East Java, Nusa Tenggara, Sulawesi and the southern parts of New Guinea where the influence of the dry south-eastern monsoon winds is most strongly felt. These forests are mixed in composition, but not particularly rich in species. When conditions are

INDONESIA'S FORESTS

Sub-alpine vegetation 3200–3800 metres

Cloud forest

Upper montane forest 2000–3200 metres

Montane forest 900–2000 metres

Rain forest 0–900 metres

unfavourable a common response for some trees is to shed their leaves. Fire is quite common in some of these areas and in some cases may be required, to stimulate seed germination by cracking open the tough outer casing of the seed, as with species of the *Leguminosae* and *Myrtacae*.

Mangrove forests are a highly specialized form of growth, found in a habitat where changes of salinity, water temperature and nutrients are a twice-daily event.

Mangrove

species have developed a series of adaptations to deal with the constantly high saline conditions which surround their roots, and for living on poor soils with low nutrient and oxygen contents. An estimated 44,000 square kilometres of mangrove forests remain in Indonesia (2.3 per cent of the land area), the largest area extant in Southeast Asia. Mangroves play a number of important environmental roles, such as protecting offshore coral reefs from excessive sedimentation and providing important feeding, breeding and nursery areas for coastal and deep sea fish, crustaceans, molluscs and other aquatic wildlife. Mangrove forests in Indonesia were little affected by large scale forest exploitation until 1975, but are now probably one of the most threatened in Southeast Asia. Conversion of mangrove areas to agriculture, brackish water fishponds, salt ponds and space for human settlement, as well as felling for conversion to woodchips and export to Japan for the production of cellulose and paper, now seriously threatens the remaining stands of forest.

Inland swamps are extensive in Indonesia and support a specific type of forest. Swamp forests are today the second most extensive type of forest within the archipelago, with almost 180,000 square kilometres remaining. Many of these grow along the lowlying eastern coasts of Sumatra and the western and southern coasts of Borneo; some parts of southwestern New Guinea are also cov-

Left: emergent rain forest tree; a strangling fig has begun to grow at the top of the trunk.

Below: contrasting environments – Irian Jaya's mountains are snow-covered all year round.

Savanna

Mangrove

ered in swamp forest. Freshwater swamp forests are frequently waterlogged and many trees have buttress roots for support. Palms are especially abundant in freshwater swamps and there is little undergrowth.

Peat swamp forests differ from freshwater swamp forests in that the former grow on dry, brittle soils that overlay a dense mixture of water, decaying plants and timber. On this substrate, trees do not need buttress roots for support. These forests are characterized by poor soils and many slender trees with abundant undergrowth. Palms are, again, a common species.

Another related type of forest, now, mainly confined to Kalimantan, is heath forest, or *kerangas,* meaning 'forested land that if cleared will not grow rice'. This type of forest is characterized by fairly small, short trees that form a single storey canopy.

Climbing out of the lowlands, different forest types are encountered that are generally more open in structure than those seen in lowland forests. As more light reaches the forest floor, there is a greater profusion of small trees, bushes and ground foliage. At mid levels there is a preponderance of oaks and

laurels. With increasing altitude, tall trees give way to smaller varieties and grasses, while herbs and ferns become more common. Members of the heather family, for example rhododendrons, are found at 2000 metres and above. There is less animal life in these regions than in the lowlands.

Montane forests, or 'elfin forests', occur at an altitudinal range of 1000-3000 metres. There are approximately 141,000 square kilometres of this forest type remaining in Indonesia – 7.4 per cent of the land area. These enchanting forests consist of dwarf, stunted trees that rarely reach more than 10 metres, and are sometimes just knee-high. The trees, often standing at angles as a result of strong winds, are usually twisted and gnarled. In contrast to the trees of lowland forests, their low branches support a single layer of foliage. Their leaves are frequently small in order to reduce moisture loss to the wind and sun. Epiphytes are common in montane forests, often festooning the trunks as well as the branches. Mosses are among the most abundant of these, together with ferns, lichens and orchids. Frequently shrouded in mist, the montane zone is also home to many species of carnivorous plant. One such plant is *Nephentes,* which relies on trapping errant insects as its main source of food.

Many of Indonesia's highest volcanic peaks are active with jets of sulfurous gases roaring from apertures in the rock within and around the craters. Where the steam condenses, pure crystals of sulphur build up in thick encrustations. In the immediate vicinity of craters, where the atmosphere is heavy with sulphurous fumes and the ground is loosely packed volcanic rubble, no plants grow. Lower down, however, typical montane vegetation includes low, compact bushes such as *Melastoma* sp. and the tiny wintergreen, *Gaultheria nummularioides,* a relative of rhododendrons.

Scattered throughout the Indonesian Archipelago are many outcrops of limestone which support their own specialized flora. These sites are prone to desiccation and plants growing in these regions must be able to overcome periodic water shortages. Trees tend to be small and scarce, but there is often a rich flora of herbs.

WHAT'S SO SPECIAL ABOUT FORESTS?

Right: primary rain forest.

Below: a slender young tree seedling with moss growing on it.

Facing page: view of lush vegetation from Temminck's plates – a mid-nineteenth century publication containing full colour plates of Indonesia's fauna, flora and natural landscapes.

THE VALUE OF TROPICAL FORESTS

Tropical forests are ancient, complex ecosystems. Those we see today support one of the most spectacular and biologically important living communities on Earth and are the result of an evolutionary process that began some four billion years ago. Over the millennia, species have evolved to meet changing environmental conditions, gradually adapting their behaviour and/or structure to allow them to take better advantage of their habitats. Some new species have evolved to meet these conditions while others, unable to change sufficiently well or in time, have become extinct. Like the vibrant, dynamic nature of the forest, the process of evolution continues: day and night.

In addition to the incalculable number of animals and plants which they support, forests worldwide are home to millions of people, providing them with food, clothing, medicines, shelter, building materials and fuel. They are also the primary source of such products for a much greater number of people who live far removed from the forest. In addition to such material goods, most forests provide many other, less obvious, services which are often not fully appreciated until the forests have been all but destroyed. Among these services are the maintenance of soil fertility through regular additions of nutrients from leaf fall, prevention of soil erosion by binding the soil around the roots of the plants, regulation of water runoff and the playing of a vital role in maintaining a stable regional and world climate.

INDONESIA'S CASE

Tropical rain forests once covered the greater part of the Indonesian Archipelago – the main exceptions being the southern islands of eastern Java, Madura, Bali, Nusa Tenggara, and parts of Maluku and Irian Jaya which bore tropical monsoon forests. Although a considerable amount of former forest habitat has been lost, Indonesia contains more tropical rain forest than any other nation in the Asia-Pacific region – an estimated 1,148,400 square kilometres – including some of the most species-rich forests on Earth. Within the archipelago, forest cover ranges from seven per cent on Java to 92 per cent on Irian Jaya.

THE SIGNIFICANCE OF BIOLOGICAL DIVERSITY

Biological diversity, or 'biodiversity' as it is often called, refers to the number of species of plants and animals and micro-organisms in the system under consideration. On another level it can refer to genetic diversity within a species, or ecosystem diversity. The biological diversity we see today in the forests, seas, deserts, mountains and snow fields is the result of several billion years of evolution.

All life on Earth is part of an intricate system which depends on and directly influences the non-living components of the planet – rocks, soil, water and air. Disturbing one part of this biosphere can disturb other parts. Nature is often far too complex for us to understand or even to be aware of some of the relationships that exist. The species and ecosystems that are the basic components of the environment are like links in a chain; if one of those links is broken the system cannot function properly. Sometimes we know that links are being broken, as a dam is constructed or the last member of a species disappears from the Earth, but for the most part we are unaware of what is happening.

The exact number of species on Earth is unknown. Scientists have already named about 1.7 million species of living organisms, but current estimates for the total number range from 5 to 100 million. Of the global total, about 1.03 million are animals and 248,000 higher plants. However, despite these impressive numbers, we can really only say that we know a little about 9000 species of mammals, 9900 birds and 260,000 plants – perhaps less than one per cent of all known species. Therefore we remain relatively ignorant about the natural richness of the Earth. As our knowledge of the importance of biological diversity increases, however, we are becoming aware of the losses to it that are taking place as large tracts of forest and wetlands are destroyed in many parts of the world.

(1) Green tree python.
(2) Young Brahminy kite.
(3) Liana.
(4) Tarsier.
(5) Proboscis monkey.
(6) Great red flying
    squirrel.
(7) Sun bear.
(8) Pitcher plant.
(9) Rafflesia.
(10) Stork-billed
     kingfisher.
(11) Tapir.
(12) Tiger.
(13) Rhinoceros hornbill.
(14) Epiphyte.
(15) White-handed gibbon.
(16) Slow loris.
(17) Orang-utan.
(18) Javan rhinoceros.
(19) Strangling fig.
(20) Rajah Brooke
     birdwing.
(21) Great argus pheasant.
(22) Monitor lizard.

1 *Eastern tarsier.*
2 *Praying mantis.*
3 *Assassin bug.*
4 *Blue-tailed pitta.*
5 *Brahminy kite.*
6 *Green python.*
7 *Sugar glider.*

Indonesia's species-rich forests harbour the world's greatest diversity of palms (477 species, of which 225 occur nowhere else), more than 400 species of dipterocarp (the most valuable commercial timber trees in Southeast Asia) and an estimated 25,000 species of flowering plants. Indonesia's riches are also apparent among the wildlife: it ranks first in the world for mammals (515 species, of which 36 per cent are endemic), first for swallowtail butterflies (121 species, of which 44 per cent are endemic), third for reptiles (with more than 600 species), fourth for birds (1519 species, of which 28 per cent are endemic), fifth for amphibians (270 species) and seventh for flowering plants.

Conserving biological diversity is not solely concerned with the immediate preservation of plants and animals that provide some useful service. One of the most important reasons for protecting biological diversity relates to the range of genetic material represented in Nature. Each individual contains millions of genes, which determine how it will develop; and there are subtle differences between genes of different organisms, allowing them to adapt and evolve to ever-changing conditions. Although we cannot witness those changes taking place, preserving genetic diversity is of vital importance. Countries such as Indonesia, which are heavily reliant on one or two main crops for sustaining the population, will always be vulnerable to virus attacks such as the grassy stunt virus which decimated many rice crops throughout Southeast Asia in the early 1970s. It was only thanks to a wild strain of rice from India that resistance to this virus was discovered – and then introduced by crossbreeding to popular varieties of rice. Similar experiences of important domestic crops being saved from widespread destruction (coffee, potato, cotton and maize), thanks to a wild plant, have been documented from around the world, and serve as constant reminders of the need to conserve Nature in its entirety.

The extinction of species has always been a natural event in the evolutionary process. But what is of great concern today is that the rate of extinction has accelerated markedly in recent centuries. Scientists believe that as many as 400 species and sub-species of birds and mammals have become extinct in the past 400 years; other estimates suggest a loss of 15-20 per cent of all species by the year 2000 – some 450,000-2,000,000 species. Few of these losses would be deliberate; by no means all would be noticed by man. And that, of course, is part of the problem. Often ignorance of the implications of our actions can push a species to the brink of extinction. Clear felling part of a forest, or draining a particular lake or wetland, can have disastrous consequences for a wide range of species that we know nothing about. Any loss of biological diversity is, in the long-term, potentially a major loss for the human population.

Why are such losses occurring? The main causes for such dramatic reductions in species numbers are associated with the steadily increasing human population and its environmental impact. The need to provide more food, and space for accommodation, industry and related activities, has resulted in widespread habitat loss. Evidence of this destructive process is most obvious and dramatic in and around tropical forests which, although they cover only 14 per cent of the Earth's surface, contain at least half of the world's species.

A loss of biological diversity affects everyone on Earth. Human beings could not exist without the abundance and diversity of Nature; all our food and many of our industrial materials and medicines are provided by plants, animals and micro-organisms – a large proportion of which live in tropical forests, or depend upon their well-being.

Conservation of biological diversity is essential to the sustainability of sectors as diverse as forestry, agriculture and fisheries, health care, science, industry and tourism. An estimated 90 per cent of the people of Indonesia live in rural areas. Their main activity is agriculture, with rice being the main staple. In addition, a range of other plants, particularly tubers, fruits and berries, most of them still growing in the wild, provide important supplementary foods through the year. Some of the country's fruit, for example durians and mangoes, are still obtained from the wild, gathered by hand and sold by the roadside and at local markets, from where it can end up in the capital, Jakarta, and other major urban centres. For others, fishing and hunting and trapping wild game are important sources of income and, for many, the primary source of protein. Recent investigations suggest that some 40 million Indonesians are directly dependent on biological diversity for subsistence. Of these, 12 million live in and around forests.

Many of Indonesia's biological resources are of considerable economic importance. More than 6000 species of plant and animal are used each day by the people of Indonesia, either taken directly from the wild or harvested from cultivated plants. Worldwide, many of the familiar plant species, that are now used in everyday life, originated in Indonesia, including cloves, sugar-cane, citrus (*C. grandis* and *C. microcarpa*), and many other tropical fruits.

Indonesia is the world's main producer of rattan – climbing palms – supplying 90 per cent of the total raw materials used worldwide. Rattans, of which there are more than 200 species, are widely

Above: basking in the sunshine, the fin-tailed lizard is a daylight predator of small mammals, birds and insects.

used in the making of cane furniture, mostly for international export markets. In 1985, Indonesia exported almost 150,000 tonnes of unprocessed rattan with a market value of about $US97 million. Within Indonesia rattans are widely used to produce mats, baskets, fish traps, dyes and medicines. The pressure from maintaining the valuable revenue from rattans, together with habitat destruction, has led to gross over-exploitation of certain species. In Kalimantan, some species have long been cultivated. This relieves pressure on wild stocks. Cultivated rattan now meets about ten per cent of market needs. No plantation rattan, however, can yet replace the wild thick *manau* rattan, the fruits of which are eaten by many animals, thus making it a very valuable plant within the forest ecosystem.

The traditional use of plants for medicine is an important activity in the tropics. The World Health Organization has estimated that 80 per cent of the people in developing countries rely on traditional medicines, generally based on wild plants and animals, for their primary health care. In

Indonesia, many plants are used for the production of *jamu* (herbal medicines). Until recently, this use was at a sustainable level. Today, however, increasing demand from industrial and pharmaceutical companies has led to some over-exploitation. Some species are now threatened – *Curcuma* sp. and

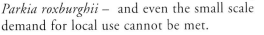

Parkia roxburghii – and even the small scale demand for local use cannot be met.

MAINTAINING THE BALANCE

Contrary to first impressions, tropical forests are fragile ecosystems. Gigantic trees perch on shallow, friable soils, although adaptations have evolved to help support these massive trees. Periods of drought, although rare, do occur in tropical forests. To cope with such events, trees may close down many of their normal operations such as fruiting, and may even shed their leaves to reduce loss of moisture to the atmosphere. The many plants and animals which live in the forests are attuned to such cycles and events and are usually able to modify their behaviour in some way to cope with natural periodic disturbances. A more serious intrusion, however – such as the removal of tree cover, the alteration of a river course or stream flow, or the removal of a particular species through over-hunting or over-collecting – can have far more deleterious, and even disastrous, consequences.

It has become increasingly apparent that complex, intricate relationships exist between very

many plants and animals within the confines of the forest; and scientists are continually discovering and detailing how these operate, connect and contribute to the overall working of the ecosystem. It is now known, for example, that certain trees produce seeds which must pass through the gut of a rhinoceros before they can germinate. Should the range of the Sumatran rhinoceros decrease further, it could mean the end for these trees, many of which may be of considerable economic potential. The durian, that 'King of Fruit', lauded by Alfred Russel Wallace who wrote, 'to eat durians is a new sensation, worth a voyage to the East to experience', also seems to rely on large mammals ingesting its seeds before they can germinate.

The plants and animals of a rain forest are mutually dependent upon one another – some to a substantial degree. These associations resemble a long chain which, intact, holds up the fabric of the forest. But if a link is broken, for example by removing a single species, the flow of events may be interrupted, perhaps irrevocably. The extent of such relationships can only be appreciated fully when one examines the minute details of the secret life of two mutually dependent species.

The flowers of the fig tree are pollinated exclusively by tiny fig wasps, each no larger than one millimetre (a pinhead) in size. When the female flowers open, newly-hatched female wasps fly to the figs, probably attracted by an odour. As they squeeze inside the immature fig they lose their wings and antennae. Wandering around inside the fig, looking for a place to lay her eggs, the wasp inadvertently transfers pollen to the flowers of the tree, pollinating it in the process. In time, the eggs develop and hatch; male wasps developing before females. These males then search for developing female pupae and fertilize them before they emerge. The male then chews a small tunnel through the fig to the outside. These tiny tunnels cause a change in the temperature and composition of the gas inside the fig, which seems to stimulate the development of male flowers and the subsequent emergence of the female wasps. As the females struggle to leave the now ripening fruit they collect pollen from the male flowers. Females leave the fruit through the tunnel constructed by the male and go in search of female figs to pollinate, beginning the cycle all over again.

Such delicate natural balances are easily disrupted. Without these tiny wasps, no figs would mature, robbing the primates, birds and insects that feed off these delicious fruit in the canopy, as well as the many forest floor dwellers who gorge on the fallen fruit, of an important food source. Unfortunately such links are being broken in Indonesia's forests as selected species are removed or driven from their natural homes as logging, hunting, mining and agricultural settlements spread through the archipelago.

INDONESIAN WILDLIFE

Above: frilled lizard.

Below: the stages in the development of an atlas moth.

Facing page: flying lizards can glide from tree to tree with the aid of a tough skin membrane supported on special ribs which grow from the animal's side.

The Indonesian Archipelago is inhabited by two distinct types of fauna of different origins. That of the west belongs mainly to the Indo-Malayan realm, while that in the east to the Pacific and Australian realms. Within the limits of the country, 47 distinct natural ecosystems have so far been identified, ranging from the ice fields and alpine meadows of Irian Jaya to a variety of humid lowland forests and from spectacular coral reefs to mangrove swamps.

Although Indonesia covers just 1.3 per cent of the Earth's land surface, it is home to some of the world's most spectacular and unusual wildlife – both plant and animal. Of equal importance is the country's breathtaking level of biological diversity: Indonesia contains ten per cent of the world's flowering plant species, 12 per cent of the world's mammal species, 16 per cent of all reptile and amphibian species, 17 per cent of all bird species and more than 25 per cent of the fish species known.

What makes biological diversity so important is that it is continually changing; as evolution gives rise to new species and new ecological conditions cause others to disappear. Evolution, however, is a laboriously slow process which may involve hundreds of thousands of years for the appearance of a new gene which might confer on its owner some advantage over fellow beings, thereby enhancing its survival chances in a continuously changing world.

At present, however, human alteration of the biosphere is having a significant impact on the Earth's biological diversity, hastening the depletion and extinction of species. The greatest losses have been predicted for tropical forests, of which an estimated 170,000 square kilometres worldwide are lost each year. Some scientists believe that about 60,000 species of the world's known 240,000 plant species, and perhaps even higher proportions of vertebrate and insect species could disappear within 30 years unless the process of deforestation is drastically reduced.

One of the features which makes the wildlife of Indonesia so interesting is the high degree of endemism. Many of the country's islands have been isolated for long periods of time. As a result, many new species have evolved – quite unlike those of adjacent landmasses. Particularly high rates of endemism are found in Sulawesi and Irian Jaya. The Mentawai Islands have a higher density of endemic mammals (although only one endemic bird species) per unit area than any other part of Indonesia.

DOSSINIA MARMORATA Fig. 1 et 2.   ZEUXINE (PSYCHECHILUS) GRACILIS, Fig. 2.
2. (ANTHRODUS) PURPURASCENS, Fig. 3.

Tab.XIV.

GAULTHERIA LEUCOCARPA.

Facing page: Livistona fan palms in the sunset at Way Kambas, Sumatra.

Left: most Indonesian orchids are epiphytes, but a few such as those illustrated here are ground dwellers. One of the jewel orchids is shown here; they are grown for their beautiful leaves.

Many of the mountain trees, and shrubs like rhododendrons and Gaultheria, belong to the heather family.

PLANT LIFE
Palms

One of the most widely used and locally appreciated groups of plants in Indonesia is the palm family: 477 species of palm occur in Indonesia, of which about ten per cent are used to some extent in a variety of activities that range from being emergency food rations to supporting national and international industries. In numerous villages in Maluku and Irian Jaya, starch from the sago palm (*Metroxylon sagu*) replaces rice as the main source of food for the population, with yields of up to 500 kilograms of wet starch being obtained per flowering stem. On other islands such as the Sangihe Islands, North Sulawesi, people consume the starch from a species of sugar palm (*Arenga* sp.). In recent times, the trunk of *Pigafetta filaris* was the traditionally selected material for constructing rice barns in Tana Toraja, Central Sulawesi. In Sumatra, Java and Sulawesi, the fruit of the scaly salak (*Salacca zalacca*) are widely sought, with yields of one tonne being recorded from a single hectare of cultivated plants each month.

Many species of palm are now treasured and planted for their ornamental value alone. With others, their leaves are widely used for thatch, their hearts as an edible food source, the leafsheath for making into containers, their wood as a source of building materials, fuel and handicrafts, their seeds as a source of animal medicine and natural dyes, their roots as a source of traditional human medi-

cine, their sap as a source of sugar and wine (as much as 20 litres of sap can be extracted a day from a single palm, for example *Borassus flabellifer*), and their thin leaf stalks as blowgun darts. The core of one species *Actinorhytia calapparis* is even pulverised and used as baby powder!

The familiar coconut palm (*Cocos nucifera*) vies with rattans and oil palm as the most widely exploited species. Cultivated in coastal areas throughout the archipelago, coconuts are a source of edible oil, fruit, drink, nuts, copra, edible hearts, leaves for thatch and weaving, timber, charcoal and other artisanal products.

Rafflesia

Most non-tree flowering rain forest plants are confined to the upper canopy. A few of the species which do grow on the forest floor extract their sustenance, not from the soil, but from the roots of other trees. One of these parasitic species, *Rafflesia arnoldii*, produces the largest flower in the world, the diameter of its bloom measuring more than one metre. For most of its life, the plant is invisible, living as a mass of tissues inside a vine of the genus *Tetrastigma*, a wild relative of the grape vine. As it matures, the parasite causes a swelling on the stem of the vine, which eventually bursts to reveal a small pea-sized bud with no leaves, stem or proper roots. The bud takes months to mature, finally opening to reveal massive maroon coloured petals, which are thick, leathery and covered in wart-like

Above: Amorphophallus titanum, belonging to the Arum family, frequently grows to more than two metres. It flowers every few years.

Above and below: growing on poor soils, pitcher plants are carnivorous plants which attract insects into their pitchers which are highly efficient traps.

Right: one of the largest epiphytes, birds' nest ferns develop on the sides of tall forest trees. As the fern grows, it retains its old dead growth, roots and root hairs. These, together with old leaves which fall into the 'nest', form a spongy mass which stores water and provides nutrients.

Facing page: the Goliath of flowers, Rafflesia arnoldii, found in Sumatra, is by far the largest flowering plant in the world.

bumps. These petals surround a deep, central cup, the floor of which is covered in large spikes. As soon as the flower opens, it gives off a particularly strong, putrid odour, like decaying meat. Attracted by the smell, flies swarm to the flower, feeding on substances produced in the plant and pollinating it in the process. After a week the flower withers and dies, collapsing in upon itself. If pollination has been successful, tiny seeds mature at the base of the flower but, in order to grow, they must be transported to another *Tetrastigma* vine. It is still uncertain how this is achieved, but presumably the seeds get carried on the feet of foraging animals – pigs, elephants, tree shrews or squirrels – and that some of these get deposited on, or near another vine, enabling germination to take place.

Carnivorous Plants

Some plants of the Indonesian forests are carnivorous. Pitcher plants (*Nephentes*) and sundews (*Drosera*) are plants typical of low nutrient soils, commonly found in heath swamp and montane forests. Although these plants contain chlorophyll, needed for photosynthesis, some food is also obtained from trapped insects. Hanging from the main stem of the plant, the vessels of the pitcher plant are modified, curled leaf tendrils which hold water. Each pitcher is covered with a lid which keeps out heavy rain. Insects are attracted to these plants by the odours they emit, and by their bright colours. Arriving at the edge of the pitcher, they enter, in search of a meal. The slippery, waxy cuticle provides no firm footing and many fall inside. At the base there is a pool of water. On one of his collecting forays on Mount Ophir, near Melaka (the Malay Peninsula), Wallace relates how he '... [being] exceedingly thirsty. ... turned to the pitcher-plants, but the water contained in the pitchers (about half a pint in each) was full of insects and otherwise uninviting. On tasting it, however, we found it very palatable, though rather warm, and we all quenched our thirsts from these natural jugs'. Insects trying to escape from the pitcher are foiled by rows of fine, downward pointing hairs growing inside the pitcher. Eventually they fall into the syrup-like mixture at the bottom of the pitcher where they drown. Glands inside the pitcher, secrete special enzymes which digest these creatures. The nutrients are then absorbed by the plant. In addition to the many corpses one might find in these pitchers, some organisms such as mosquito larvae appear capable of withstanding the plant's digestive juices and actually live in this miniature watery world. Large spiders, including the giant *Misumenops,* often lurk around the edge of the plants, lying in wait, hopeful of a meal.

Mistletoes

The most common of the 1100 mistletoes so far documented are species of *Viscum, Dendrophthoe* and *Scurrula.* These plants grow in the upper canopy of tall trees, their dense foliage usually betraying their presence. Although able to photosynthesise, they obtain much of their mineral and water supply from the host tree. Seeds are covered in a sticky substance, which even after passing through the gut of a bird, adheres to branches. As the seed germinates, its roots penetrate the bark of the tree.

Epiphtyes

The branches of rain forest trees are often decorated with numerous unkempt tufts of plants. These plants are epiphytes. They have severed all contact with the ground, relying on branches instead as a means of support. Unlike the *Rafflesia*, epiphytes are not parasites; they photosynthesise as do most 'normal' plants. This group, which contains 28,000 species, includes algae, lichens, mosses, ferns and flowering plants, including most of Indonesia's orchid species. Orchids account for about ten per cent of Indonesia's native flowering plant species. Different species exhibit different strategies of attaching themselves to a host tree and to collecting and storing rain-water and nutrients. In many species, materials such as dead leaves build up at the base and provide security for insects and frogs, adding to the diversity of these 'gardens in the air'.

Above: one of Indonesia's most threatened species, the Sumatran rhinoceros, browses on low vegetation close to rivers.

Preceding page: often heard, but seldom seen, tiny tree frogs abound in the rain forest. Their loud mating and territorial calls resonate over considerable distances.

A SAMPLING OF WILDLIFE
Rhinoceros

A three-toed footprint in the drying sand on a river bank in the Ujung Kulon National Park, West Java, is a sight many visitors hope to see. A greater reward could only be a fleeting glimpse of the animal that left these tracks – the critically endangered Javan rhinoceros (*Rhinoceros sondaicus*). Formerly well spread throughout Southeast Asia, this shy species is now found only in the forests at the extreme tip of West Java and in Vietnam; it has the distinction of being the rarest large mammal in the world. A recent survey of the park, suggests that there are only about 47 rhinos remaining. Despite their rarity, they are still threatened by poachers. Rhino horn fetches a high price in China and

Korea because of its alleged aphrodisiac powers and antipyretic (fever reducing) quality. Other threats to this tiny population include disease and the ever present danger of a catastrophe, such as an eruption from nearby Krakatau.

The smallest living member of the rhinoceros family, the Sumatran rhinoceros (*Dicerorhinus sumatrensis*), is thought to have changed little from the woolly rhinoceros which lived some 40 million years ago. This species is distinguished by a hairy, coarse russet coat and the presence of two pointed horns on the head. Once widely distributed throughout Southeast Asia, this inhabitant of low montane forests is now found only in isolated pockets of habitat in Burma, Thailand, the Malay Peninsula,

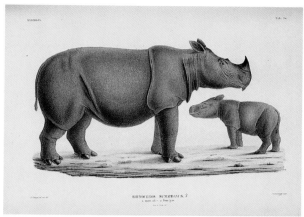

Sumatra and Borneo. The total world population is thought to be between 500 and 900 animals, but as many as ten per cent of these could be lost each year as a result of poaching pressure. Sumatra is home to an estimated 400 rhinos, but these occur over a wide area making any conservation protection efforts difficult to coordinate and enforce. The social habits of the rhinoceros and its reproductive strategy, make its future survival prospects bleak.

Hornbills

The raucous hornbills are among the most frequently encountered birds of Indonesia's tropical forests. A loud rhythmic wing beat followed by a deep whooshing sound announces the approach of a hornbill. As it alights, the sound is repeated by the arrival of its mate. Hornbills are unmistakable birds, frequently found feeding in fig trees; figs are their preferred food. Many species are predominantly black, with a whitish neck and pale fringes on the wings. The bills of most hornbills are disproportionately large in comparison with the size of their heads. A strong, downward pointing beak is adorned by a large, usually hollow, casque on the upper surface. The shape and colour of these casques vary considerably according to species; the great rhinoceros hornbill (*Buceros rhinoceros*) has a red and yellow upturned casque, similar to a banana in shape, while the wrinkled hornbill (*Aceros corrugatus*) has a much smaller, slightly pointed, ruby casque.

Besides their interesting variety, hornbills engage in a range of breeding strategies. They are monogamous and nest in trees, preferring tall dipterocarps

which offer some protection from terrestrial predators. As an added precaution, however, once the female enters a cavity large enough to accommodate herself and her future clutch, she seals the opening with a mixture of tree bark, mud and food debris. She may be assisted in this task by her mate, and, in some hornbill species, by non-breeding helpers, who bring additional building materials and help improve the fortress-like conditions for the female. Only a narrow vertical hole is left open, through which the male supplies the female and later her brood with food. In this way, the female becomes entirely dependent on her mate. When the chicks have fledged, she breaks down the tough casing covering the hole and emerges once again.

Bali Starling

Ruthless over-collecting of the beautiful Bali starling (*Leucopsar rothschildi*) almost resulted in the extinction of this species in the wild. A species

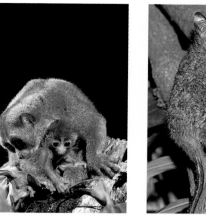

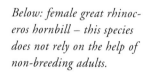

Left: Sumatran rhinoceros, from Temminck.

Above: slow loris.

The large ears and eyes of the spectral tarsier betray its nocturnl lifestyle.

Below: female great rhinoceros hornbill – this species does not rely on the help of non-breeding adults.

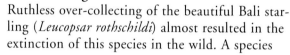

Below: Komodo dragons are usually solitary creatures, though they may congregate to feed.

Right: Komodo dragons feeding on a dead goat which has been provided in a reserve where tourists go to observe the dragons.

endemic to Bali, it is still eagerly sought by bird fanciers on account of its attractive features – a white crest and plumage with black tips on the wings and tail, and bare blue skin surrounding the eyes. Fewer than 50 birds remain in the wild in the specially created Bali Barat National Park. A concerted effort by the international zoo community and conservation organizations, has supplmented the tiny wild population with birds that have been bred in captivity in Europe and America, in cooperation with Jakarta Zoo. Unfortunately, virtually all those reintroduced have died. However, thousands of Bali starlings are now kept in captivity and the long-term success of reintroduction programmes such as this will only be assured if sufficient native habitat is maintained and if the reasons for the species' original decline are overcome.

Komodo Dragon

If Nature ever intended to provide Indonesia with the antithesis of the delicate Bali starling, she could

hardly have found a better subject than in the Komodo dragon (*Varanus komodoensis*). The dragon, or *ora* as it is known locally, may grow up to 2.8 metres in length and weigh 150 kilograms. Its size, ferocious appearance and unrestrained behaviour when feeding is thought to be the source of many early mariner tales of fire-breathing dragons prowling the islands of the archipelago. The dragon eats meat, dead or alive; it is also a cannibal and will not think twice about attacking and eating smaller dragons. Living on the island of the same name, as well as neighbouring islands of Rinca, Padar and west Flores, dragons shelter under bushes, lying in ambush for unsuspecting prey to approach. Their mouths carry a virulent strain of bacteria to which there is still no known antidote. Any animal that succeeds in escaping from the powerful jaws of a dragon will eventually die of infection, it is said. When it does, the predator will be attracted to the corpse by the stench of decaying flesh. Its acute sense of smell can detect carrion over a distance of eight kilometres. Like other lizards, Komodo dragons lay their eggs in the sand, where they occasionally fall prey to feral dogs. Hatchlings that survive climb into the trees, where they hunt insects, rodents and small birds. As they grow, their hunting skills become more refined and by the age of one year, most dragons are capable of bringing down small deer. Adults, although they prefer to feed on carrion, are capable of killing adult deer, as well as wild pigs and even water buffalo. Special protected areas, which have become major tourist attractions on Komodo and some of the adjacent islands, have been established to conserve the home of these giants.

Indonesia contains one of the most diverse collections of primates on Earth. The country boasts more than 35 of the world's 195 species and has representatives from five families and nine genera. Twenty-one of the species are endemic to Indonesia. These species are native to all regions of the archipelago except Maluku (where they have been introduced) and Irian Jaya. Both areas are separated from the Greater Sunda Islands by deep sea which primates could not cross by their own means. In evolutionary terms Indonesia is home to a wide range of primates from primitive species such as tarsiers, through to the more advanced forms of the lesser apes – gibbons and great apes (orang-utans).

Above: a female Sumatran orang-utan exhibits the great agility of this species. Baby orang-utans are encouraged by their mothers to climb at an early age.

Below: the slow loris is a nocturnal creature which bears just one young each year.

Right: feeding on young leaves and fruit, this Trachypithecus leaf-monkey keeps a constant look out for potential predators.

DISTRIBUTION AND ENDEMISM

Sumatra and Kalimantan share many primate species. All originally came from mainland Asia during the last Ice Age when the area known as the Sunda Shelf existed as a large landmass. Java and Bali represent the southeastern limit of distribution of primates that originally came from Asia. Since these islands became separated from the mainland the primates have differentiated into a wide range of varied shapes and sizes, with particular features evolving to suit the special demands of individual niches. Sumatra has several endemic primates such as *Presbytis thomasi* and *P. femoralis*. In Kalimantan different endemic species occur, such as *Presbytis rubicundus*, *P. hosei* and *P. frontata* and *Hylobates muelleri*. Some primates still found on Sumatra and Kalimantan are now extinct in Java. These include the pig-tailed macaque, orang-utan and tarsiers.

All primates now living on the islands of Mentawai and Sulawesi are endemic. The four species on Mentawai are the Mentawai pig-tailed macaque (*Macaca pagensis*), Kloss's gibbon (*Hylobates klossii*), the Mentawai langur (*Presbytis potenziani*) and the pig-tailed langur (*Simias concolor*). These primates are found sympatrically (living together) not only on the large island of Siberut but also on several smaller islands such as North and South Pagai and Sipora. Sulawesi and its adjacent islands are home to four macaque and one tarsier species. Worldwide, recent field research indicates that there may still

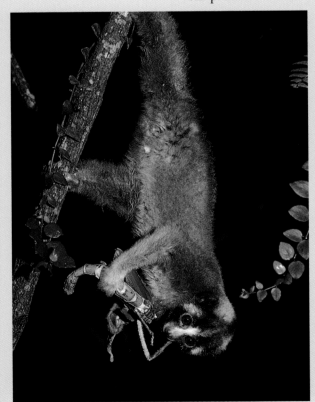

be many undocumented species of tarsier. In Lore Lindu National Park, in Central Sulawesi, studies indicate that many different species of tarsier appear to be capable of living within the same forest, each occupying a different vertical level in the forest. Populations of *Tarsius spectrum*, *T. dianae* and *T. pumillus* appear to overlap in range, occupying similar niches.

AN ASSORTMENT OF PRIMATES

A high level of endemism is exhibited by Indonesian primate species reflecting strong evolutionary change within the group. Tarsiers, however, are a family that got rather left behind in the evolutionary process and are sometimes termed 'living fossils'. This term is used because of their similarity to species which occurred long ago. Tarsiers are the smallest primate found in Indonesia; the proportions of their limbs aid their tree-hopping movement and are very similar to those of primates of the Eocene period. They are one of the smallest primates in the world with the adult male weighing only 75-120 grams. The long tail, with fine hair at the tip, is used as a support. They have a long scratching claw on the third toe, as well as a less pronounced one on the second toe. These features are used for grooming. When scratching, they bunch their toes together with the two grooming claws projecting. Enormous eyes and large ears are indications of their nocturnal habits. Tarsiers can turn their heads through 180° – and their bodies likewise, when leaping. With eyes fixed in their sockets, this is the only way for the creature to look around. Spectral tarsiers, *Tarsius spectrum*, are found in Sulawesi and the adjacent islands. They live in small territorial family groups. They are monogamous, and family sizes range from three to seven individuals. Two exceptions to the rule of monogamy are *Tarsius syrychta* and *T. bancanus* (the Bornean tarsier). *Tarsius pumilus* which is smaller, darker and has longer claws than the spectral tarsier, lives in montane forest more than 2000 metres above sea-level.

The slow loris, *Nycticebus coucang*, is another nocturnal primate species. It is small and slow moving, similar in habit to the sloths of South America. An unusual behaviour is its practice of marking its territory and routes in the canopy with urine rubbed on to trees via its hands and feet. In Indonesia it is found in Sumatra, Kalimantan, Java and adjacent islands.

Leaf-monkeys (*Presbytis* spp. and *Trachypithecus* spp.) are remarkable for variation in fur colour; that of the crown, tail, head and limbs ranging from black, white, brown and red to mixed. In Sumatra there are at least four species of leaf-monkey: *Presbytis melalophos*, *P. femoralis*, *P. thomasi* and *P. cristata*. *Presbytis cristata*, *P. frontata* and *P. rubicundus* are found in Kalimantan. Leaf-monkeys are represented in Java by *Presbytis comata* and

Above: facial expressions and features are widely used among primates as a means of communication. Threatening features include raised hair contrasting in colour to the face (Javan leaf-monkey, top), a large, bare face (black crested macaque, middle) and baring teeth (Mentawai gibbon, bottom)

Right: a young loris clings to its mother as she feeds.

Trachypithecus auratus, with the latter also occurring on Bali and Lombok. They usually live in small groups of 10 to 30 individuals, with only a few adult males present. Occasionally some species are found living in small groups of less than 15 individuals with only one adult male. Examples of this are *Presbytis comata* and *P. aygula*. The only strictly monogamous species, *Presbytis potenziani*, occurs on Mentawai.

Macaques are the most widespread genus of monkey, with a total of 20 species worldwide. Eleven species occur in Indonesia. Compared with many primates, macaques have a more complex brain and superior hand and eye coordination. With this advantage it is interesting to note that their sense of smell is less important. The long-tailed macaque (*Macaca fascicularis*) is distributed widely, whereas the pig-tailed macaque (*Macaca nemestrina*) is only found in Sumatra and Kalimantan and the Malay Peninsula. The Mentawai pig-tailed macaque (*Macaca pagensis*) shares many characteristics with the pig-tailed macaque, but is smaller. Sulawesi macaques have distinctive forms in comparison with the rest of the macaque genus.

Gibbons, including siamangs, are brachiators – species which swing from tree to tree and feed at the ends of swaying branches. The development of grasping hands, crucial for swinging from branches, has, however, been at the expense of manipulative dexterity and with a much reduced thumb they have to cup their hands to scoop up objects. They live in monogamous family groups. Gibbons are widely recognized as the sopranos of the Indonesian forests. They sing in sex-specific choruses with males mournfully heralding the sunrise; females join the chorus later in the morning. These almost magical sounds carry far over the forest canopy, often for several kilometres, and are an important means of communication with neighbouring groups of gibbons. The siamang (*Hylobates syndactylus*) is the largest gibbon, predominantly black in colour and found only in Sumatra and the Malay Peninsula. Within Indonesia, lar gibbons are found in northern Sumatra, while agile gibbons are confined to the central region. Agile gibbons are also found in west and south central Kalimantan. In Kalimantan, the Mahakam and Kapuas rivers separate the territory of the agile and Muller gibbons. A hybrid form of these two species, in terms of its morphology and vocalisation, has been identified in the upper reaches of these rivers.

ORANG-UTAN

The orang-utan is the largest primate in Indonesia and the country's only great ape. There is just one species (*Pongo pygmaeus*) but there are believed to be two sub-species: *P. pygmaeus pygmaeus* in Kalimantan and *P. pygmaeus abellii* in Sumatra. They can weigh up to 75 kilograms. The male is much larger than the female and twice as heavy. Orang-utans move slowly from branch to branch or 'knuckle-walk' on the ground. Their locomotion is a modified form of arm-swinging – suspending themselves by their arms and legs, though the arm is much the stronger limb. The orang-utan is a rare arboreal ape, confined to primary rain forest which stretches from swamp to hill and montane forest at 1000 to 2000 metres above sea-level. Orang-utans are primarily fruit-eating, but supplement their diet with leaves, bark and insects. Recent field research suggests that they may also eat small mammals and the carcasses of dead gibbons.

THREATENED SPECIES

Indonesia is home to a wide range of primate species, many of which are found nowhere else in the world. Many of these animals are now seriously threatened, primarily as a result of increased human activity in the tropical forests where these species live. Most of Indonesia's macaque species are threatened, in particular: *Macaca nigra, M. togeanus, M. brunnescens, M. maurus* and *M. pagensis*. On Java, where widespread deforestation has taken place, two species of endemic primates are currently endangered. These are the Javan or silvery gibbon (*H. moloch*) and the grizzled leaf-monkey (*P. comata*). The latter is the rarest and most endangered gibbon species. Now confined to the western part of Java, it is thought to have lost 95 per cent

of its original habitat. The total population has been estimated from a recent survey to be between only 500 to 1000 individuals. Both species are a high conservation priority.

REHABILITATION PROGRAMMES

In both Kalimantan and North Sumatra, innovative rehabilitation programmes have been designed and implemented to rescue abandoned and captive animals and return them to their natural habitat, always within the confines of a protected area. This procedure supplements the wild populations and is a way of dealing with unwanted or confiscated pets. Three rehabilitation centres have been established: Bohorok in Sumatra and at Tanjung Puting National Park and Samboja in Kalimantan.

Above: mother orang-utan and young.

Proboscis monkey.
Mentawai gibbon.
Siamang.
Crab-eating macaque.
Banded leaf-monkey.
White-handed gibbon.
Orang-utan.

6

7

Above: a babirusa wallows in a secluded muddy pool, Sulawesi.

Babirusa

One of the most bizarre mammals in the world must be the babirusa (*Babyrousa babyrussa*), a species of wild pig only found on Sulawesi and the offshore islands of the Togian group, Sula and Buru. Among its many odd features are that the upper canine teeth of the male grow upwards, penetrating the skin of the nose before curving back towards the forehead. An inhabitant of tropical forests near rivers and ponds, this species forages in the soil for leaves, fruit, roots and small animals. Little is known about their behaviour in the wild but they appear to be social animals that live in small groups of up to eight. Babirusa have few natural enemies, the python being the main predator on piglets. However, hunting by humans with nets, spears and dogs has taken its toll on the species' numbers, as has loss of natural habitat. Although legally protected under Indonesian law since 1931, babirusa are heavily hunted in some areas. They are also often one of the first species to become locally extinct after logging activities or extensive clearance of vegetation have taken place. This is probably a combined result of habitat loss and hunting pressure.

Maleo

Another species confined to Sulawesia, which shares the same forests as the babirusa, is the curious maleo bird (*Macrocephalon maleo*). Maleo display the unusual behaviour of burying their eggs on sandy beaches or in the light ash soils warmed by geothermal activity. This way, the warm soil incubates the eggs, leaving the parents free from the tedious, and often dangerous, task of sitting on a clutch. An early riser in the beautiful Bogani Nani Wartabone National Park can easily locate these shy birds by their melodious gurgling calls as the male and female arrive at a nesting site. Both birds assist with the digging of the nest, one keeping a lookout for predators while the other kicks the sand out of the hole. The female then lays her egg and the nest is carefully filled in. Maleo often excavate nests but do not lay in them. This is thought to confuse potential egg robbers who waste time searching in vain for a meal. Carefree as it may seem though, the method has its drawbacks, particularly nowadays. These eggs, about five times the size of a hen's, are a favourite food of the monitor lizard, a relative of the Komodo dragon. Their size and delicate flavour also make them much sought-after by egg poachers who later sell them at local markets. Hunting pressure and repeated disturbances at the nesting grounds contribute to the steady demise of this unusual bird.

Hunting maleo and the collection of their eggs is not a new phenomenon. Previously, however, the offtake was controlled by village leaders which usually ensured that enough were left untouched to hatch and join the adult bird population. Changing customs and a ready market for the eggs have led to increased levels of poaching which have proved difficult to control. As a result of such pressures, the maleo has become the subject of several conservation efforts; the most recent of which have been based on the collection and later incubation of eggs under controlled, protected conditions. Two facilities have been established close to the Bogani Nani Wartabone National Park; one at Tambun, the other at Tumokang. Here park rangers collect a certain number of eggs and bury them inside secure cages where conditions are similar to the local environment where they were laid. Once the chicks emerge, they are released.

Above: tube-nosed and harlequin bats.

Left: Sulawesi's unusual maleo, digging a nest.

Having broken through its tough shell, a maleo chick emerges from its earth nest. Unbelievably, it can fly as soon as it is hatched.

Adult maleo.

Above: the occurrence of many marsupials, such as the agile wallaby and the spotted cuscus, can be explained by the fact that New Guinea and the Australian continent once formed one landmass.

Below: the one-wattled cassowary.

Right: the flamboyant colours and unusual tail of the red bird of paradise attract mates.

Facing page: the male Wilson's bird of paradise. A prospecting female chooses her mate by his appearance and ability to 'dance'.

Birds of Paradise

Courtship rituals are an important aspect in the breeding behaviour of many species. Some of the most unusual and awe-inspiring rituals in the animals kingdom are those of the birds of paradise. Indonesia is home to 26 species of birds of paradise, which are only found in Irian Jaya, Maluku and Papua New Guinea. Forest-dwelling species, birds of paradise are distinguished by the flamboyant colours of the male, a deliberate gaudiness that is exaggerated by the presence of a range of ornamental feathers which differ according to the species. The smallest and most vivid member of the family, the king bird of paradise (*Cininnurus regius*) is a shimmering red colour with white undersides and blue legs. Its short tail is exaggerated by the presence of two long trailing plumes that end in green plumes. No less beautiful is the lesser bird of paradise (*Paradisaea minor*) whose rich chocolate-brown colours are off-set by an ochrous head and long, trailing white and pale yellow tail plumes that greatly exceed the size of the bird itself. When displaying, the wings are held over the back and an elaborate ritualistic dance involving wing fluttering and head movements is used to attract attention.

Though solitary by nature, during the breeding season males of many of these species congregate in a forest clearing, usually on an open perch or bare patch of ground reserved exclusively for nuptial displays, where they perform an elaborate sequence of wing movements and fluttering to attendant females. Each cock jealously guards a small patch of real estate which was probably won through conquering a rival male. Once a male has succeeded in attracting a suitor they will mate, the male later returning to his perch to woo other females. In contrast to the outrageous colours and adornments of the polygamous males, females are drab in appearance, a strategy which provides better security when sitting on a clutch of eggs and caring for chicks.

Sadly, the very virtues that male birds of paradise have evolved to attract a mate have also led to their downfall. People have long admired the beauty of these species and many tribespeople proudly valued their feathers, not only as a means of adorning clothes, but also as a form of currency in bartering for goods. Spanish explorers are thought to have brought the first bird of paradise feathers back to Europe in the sixteenth century, stimulating a major demand in the Paris fashion circles, some designers even attaching stuffed birds to the tops of hats. Increased demand for the beautiful feathers of these birds led to heavy hunting pressure and many species have been pushed towards extinction.

Cassowary

On a quiet stroll through some of the lowland forests of Irian Jaya you might, if very lucky, be surprised to be confronted by a large, human-sized bird with powerful, stumpy legs. You would also be well advised to approach no closer for these birds are among the most dangerous animals in the forest. This is the cassowary, of which three species are known from Irian Jaya. One of these, the two-wattled cassowary (*Casuarius casuarius*) is also found in northeast Australia. These flightless birds, weighing up to 55 kilograms, are quite unmistakable in terms both of their size and appearance. All species have horny casques on their heads, distinctive naked coloured patches on the face and neck and, occasionally, drooping pink wattles on the neck. The largest of these species, the one-wattled cassowary (*C. unappendiculatus*) is the largest member of the family, the female being slightly larger than the male.

Cassowaries are confined to the forest and display very unusual breeding behaviour. The female prepares a rough nest of leaves on the ground and lays between three and six huge dark green eggs. She then departs, leaving the male to incubate the eggs and look after the chicks. Cassowaries feed on fallen fruit, insects, lizards, small mammals and plant materials. Despite their ferocious reputation – they have been known to inflict serious, sometimes fatal, injuries on potential aggressors by flailing them with their long toe claws – cassowaries are generally shy birds, largely as a result of earlier (and continuing) persecution from humans. On Seram, hunters actually tip their arrows with a sharp claw from the cassowary's own feet. Some highland communities in Irian Jaya and Papua New Guinea catch cassowary chicks and raise them for a special feast or for trade purposes. At one stage, in Papua New Guinea, a single cassowary was worth as much as eight pigs, or one woman!

Left: the largest terrestrial predator in Indonesia, this tigress is joined at a stream by her two cubs. Almost fully grown and able to fend for themselves, these cubs will soon disperse to find a territory of their own, allowing the tigress to breed again.

Above: fishing cat, a shy and rarely seen member of the cat family.

Right: a young Sumatran tapir – its bold markings help to break up the body outline and conceal it in the vegetation.

Facing page: the estuarine crocodile, a predator of the mangroves, is now rare.

Young elephant.

Elephant eating swamp grass.

Below: a Mentawai gibbon scans the horizon for danger. At the slightest indication of trouble the 'on-duty guard' will warn other members of the troop.

WHAT HAS BEEN LOST?

The wildlife of Indonesia has changed considerably since humans first appeared in the archipelago. Some of this may be part of the evolutionary process, but human impact has certainly accelerated the rate of transformation. Direct hunting has played a major role in the demise of certain species, particularly ungulates such as pigs, deer and cattle, as well as primates. Trophy hunting too was an important activity in the past, particularly for elephant, rhinoceros and tiger. Loss of habitat has compounded these pressures, with populations withdrawing where possible to a few last remaining natural strongholds, frequently in the mountains.

Among the most spectacular species to have been lost are the Bali and Java sub-species of tiger (*Panthera tigris balica* and *P. tigris sondaica*). Others include the Javan wattled lapwing (*Vanellus macropterus*) and the Caerulean paradise flycatcher (*Eutrichomyias rowleyi*) of the Sangihe Islands off northern Sulawesi. Unfortunately this is unlikely to be the end of such losses: Indonesia has the dubious honour of holding the world's longest list of vertebrates threatened with extinction, including 126 birds, 63 mammals and 23 reptiles.

Among the most seriously threatened animals are the Javan rhinoceros, Sumatran rhinoceros, tiger (*Panthera tigris*), Sumatran serow (*Capricornis sumatraensis sumatraensis*) – goat-like denizens of isolated mountain slopes of Sumatra – anoa (*Bubalus depressicornis* and *B. quarlesi*) – dwarf buffaloes found only in Sulawesi – and a collection of primates, including the orang-utan (*Pongo pygmaeus*), Mentawai Islands macaque (*Macaca pagensis*), and the Javan gibbon (*Hylobates moloch*).

Other species which are recognized as being endangered include all six species of marine turtle that occur in Indonesian waters, the river (*Batagur baska*) and painted (*Callagur borneoensis*) terrapins, the saltwater (*Crocodylus porosus*) and siamese (*C. siamensis*) crocodiles, false gharial (*Tomistoma schlegelii*), Asian elephant (*Elaphas maximus*), and Malayan tapir (*Tapirus indicus*).

The greatest single threat to these, and other species, is the steady but progressive loss of habitat. Most of these species cannot live outside the forest, depending on this habitat for food and shelter. Loss of natural vegetation has been most acute in the heavily populated islands of Java and Bali where remaining forests are largely montane relicts.

In many areas, hunting continues to be a problem. Trophy hunting for tiger and leopard skins and rhino horn, is no longer the major problem it once was. This is partly due to the drastic decline in animal numbers. Improved protection for threatened species such as the Javan rhinoceros have also been of major influence in this battle. Hunting of primates, wild cattle and pigs and of many birds as a source of food is, however, a growing problem.

Despite being illegal, the removal and sale of exotic plants and animals from the wild is a significant problem in Indonesia. Birds of paradise, cockatoos and parrots are caught in Irian Jaya and Maluku, while large numbers of sea turtles and their shells, and reptile skins, are still traded each year. Delicate orchids are taken from the rain forest and considerable numbers of macaque monkeys, now extinct in Java, are captured for use in biomedical research. Greater efforts are needed to protect the remaining wildlife of the archipelago. The dangers of uncontrolled trade in wildlife products are all too obvious, and there is a need for concerted action on behalf of government and the public to ensure that the many unique and fascinating species found in Indonesia do not join the ranks of species already driven to extinction.

PEOPLE OF THE FOREST

Below: Dayak.

Facing page: a Dani tribesman from the Baliem Valley, Irian Jaya.

Human beings are an alien species in the humid tropical forest. People did not evolve in this environment, so they have had to adapt to living under conditions that were new to a creature of the open savanna and fringing woodlands. In much the same manner as other species have adapted, over thousands of years, to different living conditions, human beings have undergone physical, behavioural and cultural changes. Many forest-dwelling people are small in stature, which helps them to move freely in dense undergrowth, but is in part a consequence of their low protein and calorie intake. Compared with people of temperate climates, or those living on the open plains of the tropics, forest people drink much less and sweat less. The high humidity of the rain forest means that evaporation is low and that sweating is a less effective means of staying cool. A small, lean body is better adapted to controlling body heat than a large, rounded one. In addition, most forest-dwellers have shed their need for protective clothing against the elements of wind and cold. Few wear more than a loincloth garment made of barkcloth or leaves. Socially as well, forest-dwellers have adapted, often living in small groups that cooperate in vital activities such as hunting, a task which is frequently difficult and requires cooperation and specialization.

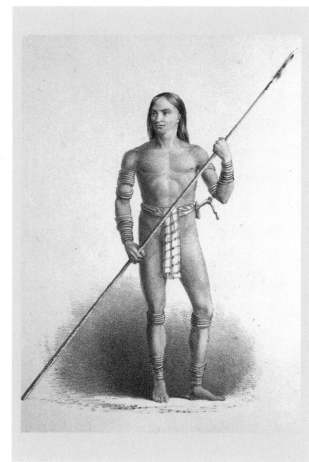

But why did human beings move into the forest in the first place? Some of the earlier people of Africa, South America and Asia were possibly attracted by the stable, favourable living conditions that rain forests offer, together with the realization that sufficient food was always available provided one knew where and how to obtain it. A principle which such groups soon learned was that of sustainable exploitation of resources – 'wise use' of natural products. Their lives depended on there always being enough food available to hunt and collect, and a number of restrictions were set by different tribes on hunting and collecting rights which enabled wildlife resources to recover from limited, often seasonal hunting pressures. These practices probably gave rise to the nomadic and semi-nomadic existence of many early forest-dwelling people.

Other forest-dwellers, however, may not have had much choice in where they settled. Many of the original inhabitants of Southeast Asia who had settled on the plains and margins of the forests were gradually pushed further inland to 'less desirable' environments as successive waves of new colonizers arrived who were often more dynamic and enterprising than their predecessors. These new arrivals were also frequently better equipped for the role of agriculturalists, armed with better tools and materials to take over and manage the land. In this way, new waves of settlers gradually assumed control of prime agricultural lands, mainly those of the lowlands. Under such pressure, the earlier inhabitants probably withdrew further inland.

The first people to make a living from the rain forest were hunter-gatherers, people who survived by a combination of fishing, catching game and gathering plant and animal foods such as fruit, nuts, tubers, leaf shoots, honey and grubs. Many indigenous tribes, especially forest- and desert-dwelling people, still live on a shifting, often seasonal basis, moving according to prevailing weather conditions and food availability, sometimes even living in response to the movements or migration patterns of wild animals – their main source of food. The bearded pig, for example, is a great migrant, though today its movements are much interfered with by development activities. Forest-dwellers in Kalimantan regularly go to the shallow river crossings to kill the pigs as they cross. Other people have adopted a more settled approach to life, but this requires a more strictly organized society and better agricultural skills. No forest group nowadays survives on wild produce alone; some crops are always cultivated – or obtained through trade.

Today, only remnants of these early settlers survive in Indonesia. The Kubu of southern Sumatra are the largest extant group of forest-dwellers, but even their numbers are steadily declining. Another group, the Punan, are settled or semi-nomadic forest-dwellers inhabiting the upper watersheds of the dwindling rain forests in Kalimantan and neighbouring Sarawak and Brunei. Few members of the Punan population have retained their traditional ways of exploiting Borneo's great forests; the men armed with blowpipe and quiver full of poison-tipped darts and the women harvesting wild sago. Today they barter forest products such as rattan

mats and wild rubber to Dayak traders in exchange for other goods. Some have even settled and now grow crops.

These indigenous people, together with other isolated groups such as the Badui of Java and the Sasak of Lombok, are part of the rich human culture of Indonesia; helping to preserve their lifestyles and cultures is as important as, and connected with, conserving the country's plant and animal diversity. Increased contact with the modern world, however, has led to a gradual but steady undermining and loss of many traditional practices and beliefs, some of which were developed many generations ago by these peoples' ancestors to ensure that natural resources were respected and not abused.

BELIEFS, SPIRITS AND RITUALS ASSOCIATED WITH NATURE

As the forest is vital to the survival of the people who use it, it is revered and respected. The forest is however, also feared as it is considered the dwelling place of numerous spirits that are potentially antagonistic towards humans who offend or treat them improperly. Many large forest trees, unusual rocks or land formations are thought to be the abode of spirits, and it is not unusual for villagers to make simple offerings at these places as they pass by. If disturbed or offended, these nature spirits can cause illness and even death. Children are believed to be particularly at risk in the forest, and Dayak mothers smear soot on their children's faces when they travel. This renders the children invisible to the spirits. Shamans called upon to diagnose disease, frequently point to forest spirits as the cause; as having attacked the individual as he passed by. Offerings, accompanied by pieces of the victim's clothing, hair or nail parings to fool the spirit into thinking its victim is present, are hung in the forest to persuade the spirit to return to its abode. The spirits of people who have died 'bad' deaths are also believed to haunt the forests. The *pontianak*, the spirit of a woman who dies in childbirth, is feared in many places. Her ghost waits at the crossroads of forest paths to attack passing males.

In Kalimantan, when the forest is cleared for new fields, offerings are made to the spirits which are being displaced in the process. Falling trees are a particular danger at such times, and they not infrequently fall on people, killing them. Such deaths are attributed to angry forest spirits, punishing people for forcing them from their abode. When land is cleared for a new village, offerings must also be made, for humans are creating a division between the civilized and the wild world, and between people and spirits. Thereafter, when any religious ceremony is held, strict taboos preventing people hunting in the forest or gathering forest produce are enforced. To associate with the untamed is to invite the forest spirits into the civilized spheres of humans, where they may create

havoc. For the Tetum of Timor, the forest is associated with the underworld where one may encounter beings who would not appear in the secular confines of the village.

The Asmat of Irian Jaya regard forest trees as symbolizing human beings. Roots are seen to represent feet; the trunk, the human torso; branches, the arms; and the fruit, the head. The sago, which provides the Asmat with their staple food, is identified with a woman, and whenever a ceremony is held sago plays an important role. During some ceremonies, including that held when the Asmat start cutting sago trees in a new area of the forest, a particularly beautiful sago palm is cut down, preferably one which is about to bear fruit and die. The stems of fallen leaves and the lower part of the trunk are removed. Decaying stems and the like are discarded to make the palm as attractive as possible. The trunk is then 'dressed' in a woman's skirt. The ritual of cutting the sago incorporates references to chasing bad spirits from the tree, and to killing during a head-hunting raid, as spears are hurled at the tree as it falls. This theme is continued as members of the men's house (*yeu*) holding the ceremony give account of their heroic deeds. The heart of the trunk is removed and later transported to the village. Finally, the large leaves are cleared away, and a leaf from the centre of the crown is set aside to make a tray for use in the ceremony. A few square holes are made in the trunk so that the capricorn beetle can crawl in and lay its eggs. The tree is left for about six weeks to give the grubs time to mature, for they form the central part of all Asmat rituals. When the sago grubs are ready the mother tree, and other sago palms, are attacked and split open to expose the grubs. The grubs – a great delicacy – are collected on the palm-leaf tray and consumed at a ceremony.

The Korowai, inland relatives of the Asmat, live in the region between the Brazza and Eilanden rivers in Irian Jaya. Building tree spirit houses was an important part of their culture. These houses were originally built to offer protection to the Korowai from rival groups, including head-hunting forays by the Asmat. They still build this style of house today.

Like shadows, Kubu hunters move silently and effortlessly through the damp, tangled forest of southern Sumatra. Clad in worn loin-cloths, the only baggage each carries is a long wooden spear, tipped with a metal blade. A pack of frantic dogs leads the group. Adhering to a lifestyle long abandoned by most of Indonesia's population, the Kubu provide an excellent example of a group which has successfully adapted to living in harmony with its natural surroundings.

While the exact origin of the Kubu remains unclear, they are physically similar to the surrounding Malay people and their speech is a dialect of Malay. It seems likely, therefore, that they have over many centuries become culturally differentiated from the Malays because of their strong orientation towards the resources of the forest. Living a deceptively simple existence, the Kubu are particularly well adapted to their complex forest environment. Today they are one of the few groups still living within and largely dependent upon the tropical forests of Indonesia.

TRADITIONAL LIFE-STYLE

Most Kubu groups practise a combination of hunting and gathering and swidden agriculture. Wild game is always an important part of their diet, but the bulk of their food is derived from either wild or cultivated plants. When living off the natural bounty of the forest, women are chiefly responsible for providing the basic food supply from a wide range of tubers, palms and wild fruit, while the men supply game as well as honey, when it is the season for the latter.

The large game, hunted by adult men, includes several kinds of deer, wild boars, tapirs, honey bears, monkeys, lizards and snakes. No encampment is complete without its unruly pack of dogs which are almost as essential for hunting – tracking, locating and cornering game – as the hunter's *kujur*. Only when a wild animal has been driven into a tree or cornered successfully will the hunter approach to make the final kill. Many forays for larger game are unsuccessful, but the hunters remain optimistic and opportunistic, seizing every chance to capture smaller prey such as porcupines and civets, turtles and tortoises, the latter being a real delicacy. The freshwater mussels, snails and fish routinely collected by women and supplemented by the ground squirrels and rats trapped by children also make up a significant food supply. Definite rules govern the ways in which different animals and animal parts should be cooked – by boiling, baking or smoking – and by whom they should be eaten.

When practising swidden agriculture, the Kubu may plant rice and maize, but also a selection of tubers and bananas which can be left to fend for themselves and be gradually harvested over many months. For these swidden plots, the ground is roughly cleared and seeds are inserted in the soil using sharpened digging sticks. Seemingly very simple, this form of cultivation is extremely efficient and can be combined with the nomadic life-style preferred by the Kubu.

In the forest, the Kubu live in small encampments, usually comprising three to eight huts. In keeping with their nomadic life-style, their houses are plain, functional and easily assembled, usually in just a few hours. Four bamboo or wooden poles are first driven into the ground and a small raised platform of split poles attached, less than one metre above the ground. A simple roof of leaves is then erected above the platform. No walls are built to provide additional shelter from the elements. When a group decides to move to another location – usually as a result of scarcity of food and general forest products in the area or because of perceived danger – their houses are simply vacated and the jungle is then allowed to reclaim its former territory. When swiddening, the Kubu make similar huts within or close to the field, or they may erect larger bark-walled swidden houses like those of the Malays.

The nomadic existence of the Kubu permits few possessions. Freedom of movement remains important, even today. Apart from basic hunting tools, the most important of which are the multi-purpose bush-knife and the two-and-a-half metre long spear the *kujur* – the meagre possessions of an average Kubu family include cooking pots, rattan mats, handmade baskets for collecting and storing tubers, rice and other crops which may be dried and easily kept, and bars of resin which are used to provide light at night.

MODERN PRESSURES

Despite their isolated existence, the Kubu are no strangers to the wider world. For centuries the Kubu economy has relied on trade with settled villagers, in particular the exchange of forest products for such vital commodities as metal and salt. Today, their medicinal plants, fruit, fish and game, rattans and dragons' blood (a natural dyestuff) are frequently traded for salt and sugar, tobacco and batteries around transmigration sites and along roads.

Below: Kubu trapping game.

Once the proud hunters of the Sumatran jungle, in recent years the Kubu have had to endure increasing pressures from the outside world. Their native forest territory has been significantly reduced as a result of logging operations and the expansion of agricultural activities by lowland farmers and corporations. The Kubu's claims to their traditional forest lands are little recognized and their protests have not met with much success to date. In addition to these mounting pressures, the construction of logging roads and modern communication arteries such as the trans-Sumatran highway, have resulted in an influx of agricultural settlers and even hunters and collectors of forest products, each of whom has interfered with the traditional practices of these subsistence, forest-dwelling people.

Although many Kubu have resisted the temptation to settle to a sedentary lifestyle, some have been forced – usually as a result of decreased levels of wildlife – to forsake their traditional way of life. Some, however, have willingly foregone the hardships of their former existence, gaining employment with logging companies or as paid agricultural labourers. Continuing loss of forest, in particular, has meant that a greater number of isolated populations of Kubu are becoming displaced as their forest home is destroyed, as the wild resources of the forest are over-exploited by outsiders and as the pressures of a modern world reach into the Kubu camps, through curious visitors, trade and settlers.

The future of the Kubu is far from clear. An estimated 5000 Kubu live in Jambi and South Sumatra provinces, clinging to their traditional way of life, and remain dependent of the forest for their survival. How long such people can continue to survive in this manner is far from certain. Unlike the vast majority of immigrant settlers, the Kubu are, by tradition, denizens of the rain forest, clearly in tune with their natural surroundings. Current estimates suggest that traditional hunter-gatherers require an average of one square kilometre of forest per person, from which to obtain most of their living requirements. The incessant expansion of agriculture and deforestation in southern Sumatra is clearly taking its toll on the environment and on the quality of the services the natural forests provide: clean, reliable water sources, flood control, regular supplies of fresh fruit and medicinal herbs – to name but a few. Traditional groups such as the Kubu are among the first to experience such effects and, in the long-term, among the most affected. Given sufficient incentive and recognition of their rightful claims to their forest homes, these modern-day guardians of the forest could play a greater role in protecting the natural environment for the benefit of everyone.

Above: a Kubu encampment usually consists of several thatched shelters in a forest clearing. Evidence of the Kubu's liking for turtles can be seen in the discarded shells on the ground and on the pole to the right.

Above: damar resin tree.

Below: artifacts made from forest products, Temminck.

NATURE'S LARDER

Most people associate forests with timber production and forests are, of course, important reservoirs of valuable timbers. In Indonesia more than 100 species of rain forest tree are commercially harvested, supporting a timber industry valued at $US4.5 billion in 1988. The vast majority of this timber (86 per cent) comes from Kalimantan's shrinking lowland dipterocarp and swamp forests.

Attention is increasingly being paid to the analysis and management of wild products, especially those emanating from tropical forests. For centuries, indigenous people have demonstrated that forests can yield much more than just timber. Many groups are practically self-reliant in terms of foodstuffs, surviving on the 'fruits of the forest', obtaining their food, shelter, clothing, medicines, and means of recreation from naturally occurring products. The vast majority of the world's population, however, remains oblivious to the importance of non-timber-forest products: their economic as well as aesthetic value, and the role that so many of these products play in our daily lives.

Non-timber products that hunter-gatherers collect every day include nuts, oils, fruit, fish, game, rattan, and a range of medicinal products. A great number of these natural products have not so far been farmed or grown in plantations, but can only be harvested from the natural forest. Many of our common medicines originated from forest plants: quinine, for example, used in anti-malaria drugs, was first extracted from the bark of the cinchona tree; rescinnamine, a tranquilizer, is extracted from *Rauvolfia* plants; and aspirin, a common substance used in painkillers, is derived from the European willow. Apart from a wide range of medicinal substances, a number of other essential products also originated in forests, including rubber, oils, glues, dyes, and some clothing and construction materials. Many of our favourite delicacies – chocolate, coffee and tea for example, as well as a wide range of fruits and vegetables – are all derived from tropical forests. Most spices, such as pepper, cloves, cinnamon, nutmeg and cardamom, are also forest products.

Bamboo and rattan grow wild throughout the archipelago and are put to a wide range of uses. They are made into fish-traps, hen coops, cooking utensils and other household items, and their strength and flexibility make them invaluable building materials for floors and bridges. In Indonesian towns, bamboo is used as scaffolding. Rattan is important commercially for the making of furniture.

A wide range of palms are exploited, the coconut being one of the most important. Other than being a source of food, it provides oil for cooking, lighting and indigenous cosmetics, among other things. The nuts of the areca palm are gathered as the main ingredient for betel chewing. Borassus palm leaves are used to make buckets and thatch, while the flowers provide sugar for palm wine, and pandanus palm leaves are woven into mats. In Minahassa, the fibres of the *gomuti* or *sagaru* palm are made into rope, and the flowers are used for palm wine. The usual way of climbing palms or tall trees to gather fruit and honey or wax from bees' nests is to make a sling attached to a coir rope encircling the tree trunk. A torch to smoke out the bees, or a container to collect palm sugar, is suspended from the climber's waist. Some individuals are able to shin up a palm tree unaided.

Clove and nutmeg trees once grew wild in eastern Indonesia; although now farmed commercially, these products were originally gathered for other

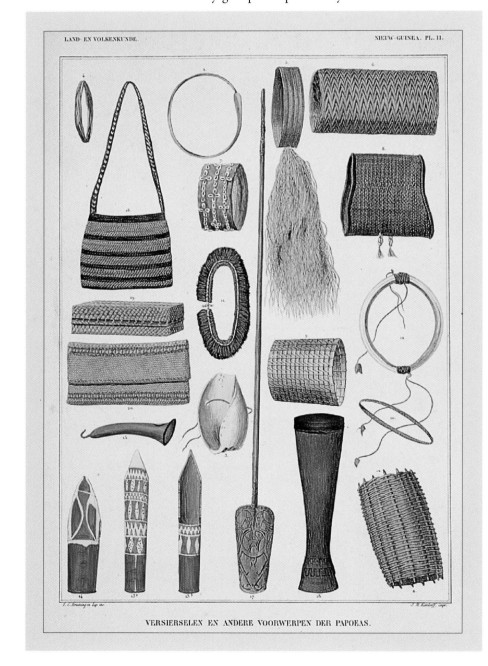

VERSIERSELEN EN ANDERE VOORWERPEN DER PAPOEAS.

purposes. Powdered nutmeg, for example, is used locally to treat overeating, alleviate dysentery, malaria and the early stages of leprosy. It was also considered an aphrodisiac and a cure for madness. Various other types of traditional medicines are obtained from the bark and roots of numerous species of tree throughout Indonesia. In Java, for example, the sap of the sana tree is used as a healing ointment and for tanning leather, while an infusion of its leaves makes a good shampoo. Another important forest product is camphor oil, obtained from trees by making a small cavity in the trunk near the ground, in which the oil collects. Crystallized camphor may be removed from the trunk once the tree has died.

Many non-timber products are of immense value to local and national economies. The sale of rattan in Indonesia in 1988 amounted to more than $US200 million. Other plants and animals have little market value but are widely used as sources of food, fuel, housing and handicraft materials. Wild pig, deer, monkeys, birds and honey have considerable local value both in terms of their nutrient value and also as objects for trade. Yet their importance is often overlooked when deciding the value and fate of a forest.

Recent studies in Southeast Asia have demonstrated that up to 80 per cent of the plant species that grow in wetlands are useful to people, not to mention the important fish and wildlife products that this ecosystem offers. Traditional uses of plants include consumption for food, medicinal purposes, construction (boats and houses) and a variety of other uses including the making of dyes, glues and fish-poisons. The lakes of the Mahakam River of East Kalimantan produce more than 30 per cent of all dried freshwater fish consumed in Java, as well as supplying local markets. In western Kalimantan, the lakes of the Kapuas River produce 75 per cent of all freshwater fish consumed locally. Mangrove-based fisheries in Indonesia earned $US194 million in export earnings in 1978, more than seven times the combined export value of mahogany forestry products. Prawn exports in 1988 alone were worth more than $US482 million.

Although individual studies highlight the economic gains of trapping wild animals or collecting wild plants, it is impossible to put a price tag on the full value of biological diversity. We still tend to think of timber as the main reason for protecting a forest whereas, in fact, the value of food and medicines, together with the many vital functions that a forest provides, certainly far exceeds the revenue from timber. One reason for this is that many resources are consumed locally and never reach the market place – tropical timber, of course, is an obvious exception. For years, economists, conservationists and planners have failed to appreciate the real value of forests. Apart from the many 'invisible' functions that forests perform (watershed protec-

tion, prevention of soil erosion and nutrient recycling, for example), we are only now becoming aware of the fragile links that forests, and the plants and animals that they habour, play in our daily lives. Finding a way to protect and preserve these resources has now become one of mankind's greatest challenges.

People rarely think of forests as sources of anything other than timber, and it is difficult for many to imagine what other possible riches these diverse natural communities might possess. Indigenous people however, who rely on forest products for their daily survival, have far greater knowledge and appreciation of the 'hidden' values of these resources. They learn the best hunting and fishing grounds, where honey can be collected, and which plants can be tapped for fresh drinking water or used as medicinal remedies. It is also in their own interests to pay careful attention to the breeding cycles and migration patterns of the many wild species which provide them with a source of food, clothing and decorative objects.

Forest products apart, the importance and value of maintaining natural vegetation cover is often underestimated in development schemes, which include clearance of forest for agriculture. In particular, the economic and social impacts are rarely taken into consideration at the planning stages of such initiatives. In the late 1980s, for example, it has been estimated that environmental disasters in Indonesia resulted in financial losses of 1.1 trillion Rupiah ($US625 million). In addition, some 5000 people are believed to have died, while another 25,000 were injured and an estimated 100,000 left homeless. Much of this devastation was the result

Above: breadfruit.

Below: sago worms.

Above: butterfly alights on the head of Andarias Pridoman, an inhabitant of the Baliem Valley.

Right: Dani displaying sacred stones found in all homes, Baliem Valley.

Asmat woodcarver, Irian Jaya.

Facing page: mountain blue swallowtail butterfly.

Butterflies, Temminck.

of flooding and landslides, usually related to the clearance of forest cover and inappropriate landuse practices. Increasing population levels have resulted in increased pressure to produce food. This has led to unprecedented levels of forest clearance, even on mountainsides where the soil is thin and susceptible to erosion. In addition, forested areas throughout the region have been felled for their valuable timbers, adding to the problems of erosion, landslides and flooding.

Biological resources are frequently threatened because the responsibility and rewards for managing them have often been removed from the people who live closest to them. Quick profits from excessive logging or overfishing are divided among a few shareholders who live far from the resource; few, if any, are re-invested in the environment, and rural communities who depend on such resources derive little benefit, except for short-term employment. Such activities can result in great hardship and disruption to the traditions and lifestyles of forest-dwelling people. Transference of some management responsibilities to these communities would provide them with an added incentive to maintain their traditional, nondestructive ways of life, and in turn attend to the well-being of the environment. In Indonesia various conservation methods are being employed, of which one of the most promising involves local people in the design and establishment of protected areas such as national parks. This strategy helps to ensure that the considerable knowledge that local people have amassed over the generations is respected and represented in the future management of the environment.

Butterfly (or other insect) farming, for example, is a low-tech, inexpensive enterprise that requires limited investment and little upkeep and has minimal environmental impact. At present the world market for tropical butterflies is worth tens of millions of dollars a year. That market includes collectors – both museum curators and individual lepidopterists – scientists engaged in research and commercial organizations such as those manufacturing wall ornaments and placemats. Some of the most sought-after butterflies are native to Southeast Asia, particular the majestic birdwing butterflies. With assistance from the government and international conservation organizations, the isolated Hatam people of the Arfak Reserve in Irian Jaya have significantly reduced their former environmentally destructive slash-and-burn activities in favour of butterfly farming. While serving to protect the local forest environment, this radical change has provided local communities with an unexpectedly steady financial income that has greatly enhanced their life-styles. Initiatives such as this, small as they are, exhibit people's concern for the present state of the environment at a very local level, as well as their willingness to act positively to bring about change.

ON THE WINGS OF CONSERVATION

Although Indonesia's tropical forests support a rich and varied assemblage of insects, few are as impressive in size or beauty as the birdwing butterflies of the genus *Ornithoptera*. One of the best known areas for these species is the Arfak Mountains Nature Reserve in the Bird's Head Peninsula region of Irian Jaya – a reserve which supports several species of birdwing butterflies, including one species and two subspecies found nowhere else in the world.

The importance of the Arfak Reserve is well recognized on account of the high level of biological diversity contained within its forests, but also for the role it plays in maintaining and stabilizing the water flow, providing dependable clean water supplies to more than 23,000 people and reducing the potential of flooding and damage to coastal fisheries. The forests also provide a wide range of foodstuffs, medicines and building materials for the region's three indigenous groups – Hatam, Meyah and Sough. The reserve is actually the traditional homeland of the Hatam people; more than 80 per cent of their land is contained within the reserve. In recent years, increasing agricultural activities, settlement and logging in and around the reserve have begun to undermine the integrity of the forest and to threaten many of the useful services which it provides to the local communities.

In 1989 the Directorate General of Forest Protection and Nature Conservation (PHPA) of the Indonesian Ministry of Forestry, with assistance from WWF, set out to manage these forest resources in a manner that would help the economic development of the local communities and thereby support protection and management of the reserve. Various options were examined and several initiatives encouraged, of which one – butterfly farming – has found considerable support from local people. Protected by law, birdwing butterflies can only be sold legally if they have been farmed as opposed to caught from the wild. In contrast to the harmful practice of catching wild adult butterflies, harvesting them does not appear to have any lasting harm on the butterfly population. In fact, if carefully managed, farming can benefit conservation as it protects and enhances the natural habitat, provides employment and income to those actively involved in the business, and helps to control illegal catching and trade.

In the Arfak Mountains, several groups of Hatam farmers were encouraged to abandon destructive slash-and-burn agricultural practices and to establish and manage a number of artificial 'butterfly gardens' on the edge of the forest. These semi-natural areas are enriched by growing the favourite foodplants of birdwing butterflies, particularly plants of the genus *Aristolochia*. Butterflies are attracted from inside the forest to the gardens where they lay their eggs on suitable foodplants. When the eggs hatch the caterpillars gorge themselves for several weeks before pupating – the final stage of metamorphosis before the adult butterfly emerges. Pupae are then harvested by the local farmers who sell them to a central cooperative. From here, the pupae are either packaged and exported, or they are raised to the adult stage in special cages when they are also harvested. This process produces 'perfect' undamaged specimens.

In the past two years more than 850 farmers have subscribed to this scheme; some 1500 gardens have already been established. A collecting station has been established and participating farmers register with the cooperative. The results of this scheme are encouraging: in the first half of 1993 alone, the butterfly farming community made about $US11,000 from the sale of pupae and butterflies to the management agency. Incentives such as this help demonstrate the value of protecting natural resources; if the quality of the forest habitat is damaged – for example through logging or degradation following slash-and-burn cultivation – the number of egg-laying butterflies declines, resulting in a loss of potential income for the local communities. This scheme is just one of many innovative approaches that are being instituted to help show local people how they can develop and maintain a better lifestyle without destroying the natural resources of their homeland.

Facing page: the Asmat of southern Irian Jaya hunt a wide range of mammals and birds, their main source of protein. This man is wearing a hat made of cuscus fur.

THE FUTURE

Developments and changes over the last few centuries have brought unprecedented exposure to the indigenous forest-dwellers of Indonesia. As settlers follow the trails blazed by logging operations into the heartland of the forests of Sumatra and Kalimantan, forest people such as the Kubu and Punan have increasingly come into contact with the outside world. This experience was not initially at their behest. Increased confrontations have resulted in considerable alterations in their living conditions, life-style and expectations for the future. What does the future hold for these people who make few demands on modern society?

Romantic and colourful as it may seem to many outsiders, living entirely within the forest and being totally dependent upon its scarce resources is a demanding existence. Disease and sickness take their toll; comforts are few. Occasional shortages of food, perhaps as a result of pollution of a stream by gold-miners or over-hunting by other settlers or poachers, compound these problems for people who traditionally have taken no more from the forest than that which meets their immediate requirements.

Increasing contact with the outside world has clearly brought many problems to groups like the Kubu. A seemingly easier way of life and the attractions of material goods have gradually drawn more and more people away from the forests and their traditional ways. The promise of what seems to be a better life beckons to an increasing number of people. Some have abandoned their traditional life-style completely, opting to live around one of the many settlements that dot the landscape of southern Sumatra. The consequences vary considerably; many are able to find employment as farm labourers or work for timber companies. Others are less successful. Once they leave the relative security and familial ties to their traditional homes, beliefs and practices, however, few seem able to retain more than a semblance of their former, traditional way of life.

Such erosion of cultural identity has led to problems in many parts of the world. This has now begun to be realized, and greater efforts are being made to include and support indigenous people in decisions affecting the long-term planning and development of natural resources and, particularly, through the establishment of protected areas. Special ethnic reserves have even been established in some countries, such as Brazil, Guatemala and Costa Rica in South and Central America, to protect the rights of such forest-dependent people. The future of the few remaining small populations of forest-dwelling people in Indonesia, together with a much larger number of people who in some way supplement their living through the extraction of forest products, is ultimately linked to the well-being of the forests.

MANAGING CHANGE IN INDONESIA'S FORESTS

Above: a well-established nursery – often a starting point for reforestation programmes using native tree species.

Right: Dayak women farmers preparing the ground and planting grains of hill rice.

The arrival of *Homo sapiens* in Southeast Asia, some 50,000 years ago, heralded a period of major change for the environment. Nowhere has their impact been greater than in the tropical forests, particularly in the lowland regions of countries such as Thailand, The Philippines, Indonesia and Malaysia. There are two main reasons why tropical forests have been so drastically affected: clearance for agricultural purposes and commercial logging for the valuable timber resources. These activities are carried out independently of each other and are conducted by different groups of people with very different goals, though ultimately they may be controlled by the same conglomerates. Their combined effect represents one of the greatest environmental threats for Indonesia, and other countries which still possess substantial areas of natural forest.

SHIFTING CULTIVATION – PROBLEMS AND PROSPECTS

People have used fire to modify the Earth's landscape for tens of thousands of years. In so doing they transformed and controlled the natural environment in countries such as Indonesia in a way unsurpassed by any other living creature. One of the main impacts of fire on the environment has been the burning of forest, primarily in the preparation of land for cultivation.

Permanent cultivation in rain forests is difficult since nutrients are quickly depleted from the soils. Another problem which settlers face is that when

disturbance to the forest is at a low level, the forest regenerates quickly, almost with a vengeance, smothering the alien crops that have been planted. With the advent of fire, however, settlers soon learned that by partially felling and then burning patches of forest, wide areas could be cleared, weeds did not recover so quickly and, most important, a reasonable number of crops could be grown with a minimum of labour and maintenance.

Shifting cultivation, also known as 'slash-and-burn' or 'swidden agriculture', is a system which provides adequate crop yields for a modest input of labour. The basic system involves the rotating use of different patches of forest every 2-3 years for growing crops. Following this period, the plot is abandoned (left fallow) and the vegetation allowed to regenerate. Meanwhile, another plot of land will have been cleared elsewhere – either a new piece of forest, or one that has already been worked in previous years. Depending on circumstances and tradition, the length of the fallow period may extend from 4-15 years, and occasionally to 30 years.

A range of shifting agricultural systems has evolved among the many cultures of Indonesia, each geared to meet local environmental conditions. As people migrate to other areas of the archipelago, these practices are spread more widely. Often, however, the techniques which suited one set of soil-forest conditions will not be appropriate for another, spelling disaster if precious topsoil is exposed and washed away under heavy rain.

The extent of forest clearance also varies consid-

erably from one culture to another, and according to the original state of the forest. For some tribes, selecting and preparing the plot is possibly of equal importance to the after-care of crops. Some traditional agriculturalists select their land according to relief, drainage patterns and the presence of particular tree species – some of which are known to grow on more fertile soils than others. Once the site has been identified, all fruit and other useful plants may be collected before clearance begins. In Irian Jaya, where large numbers of domestic pigs are maintained as family status symbols, some timber may be cut and removed to create sturdy fences which serve to keep the pigs out of the vegetable fields. In most cases, however, it is burnt and left lying on the ground for Nature to reclaim. In traditional swidden systems, care is usually taken to ensure that certain species of trees are allowed to remain and that others are cut well above the ground, encouraging fast regrowth and successful regeneration once the plot is abandoned. Where such care is taken and traditions respected, swidden gardens can be highly productive – for example through the growth and accessibility of fruit trees – and beneficial to wildlife. Newly abandoned gardens provide good forage for grazing animals, some of which in turn may be hunted by the people.

The remainder of the clearing process is fairly standard: trees are cut at the beginning of the dry season and left to dry for several months under the scorching sun and dry winds. When dry, this is burnt, eliminating undergrowth and weeds. By burning the vegetation, nutrients that are otherwise locked up in the plants are released to the soil which, together with the resulting ash, cause a temporary enrichment of minerals in the soil. The area is then lightly tilled – often only with simple wooden digging tools – and a crop planted at the beginning of the wet season in the forest's ashes.

Many crops are grown among the charred trunks of fallen forest giants – dryland rice and maize being two of the most important, together with sweet potatoes, cassava, spices and fruits. Traditional swidden systems rely on expertise accumulated over many generations; the careful selection and mixing of crops to suit particular conditions and to reduce losses to crop pests.

Shifting cultivators are often blamed for the current pitiful state of the world's tropical forests. However, as long as the human population remained relatively low, traditional shifting cultivation was not especially destructive. Extensive logging practices are often far more harmful, both through the construction of roads for moving machinery and timber and the destruction wreaked by the falling trees and soil compaction by heavy machinery. The digging of deep trenches caused by skidding logs is also damaging. By opening up new areas of forest, logging companies inadvertently 'open the door' for a range of migrants and settlers, including miners, agriculturalists and hunters. In so doing they can contribute to the demise of the forest ecosystem, as well as the sustainable livelihoods of traditional swidden agriculturalists who, under certain conditions, are recognized as being among the best qualified guardians of the natural forests.

Below: coal layers burning after the 1983 forest fire in Kalimantan.

FIRE IN THE FOREST

Long before humans discovered and learnt to control fire, it had been an important factor in shaping and maintaining the structure and diversity of many forest habitats, particularly deciduous and open savanna ecosystems. Many of the drier forests of Southeast Asia experience periodic droughts, during which trees shed their leaves in order to reduce the loss of precious water reserves. Fires are frequently an outcome of these droughts. Old vegetation is burnt off providing light and nutrients for new growth. In addition many trees rely on the effects of fire to weaken and break open their tough seed cases and stimulate germination. Many of these events are localised in scale and distribution. Occasionally, however, they may get out of control. From September 1982 until July 1983, one of the most destructive forest fires ever destroyed 35,000 square kilometres of natural forest in East Kalimantan. The fire was the combined result of hundreds of slash-and-burn cultivators; but was intensified by drought conditions induced by the El Niño effect of unusually warm ocean conditions, and exacerbated by the effects of selective logging. The fires spread quickly where dry combustible material from timber extraction littered the forest floor, also reaching into peat swamps where the dried, friable surface soil burned fiercely, exposing coal seams. Eventually the fires extinguished themselves, but the economic losses have not yet been calculated. In addition to the considerable losses to wildlife, the lives of the people were threatened and disrupted; loss of forest has also resulted in increased erosion of topsoils and subsequent sedimentation in rivers. Similar events took place on Sumatra and Halmahera during the same period, while in 1987 and 1994, other major outbreaks of fire were recorded in South Kalimantan and Sumatra. Fire, however, is a natural part of many ecosystems and there are already some signs of recovery, though full regeneration will take a long time as the scale of devastation in these instances was so great.

Above: the area given over to clove plantations in Indonesia is slowly increasing – sometimes at the expense of lowland forest.

Right: once harvested, the green cloves must be carefully dried in the sun before being packaged and transported to market.

MODERN PLANTATIONS

Large areas of Indonesia's lowland forests have been cleared of natural vegetation to allow the establishment of vast areas of tree crops such as rubber and oil palm. Such development, often referred to as the 'ultimate destruction of primary forest' requires the total removal of forest and the laying out of monocultures in straight lines which facilitate early care of the crops, as well later as harvesting.

Plantations have a long history in Southeast Asia, dating back to the nineteenth century when much of the region's wealth was based on the extensive growth of cash crops, including sugar, rubber, oil palm, cinchona, coffee, indigo, spices, tobacco and coconuts for copra. Many of these products were completely alien to the Indonesian environment. The natural home of the rubber tree (*Hevea brasiliensis*), for example, is the Amazon Basin. The plant was first brought to the region from Kew Gardens to the Singapore Botanic Gardens in 1877. Encouraged by increasing demands for rubber products in Europe, vast areas of natural forest were cleared to establish rubber plantations in Malaysia, Indonesia and Thailand. In a similar fashion, the West African oil palm (*Elais guineensis*) was first introduced to Asia via Bogor in the early twentieth century. Grown for the oil in its seeds and surrounding fruit pulp (pericarp), it too was later introduced to Malaysia and Thailand. Indonesia is currently the world's second largest exporter of palm oil, after Malaysia. Today, timber plantations are the fastest growing type of plantation.

In destroying the natural forest cover and replacing it with an immense area of trees that are uniform in size, shape and composition, plantations have a profound impact on the environment. Plantations are not entirely devoid of wildlife – some species of birds and mammal have successfully adapted to living in such habitats – but it is usually a fraction of what existed in the original forest. Mammals that can live in plantations include rats and other rodents, tree shrews, and some primates. The continued viability of plantations; the constant need to apply large amounts of fertilizer and herbicides each year, together with falling prices for many plantation commodities such as rubber, palm oil, cocoa, and coffee as a result of over-production, through mismanagement and impractical incentives and trade controls imposed by developed countries is a problem in many parts of the world. In their favour, however, plantations can often make good buffer zones around conservation areas.

RESETTLEMENT

One of the greatest problems facing the Indonesian environment, in general, and its remaining natural forests, in particular, is the existing and planned, future pattern of human settlements. The islands of Java, Bali and Madura are home to more than 70 per cent of the population, but represent just seven per cent of the country's land area. Since 1905, more than 3.3 million people have been moved from these islands to new settlements in the less-crowded parts of Sumatra, Kalimantan, Maluku, Nusa Tenggara and Irian Jaya. This ambitious programme of resettlement has been conducted through the Indonesian Transmigration Programme, the world's largest programme for voluntary, government-sponsored migration. Throughout the century, in addition to government sponsored migration, there have been many other people (estimates suggest more than through the official programme) who have moved independently.

The programme was initially designed and implemented because inappropriate land use in the highlands of Java, resulting from dense human concentrations, was causing widespread soil erosion and habitat degradation. Human life was even threatened in some places. The transmigration process was seen not only as a means of relieving overcrowding in certain parts of the country, but also as a way of promoting new industry and development in some of the remoter parts of the archipelago, particularly in Kalimantan and Irian Jaya.

Above: harvesting the tiny cloves is an arduous task.

Below: a transmigration settlement in east Kalimantan.

For some transmigrants however, expectations of their new homes were not realized. In the past, many of the sites were poorly chosen and support services were not able to keep pace with the demand from new arrivals. Insufficient attention was given to cultural sensitivities; as a result, many settlers introduced inappropriate agricultural techniques which often involved further losses of forest and wildlife. An unexpected problem also arose from 'uninvited guests' to the settlements. In addition to those officially moved, it is thought that as many as four million people have moved voluntarily within the Indonesian Archipelago, often being attracted by the possibility of a better life in transmigration areas.

Authorities have become more aware of the direct and indirect effects of such schemes in past years and recent programmes have met with far greater success. The scale of the programme has also been reduced. Yet, transmigration remains a sensitive issue in Indonesia and its role in the demise and degradation of the natural environment cannot be overlooked. The government has rightly recognized that resettlement alone is not the answer to the problem of overcrowding. Family planning programmes, as well as new initiatives for soil conservation and agricultural intensification are today linked to the transmigration programmes.

Facing page: tea plantations have consumed large areas of Indonesia's forests.

Rubber, mainly grown in Sumatra, is shown being tapped.

Coffee is widely grown in Indonesia, often in association with other tree crops such as cloves, or intercropped with maize and fruit trees.

Above: blighted by forest fires, some areas of Kalimantan are being replanted.

Facing page: valuable tropical hardwoods from Kalimantan form part of the floating traffic on the Doen River.

Following page: the sheltered shores of Baluran National Park, East Java, support a rich and varied vegetation including Sonneratia mangroves (centre) and fan palms (right).

LOGGING AND ALTERNATIVES

The demand for tropical timbers has never been greater. A decreasing reservoir of readily available timber, together with trade restrictions and increased consumer awareness of the problems related to logging in tropical forests have resulted in higher prices being paid for processed and unprocessed timbers alike. In the European, Japanese and the North American markets, a single rain forest tree can be worth more than $US1000. It is ironic that such wealth can be derived from some of the world's poorest soils. Properly managed, the vast and varied resources of the rain forest can yield unexpectedly high financial benefits to local communities and national governments. In addition, the long-term cultural, aesthetic and recreational benefits which accrue from maintaining natural forests will then be guarded.

The quest for tropical timber has had a major impact on Indonesia. From 1976 to 1980, scientists estimate that some 5500 square kilometres of forest was cleared or degraded each year – an area the size of Bali. Rather than showing any signs of abating, the rate of exploitation actually continued to increase to some 6000 square kilometres per annum from 1981 to 1985 and to an estimated 7000 square kilometres in the early 1990s. Some authorities fear it may now even be as high as 12,000 square kilometres a year. Such rates of forest loss place Indonesia second only in the world to Brazil.

Some visitors to Indonesia, aware of these figures, could well be forgiven for not expecting to see any forest during their travels. Fortunately, however, this is not the case. Despite the high rates of deforestation in the archipelago, tropical rain forests still occur extensively on all of the large islands. But for how much longer? Tattered fringes mark most of the boundaries of tropical forests in Indonesia, as constant encroachment is made by farmers clearing the land. Gradually, even these last forests appear to be retreating to safer havens within steep valleys and near mountain tops.

In the face of these pressures, however, much credit should be given to the Indonesian Government which has taken some measures to control and restrict logging operations. Although most of Indonesia's easily accessible lowland forest has been let as forest concessions, logging companies are now required to undertake reforestation programmes. The government is also planning to develop alternative means of using forests. Ecotourism, the promotion of nature and wildlife viewing, is becoming increasingly important as a source of foreign revenue. Each year, thousands of visitors come to Indonesia for its beautiful beaches and spectacular coral reefs. If encouraged, more and more of these tourists would spend some time within national parks, where they could easily explore and admire Indonesia's many extraordinary forest environments.

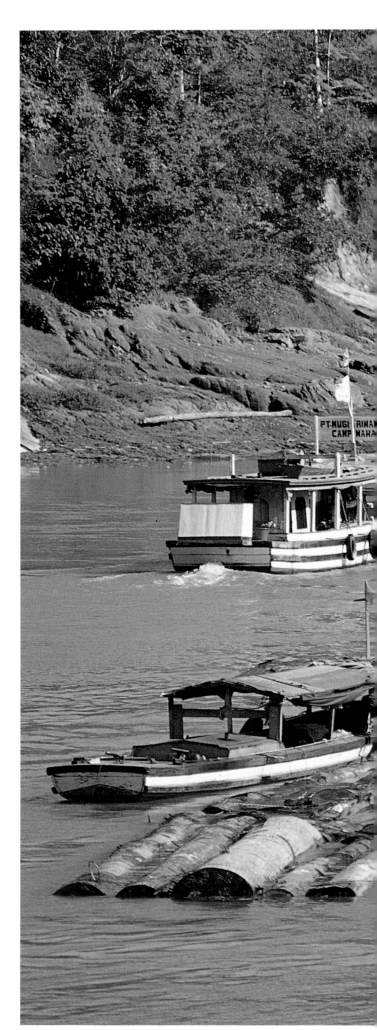

THE ROLE OF PROTECTED AREAS

The loss of forests worldwide and increasing appreciation of the wider implications have led governments to act to set aside and protect representative portions of their natural heritage. As this happens, more and more people are gradually beginning to appreciate the considerable advantages which accrue. Among these benefits are features such as: protecting important watersheds and thus ensuring regular supplies of water in towns and villages, safeguarding people's livelihoods, protecting the natural gene bank, and enjoying non-destructive forms of recreation in and around forests.

Recognizing the need to conserve its rich biological diversity, the Government of Indonesia has made a commitment to protect ten per cent of the country's land area and, eventually, some 200,000 square kilometres of coastal and marine habitats as conservation areas. But experience has shown that protection alone is not enough to secure the future of these important sites. In the past, many protect-

ed areas were established and maintained purely to protect the natural resources. The needs and desires of local communities – who were frequently better managers of these resources than outsiders since they often depended directly on them for their survival – were often neglected in the decision-making process. Recently, however, the need to involve local people in decisions concerning the management of forested areas has become much more obvious. New initiatives to link development and environmental protection have emerged in Indonesia and have been widely welcomed by rural communities. An example of such new alliances can be seen in Irian Jaya. Community involvement and traditional land use rights are of great importance to the Hatam people living in the Arfak Mountains Nature Reserve. With assistance from conservation organizations, recent developments have helped transform slash-and-burn agriculturalists into successful butterfly farmers! Realizing the value of some of the exotic birdwing butterflies that occur in this reserve, conservation organizations helped selected communities establish 'butterfly gardens' which protect important feed plants for the adults and caterpillars. Pupae are collected and taken to a special hatchery where the adults are marketed, providing an important source of income and relieving the pressure on remaining forests.

One of Indonesia's most beautiful protected areas is the recently established Bogani Nani Wartabone National Park in northern Sulawesi. Home to the maleo, babirusa, anoa, black macaque and the tiny, night-dwelling tarsier, this park consists of 3000 square kilometres of virgin rain forest. Extensive deforestation of the surrounding hills had

resulted in erosion and flooding, leading to a loss of income for lowland farmers and threatening the lives of many people. A major irrigation project developed in the lowlands was hindered by excessive deposition of soil washed off the hillsides. More than a decade ago the government took firm steps to halt and reverse the destruction caused by loss of vegetation cover, and established a national park. By protecting the forests within the newly declared national park, a major water catchment area has been secured. With this, of course, comes security for the local inhabitants and added protection for the rich and varied wildlife of the region.

Similar developments, although with a different theme, have also taken place on the tiny islands of Komodo and Bali, where the Komodo and Bali Barat National Parks, respectively, offer sanctuary to two rare and unique species – the Komodo dragon, the largest living lizard, and the exotic Bali starling. Without the protection of the reserves, these species would almost certainly perish.

Establishing and maintaining protected areas, which can be an expensive operation, is not easy. Many problems have resulted from misinterpretation of the objectives and poor planning and management. When carefully planned, however, there can be many benefits. Among the most obvious, direct benefits of protected areas are the protection of renewable resources which can be harvested for human use; support for nature-related recreation and tourism; and protection of wild species of plants and animals, many of which may have important spiritual, cultural and economic associations. Villagers around Gunung Leuser National Park in Sumatra for instance use more than 170 plants for medicinal purposes. The park helps ensure local supplies of these plants. In addition, a great many indirect benefits are achieved, including protection of soils, provision of clean, fresh water supplies, and the provision of educational and scientific research facilities.

Indonesia currently has 366 established conservation areas, including 26 terrestrial national parks. Sadly, no protected area is immune from threats to its integrity. A wide range of pressures still affect these sites, including deforestation, pollution, inappropriate management, human disturbances and, in such a geologically unsettled country as this, natural disasters. An estimated 12 million people live in and around the forests of Indonesia. Frequently it is the poorest rural people who are most dependent on biodiversity and natural habitats for their livelihoods; it is they who suffer first and most when those habitats are impoverished or destroyed. The Indonesian Government has clearly demonstrated its intention to protect the most important parts of its biological diversity and some of the most spectacular parts of its country. This commitment is a clear symbol of the recognition of the importance which biological diversity plays in our lives.

PARKS

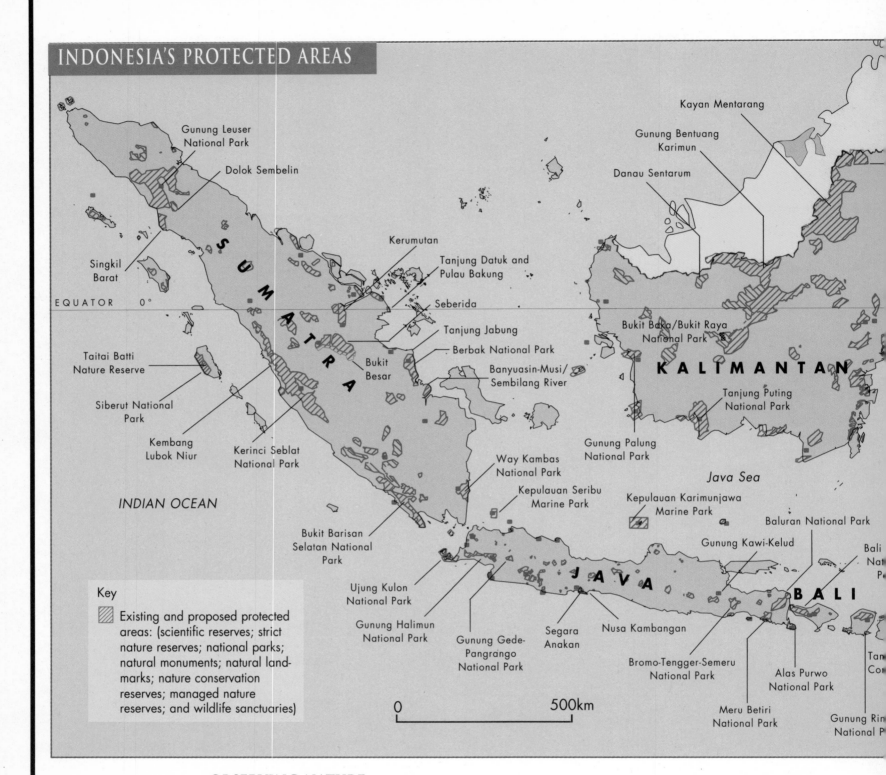

INDONESIA'S PROTECTED AREAS

Kayan Mentarang

Gunung Bentuang
Karimun

Danau Sentarum

Gunung Leuser
National Park

Dolok Sembelin

Kerumutan

Tanjung Datuk and
Pulau Bakung

Seberida

Singkil
Barat

EQUATOR   0°

Tanjung Jabung

Berbak National Park

Bukit Baka/Bukit Raya
National Park

KALIMANTAN

Taitai Batti
Nature Reserve

Bukit
Besar

Banyuasin-Musi/
Sembilang River

Tanjung Puting
National Park

Siberut National
Park

Kembang
Lubok Niur

Kerinci Seblat
National Park

Way Kambas
National Park

Gunung Palung
National Park

Java Sea

INDIAN OCEAN

Kepulauan Seribu
Marine Park

Kepulauan Karimunjawa
Marine Park

Baluran National Park

Gunung Kawi-Kelud

Bali
Nat
P

Bukit Barisan
Selatan National
Park

JAVA

BALI

Key

Existing and proposed protected
areas: (scientific reserves; strict
nature reserves; national parks;
natural monuments; natural land-
marks; nature conservation
reserves; managed nature
reserves; and wildlife sanctuaries)

Ujung Kulon
National Park

Gunung Halimun
National Park

Gunung Gede-
Pangrango
National Park

Segara
Anakan

Nusa Kambangan

Bromo-Tengger-Semeru
National Park

Alas Purwo
National Park

Tam
Co

Meru Betiri
National Park

Gunung Rin
National P

0   500km

OBSERVING NATURE

Indonesia is immensely rich and diverse in terms of the
animal species it contains, but actually spotting wildlife is
not easy. Most of the terrestrial parks consist of dense
tropical vegetation where animals can easily hide. In
addition, many species are shy and elusive, either by
nature or because of hunting. Expectations of seeing
animals should be low – any sightings will then come as a
pleasant surprise! Visitors should be careful not to
underestimate the difficulty of exploring most parks due to
the heat, humidity, high rainfall and rugged terrain.

In addition to these natural difficulties, the infrastructure
of wildlife tourism in Indonesia is still limited. In general,
neither the Perlindungan Hutan dan Pelestarian Alam
(PHPA), the Directorate General of Forest Protection and
Nature Conservation, the government body in charge of
national parks and nature reserves, nor tour operators,
understand what wildlife tourists expect. The standard of
guiding is low, with park rangers and private guides
having limited knowledge of wildlife and how to spot it.

For the best results, excursions should always be made in
groups and everyone – guides and tourists – should move
slowly and very quietly. Smoking, chatting, and rapid
movement will reduce the chances of seeing anything.

The best time of day for seeing wildlife in all the parks
(except the marine ones) is early morning; most animals
also have a period of lesser activity in the late afternoon.
Many tour operators offer day trips to national parks
because of the lack of decent accommodation: such trips
are of little value. To see much wildlife it is essential to
spend at least one night in a park, venturing forth as it
gets light. The basic kit needed for a reasonable night in
the spartan accommodation available in most Indonesian
parks is: mosquito net, sleeping-bag sheet liner or sarong,
tikar mat, torch and bottled water. Food is generally not
available, so emergency rations should be taken.

These warnings are intended to prepare, not dissuade!
Spending a few hours in a tropical forest is an awe-
inspiring experience. Just to feel this incredibly complex
ecosystem filling all the senses is worth any number of

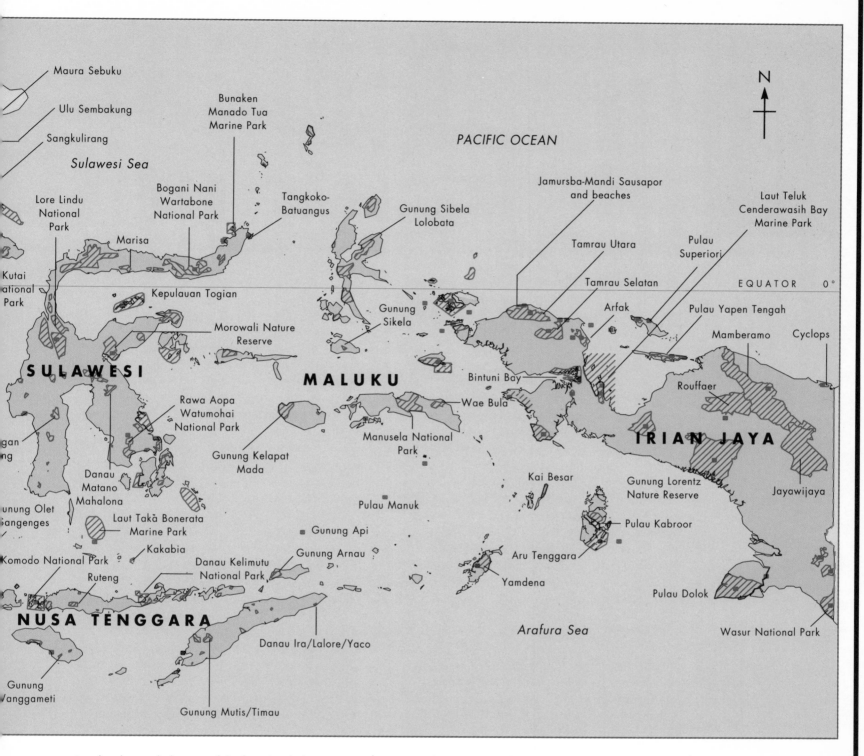

Maura Sebuku

Ulu Sembakung

Sangkulirang

Sulawesi Sea

Bunaken
Manado Tua
Marine Park

PACIFIC OCEAN

N

Jamursba-Mandi Sausapor
and beaches

Laut Teluk
Cenderawasih Bay
Marine Park

Lore Lindu
National
Park

Bogani Nani
Wartabone
National Park

Tangkoko-
Batuangus

Gunung Sibela
Lolobata

Tamrau Utara

Pulau
Superiori

Marisa

Kutai
National
Park

Kepulauan Togian

Tamrau Selatan

Arfak

EQUATOR   0°

Pulau Yapen Tengah

Morowali Nature
Reserve

Gunung
Sikela

Mamberamo

Cyclops

SULAWESI

MALUKU

Bintuni Bay

Rouffaer

Rawa Aopa
Watumohai
National Park

Wae Bula

IRIAN JAYA

gan
ng

Gunung Kelapat
Mada

Manusela National
Park

Danau
Matano
Mahalona

Kai Besar

Gunung Lorentz
Nature Reserve

Jayawijaya

unung Olet
Sangenges

Laut Takà Bonerata
Marine Park

Pulau Manuk

Pulau Kabroor

Kakabia

Gunung Api

Gunung Arnau

Aru Tenggara

Komodo National Park

Danau Kelimutu
National Park

Pulau Dolok

Ruteng

Yamdena

NUSA TENGGARA

Danau Ira/Lalore/Yaco

Arafura Sea

Wasur National Park

Gunung
Wanggameti

Gunung Mutis/Timau

minor hassles, and glimpses of the forest's inhabitants are highly rewarding: a malkoha among the branches hunting for insects; a palm civet feeding unconcernedly, unaware of being observed; or a family of gibbons at close range, calling out in their melodious whoops.

ORGANIZATION OF PROTECTED AREAS

Protected areas in Indonesia are categorised into national parks, game reserves, strict nature reserves, hunting preserves, protected forest and recreation parks or forests. The categorisation is according to size, uniqueness of the ecosystem and function. All are under the jurisdiction of the Ministry of Forestry, with the PHPA responsible for administration of conservation and recreation functions.

The recreation parks and forests *(taman hutan raya* and *hutan wisata)* are generally of little biological significance but are important as a leisure resource, particularly for domestic tourists. Access to the strict nature reserves *(cagar alam)* is restricted and special permits have to be obtained (although in practice staffing levels are too low to control

visitors). The national parks *(taman nasional)* are designed to protect biota of national and international significance and are assuming increasing importance as recreational resources for both domestic and international tourists, contributing to Indonesia's foreign exchange earnings through revenue from the latter group. All of the national parks have been gazetted since 1980, often incorporating older protected areas. Permits to visit the national parks can generally be obtained from PHPA offices at the entrance to each of the parks or in the nearest town. Since 1993 a small entrance fee has been charged.

There are over 350 protected areas throughout Indonesia, including 26 terrestrial national parks and five marine parks. The 21 parks and reserves described in this section have been chosen to give a representative sample of Indonesian fauna, flora and habitats, best wildlife viewing and least primitive facilities for the visitor. They include those which are most easily accessible from the main centres of the archipelago.

CONSERVATION OF INDONESIA'S NATURAL WEALTH

Above: elephant in Way Kambas National Park, Sumatra.

Reading about Indonesia's natural wealth could lead to a sense of complacency and the assumption that everything is fine in this Garden of Eden. This is not so. Indonesia's environment is threatened from many different sides. Indonesia is the fourth most populated country in the world, after China, India and the United States of America, and the third most populated developing country. The current population of almost 190 million people is expected to continue to grow until the year 2030 when it may level off at about 250 million. This large population inevitably places great demands upon the land, and this is nowhere more obvious than in Java where more than 60 per cent of the population is concentrated. Since the late 1960s, with transmigration programmes, agricultural developments, exploitation of natural resources and general urban development, all regions of the archipelago have been affected to some degree.

Thanks to a far sighted scheme, led by the Directorate General for Forest Protection and Nature Conservation (PHPA), Indonesia now has over 350 protected areas. Lack of human and financial resources is a major handicap to effective management, but a number of interesting and successful conservation projects have been initiated. Many of the protected areas have key 'flagship' species at their head, such as the orang-utans of Gunung Leuser, tigers at Kerinci Seblat and elephants at Way Kambas. Others, such as the Kayan Mentarang Nature Reserve in Kalimantan, and the proposed Gunung Lorentz National Park in Irian Jaya, are centres of outstanding biological and cultural diversity and thus warrant protection.

Park management today focuses less on the species and ecosystems which the parks were set up to protect, and more on the people who rely upon their resources. Demonstrating how protected areas can contribute to and even enhance people's livelihoods is now the cutting edge of modern conservation. Many of today's conservation programmes involve agriculture or agro-forestry schemes to support local people. They may also involve commercial activities, such as the growing of cinnamon or extraction of rattan (Kerinci), farming of butterflies (Arfak), fish farming (Cyclops) and the extraction of oils from local plants (Wasur). As the following examples show, innovative methods are being used to tackle some of these problems and to strengthen conservation efforts.

CANTEEN IN THE TREETOPS

The rain forests of northern Sumatra might seem an unlikely place to open a restaurant, particularly one where the clients are not encouraged to come back and where the menu is kept deliberately boring; the same day after day. Yet business is good and the service is eagerly supported.

These 'canopy cafés' are at the heart of an ambitious conservation programme for the orang-utan (*Pongo pygmaeus*). Many young orang-utans are captured and sold as pets. When this happens, it usually means that hunters have already killed the infant's mother and the orphans are unable to look after themselves. Baby orang-utans are attractive playmates but as they outgrow their juvenile charms and become more unruly, most are abandoned or confined to cages where they lead a miserable existence. The Bohorok Rehabilitation Centre was established in 1973 on the periphery of the Gunung Leuser National Park, North Sumatra, to return once captive animals to the wild. The centre was established with funds from WWF and is now completely managed by the PHPA. Since it first opened, more than 150 wild juvenile orang-utans have benefited from this restaurant and have been returned to the forest.

Rehabilitation, however, is a slow and expensive process. When animals are first brought to the sanctuary, each must spend several months in quarantine to ensure that they are in good health and that no infectious diseases will later be transmitted to wild animals. Surprisingly, these most agile of apes also have to be taught to climb. They are gradually encouraged to climb on ropes and branches to build up their strength, to construct simple nests, and to forage and experiment with eating different foods. Gradually they are introduced again to the forest, initially from the shoulders of a park guard and later by spending short periods of time playing amongst the vegetation. Eventually they are released near to a feeding station where copious amounts of bananas and milk are supplied to all-comers. These items are initially intended to complement natural foods the animals find in the forests but the diet is kept deliberately boring to encourage the animals to look for choicer items in the forest. Twice a day, rehabilitation animals return to these platforms, swinging down from the treetops for their rations. This opportunity provides park rangers with an easy way of monitoring the progress and health of the rehabilitated animals.

In addition to these orphaned animals, another source of clients for the centre has been juvenile and sub-adult animals captured in forests which were about to be logged. Depending on their age, these too are released around the feeding stations or further inside the forest. Initiatives such as the rehabilitation programme at Bohorok play an important role in raising conservation awareness and in solving the problems of orphaned or abandoned orang-utans. Any visitor to Bohorok will find it particularly gratifying to witness the success of such initiatives and marvel as a young female orang-utan – released just a few years ago – returns to the feeding stations carrying a tiny baby. That this baby can grow up in the relative safety of the national park is a tribute to the dedicated work of the research staff and park rangers, and the PHPA.

LEARNING FROM TRADITION

Peering down from the summit of Gunung Kerinci, Indonesia's highest peak outside Irian Jaya, many of the country's conservation problems are laid out in the vast stretch of forest below, surrounded by agricultural lands and settlements. The ragged, tattered edges of the forest signal the constant pressure of agricultural incursions on this habitat.

Kerinci Seblat National Park is the largest conservation area in Sumatra and includes some of the largest unbroken stretches of closed canopy forest along the spine of the country. The park extends across four provinces and supports a wide range of wildlife, including most of the country's large mammals – elephant, tiger, Sumatran rhinoceros, clouded leopard, serow and tapir. Logging and agriculture practised by newcomers are widespread; clearance of land for cinnamon plantations (which earned Indonesia some $US22 million in exports in 1989) has become a particular threat. Conservation of remaining forests within the park is a high priority as they are crucial for the protection of the watersheds of two of the most important rivers in Sumatra, on which over 3,000,000 people and 70,000 square kilometres of agricultural land depend.

Working with local communities, park authorities, provincial and local governments, PHPA and WWF have designed an innovative conservation programme intended to improve the living conditions of local communities in a manner which will also help ensure long-term protection of the national park. Among the activities has been the rehabilitation of degraded, derelict lands and introduction of agro-forestry schemes to provide food and cash crops, as well as animal fodder and building materials. Support has also been provided to encourage the maintenance and development of traditional village woodlots in which the forest is protected according to local customs and traditions. Careful management and replanting within the woodlot have enabled the community to harvest fruit and timber products without destroying the ecological balance of the forest. In addition, water from the woodlot has been used to develop a community fishery project using local fish species. Recognition of the project's achievements was gained in 1993, when the President of the Republic of Indonesia presented the Kalapataru – Indonesia's top environmental award – to Darius Khatib, the customary leader of the Keluru Community, for development of the Temedack Customary Village Woodlot Project. Following the success of this project, support for similar initiatives has been widespread, with more and more villages subscribing to these practices.

Elsewhere in the park, WWF has encouraged the development of ecotourism through support of local home-stays and the development of the Eco Rural Travel Corporation. In the first half of 1993, more than 500 domestic and 200 foreign tourists benefited from these activities – particularly guide, accommodation and related services – providing a valuable source of income to rural communities and helping demonstrate further the importance of maintaining the natural resources of the region.

Left: mother and baby orang-utan, Bohorok Rehabilitation Centre, Sumatra.

① *Agamid lizard.*
② *Damselfly.*
③ *Elephants.*
④ *White-winged wood duck.*

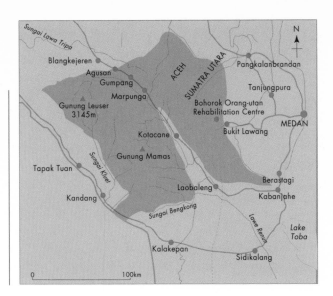

GUNUNG LEUSER

Gunung Leuser is one of the most important parks in Southeast Asia because of its size and diversity. It covers 9500 square kilometres and ranges in altitude from sea-level to mountains, with Gunung Leuser the highest at 3145 metres. Twelve major rivers flow from the park, supplying domestic and agricultural water to more than two million people.

Forty-five per cent of the 9000 plant species known for the West Indo-Malayan region are found in the Leuser ecosystem. The trees are mostly dipterocarps. The large parasitic flower *Rafflesia* occurs here. Various fruit and other trees with commercially valuable crops grow wild, including camphor, durian, banana, citrus, rambutan and cinnamon.

Leuser is home to 54 per cent of Sumatra's terrestrial species and is one of the few places where viable populations of some of the rarer species remain. It is a stronghold of the endangered Sumatran rhinoceros and the orang-utan: the Bohorok orang-utan rehabilitation station is on its eastern border. Other spectacular mammals among the 105 species present are the Sumatran elephant, tiger, serow, siamang, white-handed gibbon, Thomas' leaf-monkey, pig-tailed macaque and sunbear. There are at least 95 species of reptile and amphibian, including crocodiles and the false

gharial, and 313 bird species, including nine hornbills and five pheasants, of which the Argus pheasant with its distinctive call is the most commonly heard.

To the east of Gunung Leuser are the lands of the entrepreneurial, mainly Christian, Karo Bataks, while within the park and to the north are the Islamic Alas and Gayo peoples. The Alas River bisects the park from north to south. Along its upper reaches there is serious encroachment of the protected area by settlers who farm the flat land along the valley and, increasingly, the steep slopes beyond. This habitat disturbance has serious implications for some important species, notably the elephant, which is now divided into two populations within the park. A European Union funded programme is currently attempting to deal with the poverty and land needs of local people by providing alternatives to exploiting the park's resources. One successful project has encouraged villagers to police their own sections of river and prevent outsiders from poaching fish. Depleted fish stocks have recovered since the introduction of this scheme.

Although 90 per cent of Gunung Leuser lies in the province of Aceh, the main points of access are via North Sumatra, starting from Medan. The most

popular parts of the park are the Bohorok orang-utan station near Bukit Lawang, where there is a good range of accommodation, and the Kutacane area, where rafting trips down the Alas River start and from where treks into the forest can be made. The quality and range of tourist facilities are improving as tourism becomes better developed.

KERINCI SEBLAT

Kerinci Seblat is Indonesia's largest national park, covering 14,846 square kilometres of mountainous territory in the Bukit Barisan range in western Sumatra. The park is notable for its high levels of biological diversity and its spectacular scenery of lakes, forests and high peaks, including 3800 metre Gunung Kerinci, the highest mountain in

Indonesia outside Irian Jaya. It is also an important watershed for two of the largest rivers in Sumatra. Kerinci is still an active volcano, having last erupted in 1934, and there are several other volcanic outlets in the park. Excellent possibilities for hiking exist in Kerinci Seblat, including treks up Gunung Kerinci and other peaks.

Biologically Sumatra falls into two distinct sections: one to the north and one to the south of the vast Lake Toba. The lake is the most dramatic legacy of a volcanic eruption which

ocurred about 75,000 years ago, and which devastated Sumatra and created a strong barrier, so that some species occur only in the north or the south. Kerinci-Seblat protects a representative selection of the southern fauna.

Habitat types include lowland dipterocarp forest, montane forest, alpine vegetation, crater lakes

and the highest freshwater swamp in Sumatra. Many of Sumatra's 26 species of rhododendron are found on the mountain slopes, and the world's largest flowers, the parasitic *Rafflesia arnoldii* and the two-metre high *Amorphophallus titanum* also occur.

Mammals of Kerinci include all the major Sumatran fauna, notably the endemic giant Sumatran rat, Sumatran rhinos, tigers, elephants, sunbears, tapirs and dark-handed gibbons. These last two species occur only to the south of Lake Toba,

while the white-handed gibbon and orang-utan are found only to the north.

Bird watching can be excellent because of the variety of habitat and altitude range. Sumatra shares much of its avifauna with mainland Asia, Borneo and Java, with 580 species of bird and only 14 endemics (compared with 328 species and 88 endemics on Sulawesi). One Sumatran endemic, the Kerinci scops owl, has been recorded only near Gunung Kerinci.

Despite its size and importance, successful administration of the park is severely challenged by several factors. Its territory spreads over four different provinces (West Sumatra, Jambi, Bengkulu and South Sumatra), which gives rise to jurisdictional difficulties. Sungai Penuh and several villages contain 280,000 people, so population encroachment on the park's boundaries is a problem. The PHPA, with assistance from WWF, is tackling some of these problems by trying to settle disputes over land rights and boundary issues.

The usual access route to Kerinci Seblat is by plane to Padang and then by road (an 8-12 hour drive) to Sungai Penuh, where there are several small, rather basic hotels.

TAITAI BATTI

The Taitai Batti Reserve was established to protect the wildlife of the Mentawai islands, of which Siberut – where Taitai Batti is located – is the largest. The reserve covers an area of 565 square kilometres. The whole island of Siberut was declared a Man and Biosphere Reserve in the early 1980s in an attempt to preserve the region's unique wildlife and human culture. Today the reserve is part of Siberut National Park.

Lying 100 kilometres off the west coast of Sumatra, the Mentawaian chain of islands has been separated from the mainland for around 500,000 years. This has allowed the wildlife to evolve in isolation from that of the rest of mainland Asia. The result is a high level of endemism, with 11 endemic mammals, including four primates, five squirrels, a tree-mouse, and a bat. However, it is rare to see primates because they live at low densities and are shy of humans due to hunting. The most frequently heard of the four primates is the black Mentawai gibbon; the other three species are the Mentawai macaque, Mentawai leaf-monkey,

and snub-nosed monkey.

The swampy terrain, numerous rivers and thick vegetation make travelling around the island extremely arduous. The island does not offer very good bird watching, although keen bird watchers will want to try and see or hear the Mentawai scops owl, the only endemic species.

The human inhabitants of Siberut are no less interesting than the wildlife. By their language and customs the Mentawians are thought to be most closely related to tribal groups in Vietnam. Traditionally living in extended family groups in a clan house, they obtain most of their needs from the forest, including sago which is their staple. Despite the island's biological prominence as a Man and Biosphere Reserve and the considerable attention it has received from groups supporting the rights of cultural minorities, many elements of the Mentawaians' ancient way of life have now disappeared, due to the well-meant activities of missionaries and government officials, and to the actions of logging concerns keen to exploit Siberut's natural wealth of timber. Cultural traditions have been maintained to a greater extent in the central and southern parts, where both men and women are heavily tattooed and bark-cloth is still used for clothing. Here there are frequent performances of ceremonies by medicine men (*sikerei*) to banish illness and bad spirits.

Access to Siberut itself is not difficult: ferries leave regularly from the west Sumatran city of Padang. However access to the interior is very much harder, necessitating long and demanding treks on foot and uncomfortable canoe journeys. The only accommodation available in the interior is with villagers.

WAY KAMBAS

Way Kambas is one of the oldest reserves in Indonesia, declared in 1937, and upgraded to national park status in 1989. It covers a triangle of marshy lowlands along the eastern coast of Lampung, in southern Sumatra, measuring some 1300 square kilometres in area. Much of its territory has been damaged by human interference, but it is nonetheless important because it protects some of the few stands of lowland dipterocarp forest remaining in a Sumatran reserve, and has excellent examples of non-peat swamp forests. The extensive mud flats and mangroves along the coast are important habitats for birds.

Rainfall is lower than in the mountainous areas of Sumatra further north and there is a marked difference between the wet season (November-March) and the dry season (July-September) when little rain falls.

Way Kambas is the centre of an elephant training programme, initiated in the mid-1980s as a solution to the wild elephant problem. Of all the wildlife displaced by the clearance of vast areas of southern Sumatra for agricultural use, elephants have been the most persistent nuisance, trampling crops and even attacking peoples' homes. Villagers complained that the elephants could do as they pleased and that they were not allowed to prevent them destroying their livelihoods as elephants are a protected species. Surplus elephants were therefore captured and domesticated; graduates from the 'school' now feature in zoos and circuses and provide safari rides for tourists at Way Kambas. Trained elephants are also used to keep wild elephants away from human settlements. Plans to use them in the logging industry as a less damaging alternative to heavy machinery have not materialised.

There is a good chance of spotting wildlife in Way Kambas National Park: long-tailed and pig-tailed macaques, siamangs and agile gibbons, wild pigs, and perhaps some of the 300-strong population of wild elephants are among the creatures which can be seen, as well as smaller species such as squirrels and monitor lizards. Some rarer animals reported to be present include tiger, clouded eopard, porcupine, and tapir.

Bird watching is good due to the relatively extensive network of trails and quiet rivers, and to the open, logged-over areas. Swamp grasslands in the south are home to milky storks, egrets, herons, bitterns, terns, pygmy geese and whistling ducks. The park is one of the few places where the endangered white-winged wood duck breeds.

Access to Way Kambas is from the village of Tridatu, about three hours' drive from the main Java-Sumatra ferry terminal at Bakauheni or from Tanjung Karang. Simple accommodation is available.

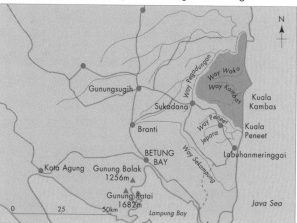

❶ *Wild pig.*
❷ *Scarlet earth ginger.*
❸ *Javanese edelweiss.*
❹ *Reef fish.*

UJUNG KULON

Ujung Kulon is of international conservation importance because it contains the world's only viable population of the highly endangered Javan rhinoceros. Its importance was reflected in its designation in 1992 as a World Heritage Site. Linked to the rhinos' survival is Ujung Kulon's other claim to fame: within its boundaries lies the volcano Krakatau, whose dramatic eruption in 1883 is well documented. The tidal wave resulting from the explosion swept over Ujung Kulon and wiped out the human settlements; they were never re-established. Much of the forest and animal populations were also destroyed, but a few rhinoceros survived on higher ground and later recolonised the peninsula.

Occupying 786 square kilometres in the far west of Java, Ujung Kulon is covered mainly with lowland forests, coastal forests and mangroves, with small patches of open grassland. The northern coast is sheltered and fringed with sandy beaches and mangroves, while the southern is dramatic and rocky. The rainy season, from October to March, brings rough seas which make access difficult.

Great efforts by the PHPA, aided by WWF and Minnesota Zoo, have ensured the survival of the last 50 or so rhinoceros. The possibility of moving some of the rhinos to another protected area has been debated, to avoid the danger of another eruption or other natural disaster extinguishing this vulnerable species. However, given the difficulty of moving the rhinos safely, it is currently considered best to leave them where they are.

Ujung Kulon is also important for the conservation of other species, notably banteng (wild cattle), leopard, wild dog and the Javan leaf-monkey. More common species are long-tailed macaques, monitor lizards, rusa and barking deer, and wild pigs. There are persistent but unsubstantiated reports of tigers. Confusion can arise because the Indonesian word for tiger (*harimau*) is sometimes used for 'leopard'. It is important to ensure that the speaker distinguishes between a 'spotted tiger' and a 'striped tiger'!

Around 260 bird species have been recorded. Among the easiest to see are green peafowl, southern pied and rhinoceros hornbills, white-bellied sea eagles, dusky herons and blue-throated bee-eaters. Good bird watching is possible along the trails of the peninsula and Peucang Island.

The volcano Anak Krakatau appeared in the sea between the shattered remnants of the original Krakatau and is the site of continuing studies of how plants and animals colonize virgin land. Volcanic activity can reach dangerous levels and access to these islands is frequently denied.

Access to Ujung Kulon and Krakatau is by sea from Labuan, on the mainland of Java, or on foot via Taman Jaya. Excellent accommodation is available on Peucang Island in bungalows operated by a private concessionaire. More basic accommodation is run by the PHPA on Peucang and Handeleum Islands.

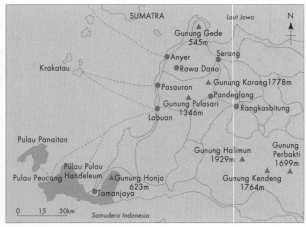

GUNUNG HALIMUN

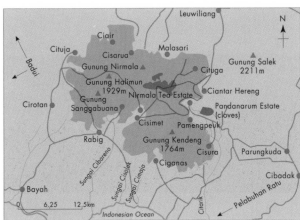

Gunung Halimun is a little known national park of 360 square kilometres in the centre of West Java. It is one of the few patches of primary forest left in this developed island, yet it can be reached in 3-4 hours from Jakarta. Rather surprisingly, it has escaped major damage, which may be due to the natural conservatism of the agricultural people surrounding it and their beliefs in spirits inhabiting the mountains (although such taboos have not generally saved other forests), or to the protection offered by the management of a tea estate located in the centre of the reserve. The area was designated a nature reserve in 1987 and a national park in 1992 in order to safeguard a major watershed as well as an increasingly rare ecosystem.

The park ranges in altitude from 500 metres to the peak of Gunung Halimun at 1929 metres. Rainfall is extremely high, up to 6000 millimetres per year; the least wet months are usually May to October. The classic stratification of rain forest vegetation can be seen here, with plants taking advantage of every possible growth site. The upper branches and trunks of the larger trees are festooned with epiphytes, including orchids; strangler figs are common.

Some of the original Javan fauna still exists here. One of the larger species present is the endemic Javan gibbon, whose stirring calls ring out in the early morning; other primates present are the Javan leaf-monkey and long-tailed macaque. The park also has populations of leopard, leopard cat, barking deer, mouse deer, colugo, small-clawed otter and Malay badger.

Halimun is a good place for bird watching, partly thanks to the estate road which allows excellent views into the forest. The secondary growth where the forest opens out on to the tea plantation is also very productive. Of the 147 species recorded, 14 are endemic to Java. Feeding flocks of any of 20 or so different species often cross the path, and even inexperienced bird watchers will be fascinated by the more colourful forest birds: scarlet sunbirds, Javan firebreasted flowerpeckers and blue-winged leafbirds are easily spotted. Many species are easiest to identify by their song, such as the barbets and the crested serpent eagle, the most commonly heard eagle over Java.

The park is threatened by gradual deterioration because of fuelwood collection and uncontrolled hunting of birds and other animals. As with most Indonesian parks and reserves, protection is inadequately enforced.

Access to Halimun is from the road between Bogor and Pelabuhan Ratu, turning west at Parungkuda. The local people know the area as the Nirmala tea estate. Accommodation is sometimes available in the plantation mess, but it may be necessary to camp.

GUNUNG GEDE-PANGRANGO

First protected by the Dutch in the mid-nineteenth century as a hunting preserve, Gunung Gede-Pangrango National Park is one of the few remaining areas of original forest in Java. The second smallest national park in Indonesia at only 150 square kilomteres, it is now an

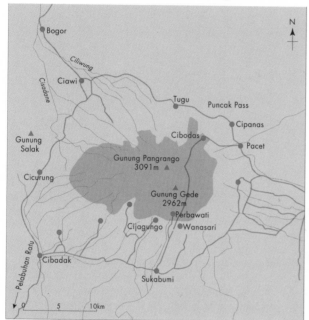

important recreational resource for the huge Jakarta conurbation; it also helps to protect the source of several large rivers which provide water to the surrounding densely populated agricultural and residental areas, including the Ciliwung, Jakarta's main river.

The principal geological features are the twin volcanic peaks of Gunung Gede (2958 metres) and Gunung Pangrango (3029 metres). Although

Pangrango is extinct, Gede is still active: sulphurous fumes emanate from its crater walls and hot springs bubble on the slopes. The wettest months are December to March, and temperatures drop dramatically with increasing altitude. At the summits, night-time temperatures can fall below freezing, and hailstorms can occur.

The park's flora and fauna are probably the best studied in Indonesia due to its accessibility: zoologists and botanists have congregated here since colonial times. The labelled plants of the neighbouring botanic gardens of Cibodas give a good introduction to the flora. Trails lead up the mountain slopes through sub-montane, upper montane and sub-alpine moss forests and allow an excellent view of how vegetation changes with altitude, both in stature and variety, with smaller trees and fewer species growing at higher elevations. The best known plant in the park is the Javanese edelweiss, whose white flowers and greyish foliage are conspicuous on open areas at the top of the mountains.

Formerly home to the Javan rhinoceros and the now extinct Javan tiger, the park still harbours other interesting large species, particularly the leopard, Javan leaf-monkey, and the endemic Javan gibbon and Javan warty pig.

Some 260 bird species have been recorded from Gunung Gede-Pangrango, including 20 of the 23

Javan endemics. The Javan kingfisher, pearl-cheeked babbler, red-fronted laughing thrush, white-bellied and red-tailed fantails and Kuhl's sunbird are amongst the most easily seen. Generally, this park is a good place for spotting forest birds. The rare peregrine falcon lives on the crater walls of Gunung Gede.

The park is located two hours south of Jakarta and becomes very crowded on Sundays and public holidays. Accommodation is available near the park, and at campsites within it. There is a good network of trails, although these are rather littered at lower elevations. The mountain trails are closed during the wettest months, December to March, to prevent erosion.

KEPULAUAN SERIBU (THOUSAND ISLANDS)

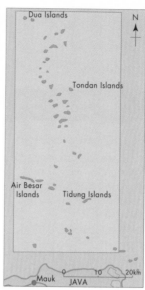

The most accessible national park from Jakarta, Kepulauan Seribu Marine Park is performing an increasingly important role in the provision of leisure facilities and also in the protection of fisheries resources. There are important nesting grounds for sea turtles.

The park's 11,000 square kilometres cover 110 coral atolls stretching 50 kilometres into the shallow sea north of Jakarta. Visibility can be poor, especially in the rainy season (December-April) when rough seas can also make the islands harder to reach.

The PHPA has been working with the WWF to implement a conservation awareness programme within the park, including the creation of a zoning system with different areas designated for recreational and fisheries use or as core zones, where no human activity should take place. However, there are still several threats to the fragile coral ecosystem. Park staff lack the resources to prevent fish-bombing and poisoning and the aquarium trade is a particular culprit in its demand for reef fish. Ocean currents bring polluting effluent from the heavy industries around Jakarta. The reefs around the populated islands have largely been destroyed through anchor damage and sewage and soil run-off, while tourist resorts are having a negative impact on the very resource they depend upon, by mining coral blocks for building, dredging mooring sites, and inappropriate waste disposal. Most tourists – including divers – are unaware of the area's protected status and collect shells, sponges and other marine organisms.

Despite these problems, some of the reefs are still in good condition and well worth a visit. Some of the most popular dive sites are around Kotok, Malinjo and Cina islands, with Piniki, though located a little to the east of the main group of islands, also worth a visit. There is a wreck dive at the island of Papa Theo – named after the ship which ran aground there and sank in 1982.

There are resorts on several of the islands, the most popular being Pantara Putri, Sepa,

Pelangi and Kotok. Of these, Pantara is the most up-market. The resorts all have dive shops with equipment for hire and dive buddies. The islands are easily reached by ferries, speedboats and hydrofoils leaving Jakarta from the Ancol Marina. The journey takes 1-3 hours, depending on the mode of transport and the particular island being visited. Weekends are busy and it is best to book in advance; most of the larger Jakarta travel agents assist in reserving accommodation.

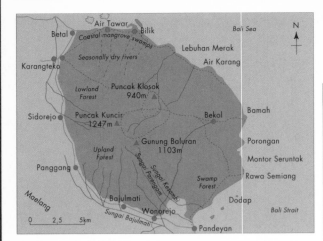

1 *Strangling fig.*
2 *Dayak man.*
3 *Orang-utan.*
4 *Screw pines.*

BALURAN

Located in the northeast corner of Java, Baluran's 250 square kilometres offer an unusually diverse range of habitats over a compact area, from coral reefs and mangroves to savanna grasslands and monsoon forest. The park is an important natural area in the heavily cultivated and increasingly industrialised province of East Java. This is one of the hottest and driest parts of Java, with a rainfall of 900-1600 millimetres per year compared with 2000-6000 millimetres for West Java. The wettest months are January to April.

The low rainfall means that the vegetation is very different from the evergreen rain forest of western Indonesia. Most of the trees in Baluran are deciduous, and the sparsely wooded savanna is unique in Java – although it is clear that savanna ecosystems were created by regular burning over the centuries. Several exotic species occur on the savanna, including acacias, tamarinds, and the lantana shrub whose pretty yellow and pink flowers belie its nuisance value as a toxic and invasive weed.

Because of the relatively open vegetation the attractive panorama of Baluran volcano (1556 metres) can be fully appreciated, and the savanna allows for good wildlife viewing, particularly as several watch-towers have been built. Baluran is an important habitat for banteng, although the most common large animals are feral water buffaloes.

These were once thought to compete with banteng for food and water, so over the years a number have been domesticated and distributed to local villagers, though hardly any have been caught in recent years. The banteng are more difficult to see, especially during the wetter months when they do not need to come down to water-holes on the savanna. Large groups of rusa deer can be seen, as well as the smaller and more solitary muntjac, or barking deer. Wild pigs are rather too frequently encountered, having become something of a nuisance at guesthouses

where they forage for food. Long-tailed macaques scramble about on the beach, living up to their alternative name of crab-eating macaques. Rarer and more interesting is the Javan lutung, which occurs here in black and red forms.

The varied habitat over a small area allows for good bird watching, and at least 160 species are present. Green peafowl, green jungle fowl, yellow-vented and sooty-headed bulbuls, pied fantails, black-naped orioles, black-winged starlings and spotted doves are all common near the guesthouses.

Baluran is subject to considerable encroachment from villagers living around the park, but is nonetheless a delightful place to visit – although it can become rather crowded at weekends and on public holidays. Just off the main Surabaya-Banyuwangi road, it is only an hour's drive from the main ferry terminal to Bali. There are several reasonably well-equipped guesthouses. **1**

BALI BARAT

Bali Barat is best known to tourists for the world-class coral reefs off Menjangan Island. However, its main significance for conservationists is as home to the last wild population of Bali starlings, of which less than 50 remain. An ambitious programme is under way, through which captive-bred

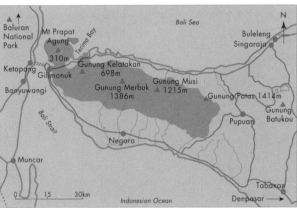

starlings are released into the wild. Some have successfully mated with wild birds and reared young.

Comprising nearly 780 square kilometres of West Bali, the mud flats, mangroves, coastal forest, savanna, monsoon and riverine forest of the park provide an excellent variety of habitats for bird species. Stands of coconut and kapok trees provide further roosting and nesting places. The highest elevation is 1386 metres. Between May and November the climate is dry; the wettest months are from January to March.

Ornithologists have been attracted to the park by the chance of spotting the Bali starling (though access to their area is restricted), and as a result the bird life has been studied quite extensively, with around 170 species recorded so far and new species constantly being added. In recent years a huge west-east migration of raptors has been observed in October as the seasons change in the northern and southern hemispheres. Large numbers of oriental honey-buzzards, Japanese sparrowhawks and

Chinese goshawks use the thermals over Bali to aid their journey along the Indonesian archipelago to the east and south.

Bali's mammal fauna is impoverished compared with the other islands of the Greater Sundas, but nevertheless offers something of interest to the

casual visitor. Long-tailed macaques (sometimes called temple monkeys) line the road through the park begging for tit-bits, and Javan lutungs can also be encountered. During the dry season the normally shy and solitary muntjac, or barking deer, can be easily seen. Rusa deer and wild pigs are common, as are squirrels.

There is excellent snorkelling and diving off Menjangan Island, with steep, rugged walls, undamaged coral and gentle currents. All the dive operators on Bali offer day trips to the site.

There are several villages within the park boundaries. These are a direct threat to the Bali starling via poaching and indirectly because of habitat clearance. As everywhere in Bali there are many shrines and temples; notably Jayaprana's Grave, at the top of a long flight of steps. A path into the forest behind the shrine offers access to the park.

There are several access points from the main Gilimanuk-Lovina road which runs through the park. Small guest-houses in the park or at Gilimanuk offer simple lodgings.

KUTAI

The wildlife of Borneo is  particularly rich because during the ice ages land-bridges connected the island with mainland Southeast Asia and plant and animal species were able to spread across. Lying below the typhoon belt and along the Equator, the island's stable climate

has also contributed to the exceptional diversity of plant species. Lack of volcanic activity has resulted in poor soils.

Kutai is in East Kalimantan, one of the fastest developing regions of Indonesia, and is of high conservation priority because it includes extensive lowland forest, one of the most threatened habitat types on Borneo. The park is 2000 square kilometres in area and extends from sea-level to Gunung Tandung Mayanag, at 397 metres.

Average monthly temperatures are 26-27°C. The west monsoon (December-February) brings the heaviest rainfall, with relatively low rainfall during the east monsoon (June-August). The driest months are September to

November. Occasional periods of prolonged drought in East Kalimantan are probably related to the El Niño oscillation. A particularly severe drought in 1982-1983 was exacerbated by logging and slash-and-burn clearance and resulted in a devastating fire which damaged a vast area, including over 50 per cent of Kutai.

The park's rich flora is contained in six main forest types, including mangroves, freshwater swamp forest, heath forest, and ironwood forest. Borneo is the centre of distribution of dipterocarps, with 267 species and 155

endemics. Kutai contains a substantial proportion of these: altogether, more than 500 tree species are found within the park.

Around half of Borneo's mammals are found in the park, including 11 of the country's 13 primates. Kutai is especially important for protecting the endangered eastern race of the Bornean orang-utan. There are two species of gibbon on Borneo; the Bornean in the north and east and the agile in the south and west. The Bornean gibbon was part of an earlier wave of migration from the mainland; by the time the agile gibbon arrived it was prevented from spreading over the whole of the island by river barriers,

and the two groups evolved into separate species. Other large species in Kutai are the banteng, clouded leopard, marbled cat, salt water crocodile, sambar deer, *muntjac*, mouse deer and Malayan sunbear. Nearly 80 per cent of the bird species found on Borneo are present.

A visit to Kutai could be combined with an introduction to some of Kalimantan's many tribal groups, known collectively as Dayaks. Longhouses and other aspects of their colourful culture can be seen most easily along the Mahakam River.

The park is 80 kilometres north of Samarinda, the provincial capital, and is accessible by road, by plane to Sangatta and by sea. Accommodation is basic and limited to two places: the Teluk Kaba and Mentoko research stations.

TANJUNG PUTING

Tanjung Puting offers important protection to a wide variety of Bornean lowland fauna and flora, and is best known to the outside world because of its orang-utan rehabilitation centre. The park covers a 3550 square kilometre area of low-lying alluvial land on the southern coast of Central Kalimantan, with the highest elevation just 11 metres.

Around one-third of the vegetation is tropical heath forest with low- to medium-

sized trees, amongst which pandanus, palms, epiphytes and pitcher plants are common. Another habitat type found within the area is peat swamp forest. Three rivers run through the park with freshwater swamp forest along their banks. There are mangroves and nipa palms along the estuary.

Two particularly important mammals in Tanjung Puting are the Irrawaddy dolphin, occurring in the Kumai River, and the dugong, found in the waters of Kumai Bay. The park also has substantial populations of a number of primates, including the orang-utan. Wild orang-utans are rarely spotted, but semi-tame ones can be encountered at the well-known Camp Leakey rehabilitation centre on the eastern tributary of the Sekonyer River, and at Tanjung Harapan where baby orang-utans are held

in quarantine. Easier to observe in the wild than orang-utan, are proboscis monkeys, which congregate in trees along the rivers, particularly in the mornings and late afternoons. There is a proboscis monkey research centre at Natai Lengkuas, on the Sekonyer River.

Other primates are the maroon and the silvered leaf-monkeys, long-tailed macaque, and agile gibbon, whose range is limited to southwestern Borneo: the Kapuas and Barito rivers to the north and east form a natural barrier to its distribution. Ground-living species include sambar, Bornean yellow *muntjac*, lesser mouse deer and bearded pig, while arboreal species include the western tarsier, slow loris and flying lemur. Clouded leopards and leopard cats are present, as are the giant squirrel, long-tailed and common porcupines, yellow-throated marten, hairy-nosed otter and binturong.

Some 210 species of bird have been recorded

here. Of greatest conservation significance is the woolly-necked stork, one of the world's rarest storks; other notable species are the Javan white-eye, dusky-grey heron (rare elsewhere in Borneo), wandering tree duck, sacred and ruddy kingfishers, hook-billed bulbul, and white-throated babbler.

The park's viability as a sanctuary for wildlife is threatened by human exploitation, which has caused numerous patches of scrub and *alang-alang* (coarse grass) to develop. Transmigration settlements to the north are sited on such poor soils that agricultural success is minimal, forcing the transmigrants to use other resources available to them – including those of Tanjung Puting.

Access to Tanjung Puting National Park is via Pangkalanbun and a half-hour drive to Kumai. Boats can be hired for the trip up the river. Rimba Lodge, an hour from Kumai, provides good standard accommodation.

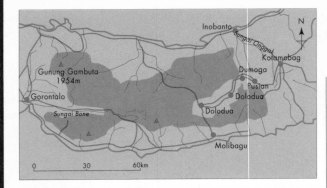

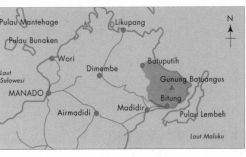

1. *Spider on an orb web.*
2. *Bear cuscus.*
3. *Kauri pine and lichens.*
4. *Sea anemone.*

BOGANI NANI WARTABONE

The Bogani Nani Wartabone (formerly Dumoga Bone) National Park covers 2870 square kilometres in northern Sulawesi. It was set up to protect the catchment areas of important rivers and to reduce flood damage to Gorontalo and the surrounding populated areas.

Much of the park consists of narrow valleys and steep mountains, the highest peaks rising to almost 2000 metres. North Sulawesi is subject to considerable volcanic activity as it lies along the juncture of two tectonic plates: the Australian/Papuan plate is gradually moving northwards and dips underneath the Asian plate. Rainfall is fairly evenly distributed throughout the year, with wetter periods from November to January and March to May and drier spells in February and from June to October. A deep ocean trench lies between Borneo and Sulawesi; the latter was not connected to the Asian landmass during the last Ice Age, as the Greater Sundas were. The vegetation is therefore less rich in species than it is in Borneo and Sumatra. Bogani Nani Wartabone does, however, contain a good range of vegetation types: lowland primary forest, lowland vegetation on alluvial soils (much disturbed by farming), lower montane and moss forests.

Because of its long isolation, Sulawesi's fauna has evolved an exceptionally high level of endemism: 61 per cent of the mammals are endemic, as are 34 per cent of its birds. The composition of the fauna and flora is also of interest because it contains species of both Asian and Australian origin. The park contains most of the fauna of the region, including over 200 bird species. One of the most interesting for the casual visitor is the maleo, which lays its eggs in light soils to be incubated by volcanic heat.

The park is also home to 110 mammal species, including 50 bats. The largest of the endemic mammals are the babirusa, two species of macaque (the Sulawesi in the west and the crested in the east), and the anoa. There is some doubt as to whether there are one or two species of this dwarf ox: some sources distinguish between mountain and lowland species. The tarsier, Sulawesi wild pig and the marsupial bear and dwarf cuscuses are frequently seen. Cuscuses are derived from the Australian biogeographical zone, while all other Sulawesi native mammals have Asian origins.

The people of the area are mostly Christian and are prosperous thanks to the cultivation of cloves and coconuts; the villages are neat and pretty and the roads well-surfaced.

The park can be reached in 4-5 hours' drive from Manado. The main entrance is at Toraut, which also functions as a research station with limited accommodation.

TANGKOKO-BATUANGUS

The 87 square kilometre National Park of Tangkoko-Batuangus faces east from the tip of North Sulawesi. Encompassing a range of habitats within a relatively small area and with rich forest, especially at the lower altitudes, the reserve is important for the protection of several of Sulawesi's endemic species. This is one of the best places in Sulawesi to see wildlife, and several treks of varying difficulty can be made within the reserve.

The altitudinal range is from sea-level to the summit of Gunung Dua Saudara, at 1351 metres. Habitat types include coral reefs, savanna grasslands and lowland, sub-montane

and moss forest. There are at least 18 sites of volcanic activity in Northern Sulawesi, including one volcano within Tangkoko which last had a major eruption in 1839.

The high soil fertility resulting from the volcanic activity has produced a large number of fig trees and other fruit-bearing trees. These support good populations of macaques and other frugivores. Crested macaques live here at a density greater than any other primate in Asia, with around 300 per square kilometre. This is probably the best place in Sulawesi to spot Indonesia's smallest primate, the spectral tarsier, which is active at night; the bear cuscus can also be seen here more easily than in most places, and squirrels are common.

Certain fruit-eating birds also live at a high density in the reserve, including the red-knobbed hornbill, one of two hornbills endemic to Sulawesi. Tangkoko's best known avian inhabitant is the maleo, which lays its eggs in thermally heated sand-pits. These are now less numerous than before because of over-exploitation of the large and nutritious eggs by villagers. Thanks to training by WWF fieldworkers in the late 1970s, some of the PHPA rangers at Tangkoko are skilled at bird identification and are helpful to visiting bird watchers.

The beaches and reefs of Tangkoko are worth exploration. They are formed of black sand of volcanic origin, and are used as nesting sites by the green turtle and the rarer leatherback turtle. Rock-hopping blenny fish are common on the wet basalt rocks, clinging on with their ventral fins. Close to the beach are coral reefs.

Tangkoko is only 40 kilometres from Manado, the capital of North Sulawesi. Limited accommodation is available.

LORE LINDU

Lore Lindu National Park occupies 2310 square kilometres in Central Sulawesi south of the provincial capital, Palu. The park's essential function for the local human population is in protecting the watershed of rivers irrigating agricultural areas, including the Palu Valley – the driest place in Indonesia with only 700 millimetres of rain per year.

Most of Lore Lindu lies at over 1000 metres. Mountain peaks include Gunung Rorakatimbu (2610 metres) and Gunung Nokilalaki (2355 metres) which is popular with hikers. The southern boundary of the park is

formed by the Lariang River, the longest in Sulawesi at 225 kilometres, and the 32

square kilometre Lake Lindu in the north is both an attraction and an important habitat for various endemic fishes. During the rainy season, from November to March, trails can become impassable.

The principal vegetation type is montane forest. Sulawesi represents the easternmost limit of the eucalyptus, with just one species, *Eucalyptus deglupta*, which is fairly common in the forest and noticeable because of its size and its peeling, colourful bark.

Most of the endemic mammals of Sulawesi occur within Lore Lindu, including anoa, babirusa, bear and dwarf cuscuses – although none of these are easily seen. More commonly encountered are troops of Sulawesi macaques which are one of the four species of black tail-less macaque found in Sulawesi. The four species are located in the southern, southeastern, central and northern parts of the mainland.

Thirty-four per cent of the 260 species of bird found in Sulawesi are endemic (see Bogani Nani Wartebone entry). Lore Lindu is one of the best places in Sulawesi for bird watching because it covers the complete altitudinal range of every land-based species in the island, with the area around the park headquarters at Kamarora particularly productive.

Around the eastern and southern edges of the park are broad, grassy valleys where ancient, mysterious stone vats and megalithic statues stand dotted about. These remains are the principal attraction for tourists to the park.

As with most Indonesian national parks, Lore Lindu is subject to the usual threats of hunting of protected species and illegal collection of forest products. A proposed dam and hydroelectric plant on

Lake Lindu is a further threat to the park's biota.

The northern parts of Lore Lindu can be reached by road in 3-4 hours from Palu, and occasional flights operate from Tentena to the Bada Valley, in the south. The traditional trading routes within the park, still in daily use by caravans of pack-horses, make excellent hiking trails. With the combination of forest, mountains, rivers, a lake and cultural attractions, this is an interesting park to visit. There are guesthouses at the park's headquarters at Kamarora, and it is possible to stay with villagers in other places. ❸

BUNAKEN MANADO TUA

The fabulous coral reefs of Bunaken Marine Park are internationally renowned as Indonesia's premier dive site. The park's 890 square kilometres also form an important protection zone for fisheries resources.

Most of the park consists of five continental islands off the north coast from Manado, at the tip of the North Sulawesi peninsula. The islands comprise several marine habitats: a barrier coral reef, fringing reefs, lagoons, seagrass meadows, mangrove forests, oceanic waters and deep ocean trenches. A smaller protected area lies on the mainland, south of Manado and includes

additional habitats important for nesting sea turtles and dugong.

Visibility in the water is normally 12-25 metres; less than along some other tropical reefs due to the high levels of plankton. Visibility can be poor during the wetter months when storms can cause soil run-off. Currents are in general slight.

Upwellings of currents from deeper levels carry nutrients to the reefs, and partly account for the diversity of life forms they support. The most popular dive sites are off Bunaken Island, where the reef falls steeply away to a depth of 1000 metres. The wall topography offers a tremendous assortment of habitats for marine organisms to live in, and divers to explore: slopes, overhangs, gullies and caverns. The surfaces are crowded with soft and hard corals, sponges, filter feeders and others. The fish are equally diverse, from razorfish and clown anemone fish to the much larger barracuda and sharks. There are also

good numbers of invertebrates and other marine animals: cleaner shrimps, colourful nudibranchs, moray eels and sea snakes. Divers can spot sea turtles, particularly the green and hawksbill; sightings of dugongs are rare.

All the islands are inhabited. The residents include several groups of nomadic Bajau. The reefs are under some threat by destructive fishing methods such as poisoning and bombing, and with increasing tourist use there is evidence of diver and anchor damage. Efforts are being made by the WWF, among others, to encourage the park's residents to use their resources sustainably.

Bunaken is easily accessible, with daily flights to Manado. A number of good dive resorts offer accommodation and competent dive services. ❹

MOROWALI

Morowali Nature Reserve is in the eastern part of Central Sulawesi, one of the least explored of Indonesia's provinces. The reserve covers 2250 square kilometres and extends from the coast to steep mountains, with Gunung Tokala the highest at 2630 metres There are five major rivers, several lakes and at least one cave system. Prior to 1980 the area was designated as a transmigration site. The reserve's protected status and much of what is known of the flora, fauna and topography is due to the work of scientists on the British expedition

Operation Drake.

The main habitat types are tidal swamps, alluvial plains and valleys, floodplains, peat swamps, and sandstone and limestone mountains. The reserve's importance lies in its tracts of forest on mineral-poor ultrabasic soils, of which the largest areas in the world occur in eastern Sulawesi, and in its extensive alluvial plains, which elsewhere in Indonesia have mostly been converted to agricultural use.

The vegetation varies greatly because of the different soil types and land forms. Stands of

casuarina trees are typical of the braided floodplains, while the ultrabasic soils of the forested areas produce relatively low and scrubby vegetation. Indicative of the low mineral content of the soil is the large number of pitcher plants. Patches of *alang-alang* within the

reserve indicate the failure of the forest to regenerate after prolonged clearance for swidden agriculture.

Morowali contains most of the Sulawesi endemic mammals, including anoa, babirusa, tarsier, two cuscuses, and the black macaque, although they are thinly spread and rarely encountered. This may be due to the deficiency of plant nutrition available in vegetation on the ultrabasic soils, or to hunting pressure from the inhabitants of the reserve. There are good nesting grounds for maleo in the sandy riverbank soils.

The principal point of

interest for visitors is the Wana people, who still pursue their traditional subsistence life-style, obtaining most of their needs from the forest and clearing a new area of forest every couple of years to plant cassava and other crops. The families closest to the coast now indulge in limited trading with the outside world, acquiring items such as clothes, enamel plates, and kerosene; but there are still groups in the highlands who remain so isolated that they use bark-cloth for their clothes rather than woven textiles.

Access to the reserve is by road to Kolonodale and by boat across Tomori Bay. Accommodation can be arranged with villagers.

① *Flying foxes.*
② *Goliath birdwing of Seram.*
③ *Icefields, Gunung Jaya.*
④ *Blyth's hornbill.*

KOMODO

Komodo National Park is home to the world's largest lizard, the Komodo dragon. The 750 square kilometre park includes Komodo, Rinca, Padar, many smaller islands and the surrounding seas. Distant from both the Australian and Asian centres of species distribution and never part of a major landmass, this part of the Lesser Sundas contains a somewhat impoverished fauna.

The terrain of the islands is stark and mountainous with few flat areas. The highest point is Gunung Ara, on Komodo (720 metres). Rain generally falls only between November and March and the vegetation consists mainly of coarse grass dotted typically with *ziziphus* trees and lontar palms, with thicker stands of trees along water courses. The frequent occurrence of fire contributes to the sparse tree cover. There is little surface water on any of the islands in the dry months.

The avifauna reflects the park's location in Wallacea, where Asian and Australian biogeographical zones overlap. Australian species, such as sulphur-crested cockatoos and noisy friar birds, occur alongside jungle fowl and

monarch flycatchers of Asian origin. Also present and easily seen is the brush turkey (or scrub fowl) which lays its eggs in piles of rotting vegetation where they are incubated by the heat of decomposition.

There are thought to be around 7000 Komodo dragons left, weighing up to 150 kilograms and reaching a length of almost three metres. The dragons were formerly believed to eat mainly carrion, but they are now known to be effective hunters of live prey, charging swiftly at herbivores such as rusa deer, wild pigs and even horses, from lairs in the long grass. Their saliva is particularly poisonous so even if the animal escapes with a bite it is likely to die later from blood poisoning. The species faces few threats to its survival apart from some competition from humans for its prey species.

Other Komodo wildlife includes colonies of fruit and cave bats and marine animals. Dolphins are often observed and more rarely whales, manta rays and sea turtles. There is good snorkelling and diving on coral reefs around the islands, including some just outside the national park, accessible from Labuan Bajo (Flores). Straits between the islands form channels between the

Pacific Ocean to the north and the Indian Ocean to the south; currents can be extremely strong.

There are fishing villages of traditional stilted houses on Komodo and Rinca. Access to the park is from Flores or Sumbawa by chartered boat or ferry; there are rather basic PHPA guesthouses on Komodo and Rinca.

MANUSELA

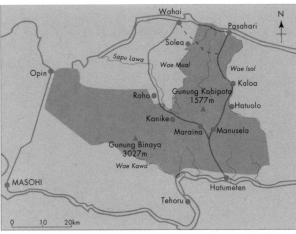

Manusela is the only national park in Maluku and occupies a 1890 square kilometre segment of the island of Seram, stretching from the north coast to the south. It protects a unique habitat of Malukan rain forest and several endemic plant and animal species and covers an unusually wide altitudinal range of primary rain forest, from sea-level to the tree line.

The dominant geological feature of the park – and indeed of the whole island – is a huge limestone massif culminating in Gunung Manusela at 3019 metres. Rain falls throughout the year, with the northern side wettest during the west monsoon and the southern side receiving most rain during the southeastern monsoon.

Manusela lies within Wallacea (the overlap zone of the Asian and Australian biogeographical regions) and is floristically impoverished compared with the areas on either side of it. Despite this, there are many features of

interest. The eastern limit of dipterocarp trees is here, with just two species represented, compared with over 260 in Borneo. They include the Malukan endemic *Shorea selanica*, which comprises 30 per cent of the trees in some parts of the park. The eucalypts have around 500 species in Australia but only one occurs in Seram; *Eucalyptus deglupta*.

The absence of a land-bridge at any time connecting Seram with larger landmasses restricted colonization by terrestrial animals. The island has 26 species of bat and only eight indigenous non-flying mammals: five rodents and three marsupials, consisting of the grey and spotted cuscuses and the Seram long-nosed bandicoot. Introduced mammals include the Malay and common palm civets, wild pigs, and rusa deer.

The avifauna is distinctly more Australian than Asian. Included in the 196

bird species recorded are 15 endemics. Notable endemics are the salmon-crested cockatoo and the grey-necked friar bird. Also present are the very rare purple-naped lory, the scrub fowl, and the giant, flightless cassowary, which was probably introduced.

The herpetofauna is strongly Australo-Papuan. As reptiles cross seas better than amphibians, the former are better represented, with lizards (especially skinks) predominating. The reticulated python is found here at the eastern limit of its range, while the amethystine python is an Australian species at its western limit.

The human population is culturally diverse, and includes representatives of the original inhabitants of Seram plus Malays, Chinese, Buginese and Javanese. The arrival of the Europeans in the sixteenth century culminated in the

disappearance of the original cultures, and the population of the interior is steadily declining as people relocate to the coast.

Access to Manusela can be achieved by boat from Ambon to Wahai, and then on foot. There have been several expeditions to the park run by Operation Raleigh and other British groups.

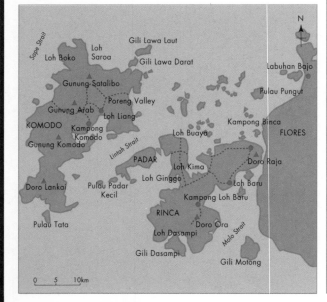

LORENTZ

The Lorentz Reserve stretches from the southern coast of central Irian Jaya to the peaks of the Jayawijaya range, including the 5039 metre summit of Gunung Jaya, Indonesia's highest mountain. The largest protected area in Indonesia at 21,500 square kilometres, it comprises all the major vegetation types found in Irian Jaya, from mangroves and swamp forests to montane, sub-alpine and alpine zones. It has been proposed as a World Heritage Site by The World Conservation Union because of its uniqueness.

From the south the mountains rise steeply, in some places in a series of vertical walls, while north of the Jayawijaya peaks there is a vast plateau. The reserve includes one of only three equatorial glaciers in the world.

New Guinea shares the Sahul Shelf with Australia, and the native fauna was formerly believed to be predominantly Australian. Recent surveys however have shown the Asian influence to be the stronger. Only 34 per cent of the 154 mammals are monotremes or marsupials, while 32 per cent are bats and another 32 per cent are rodents, all originating from the Asian region. Over three-quarters of Irian's mammals occur in Lorentz, including both monotremes (the short-beaked and long-beaked spiny anteaters) and representatives of the endemic genera of marsupial mice. In the absence of primates in New Guinea, a group of kangaroos has evolved the ability to climb trees and eat leaves. There have been persistent reports that the Tasmanian wolf (a marsupial carnivore thought to be extinct) may be present in the highlands of Irian Jaya, including Lorentz.

The 643 species of bird in Irian includes 269 endemics. The avifauna is predominantly Australian, and includes honey-eaters, parrots, bower-birds, crowned pigeons, hornbills, sunbirds, eagles, kingfishers, and some 26 species of birds of paradise.

There are a number of human settlements within or near the reserve, but none is as intrusive or damaging as the huge Freeport copper mine in the Jayawijaya range just south of the glaciers. The reserve's boundaries officially include the mine and associated towns and roads, as well as much of the concession. A large mountain composed mainly of rich copper ore has already been removed by open-cast and underground mining, and further massive operations are planned. The mine has been blamed for the shrinking of the glacier, although other theories suggest that global warming or a natural cycle of growth and retreat may be the cause.

Access to Lorentz is difficult. The reserve can be explored on foot from the north (all trekking is strenuous) and by canoe from the south, after first reaching villages by light plane. Accommodation is with villagers.

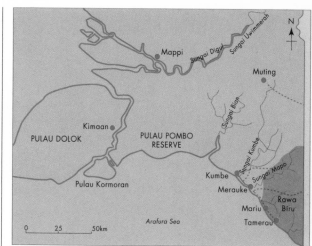

WASUR

Wasur lies at the southeastern extremity of Irian Jaya, against the Papua New Guinean border. It is one of Indonesia's newest national parks, having been declared in 1990, and it is one of the best for seeing wildlife because of its open terrain and ease of access. Covering 4260 square kilometres, the park was set up to safeguard fresh water supplies for the nearby town of Merauke and to reduce uncontrolled hunting.

Wasur is completely flat. Principal vegetation types are mangrove and coastal forest, light forest of fire-resistant *Melaleuca leucodendron* trees, mixed monsoon forest with open grassy areas, and vast savanna grasslands interspersed with reedy swamps. In places huge, termite mounds, some over three metres high, are a striking feature of the landscape. The climate is monsoonal, with a dry season from June to November and a wet season from December to May. The temperature range is 16-36°C, and during the southern hemisphere summer the temperatures can be pleasantly cool.

The park is home to nearly 400 species of bird, including large populations of migratory waders and shorebirds from Australia. Even brief excursions should reveal a substantial number: white-necked herons, bustards, brolga cranes, palm cockatoos, rainbow lorikeets and wattled lapwings are among the most frequently encountered.

Of the 80 mammal species the most obvious is the agile wallaby, large numbers of which bound about the bush. Introduced rusa deer and wild pigs have become an integral part of the park's ecology. Harder to see are smaller marsupials such as bandicoots, sugar-gliders and cuscuses, some of which are nocturnal and can be spotted at night with a strong torch.

Wasur is the ancestral homeland of the Marind and Kanum peoples. Although decades of contact with missionaries, government officials and traders have meant the disappearance of many of their customs, their way of life is still interesting to outsiders. Sago is their staple food, while additional crops are cultivated in gardens. Protein comes from river fish and domesticated pigs and from hunted birds and other prey. There are several threats to the park, mainly because its accessibility has rendered it vulnerable to human exploitation: there is a substantial amount of hunting, sand is quarried for roads and some areas have been converted to cattle ranches. Transmigration settlements to the north pose a further threat. The WWF is running an ambitious management programme, working with various sectors to prevent over-exploitation.

The park boundary, half-an-hour's drive from Merauke, is serviced by several flights a week from Jayapura, the capital of Irian Jaya. The Trans-Irian Highway bisects the park and provides excellent access. Trails can be explored on foot or on horseback. Simple accommodation is available in some of the villages.

Contributors

The Author
DR DAVID STONE

With a particular interest in Southeast Asian wildlife and forest ecology, Dr Stone, a zoologist, has travelled extensively in Indonesia and Malaysia. As a conservation officer and scientific editor with the World Wide Fund for Nature in the late 1980s, he was responsible for the development and monitoring of a wide variety of projects, ranging from those concerned with species conservation to those promoting sustainable rural development, in a number of locations. Now, as a freelance consultant, he works closely with a number of international agencies including IUCN, the United Nations Environment Programme and WWF. He is a regular contributor to international natural history magazines, nature adviser to a major international travel guide series and has published a wide range of scientific and popular articles and books. Dr Stone is currently working on a book on the natural history of New Guinea.

Feature Writers
JANET COCHRANE

Janet Cochrane, contributor of the Parks section on Indonesia's national parks and reserves, has worked in conservation and tourism in Indonesia since 1979, initially working for an environmental group based in Indonesia, and subsequently writing travel articles and leading tours throughout the country. After a three-year interlude with the BBC World Service, she began carrying out ecotourism consultancy work for WWF and other conservation bodies, looking for ways of involving local people in tourism in protected areas.

DR CHRISTOPHER HAILS

Dr Chris Hails, author of the feature entitled *Conservation of Indonesia's Natural Wealth*, is based in Switzerland where he is Director of the Asia-Pacific Programme for the WWF, the largest private conservation organization in the world. Prior to this appointment, he worked for much of his professional life in Southeast Asia where he researched and taught zoology at the University of Malaya in Kuala Lumpur. Following this he was employed by the Ministry of National Development in Singapore, working on conservation problems. He has many scientifc and popular publications to his credit, including *Birds of Singapore*.

DR SOEDARSONO RISWAN

A senior botanist at Bogor Herbarium in Java, Dr Riswan is a specialist of forest ecology. His interests include studying human impact on tropical forests, conservation ethnobotany, medicinal plants and traditional land use systems. His latest publications focus on rain forest types in the Manusela National Park, drift fruits and seeds on Anak Krakatau beaches and the use of traditional knowledge as a guide to useful products. Dr Riswan has contributed the feature entitled *Coming to Terms with How a Forest Works*.

FELIA SALIM AND DESI HARAHAP

Both Felia Salim and Desi Harahap work for Sejati, an organization based in Jakarta, which works with traditional societies throughout Indonesia, researching and documenting ways of life and disseminating information on what are, in some cases, cultures under pressure from modern developments. Sejati aims to foster mutual understanding between indigenous communities and developed societies throughout the archipelago and to advocate the value of traditional cultures, particularly regarding the important issue of environmentally sustainable practices. These two writers have contributed *Wisdom from the Sea: The Bajau*.

DR JATNA SUPRIATNA

The feature *Primates of Indonesia* has been written by Dr Jatna Supriatna, Indonesia's leading primatologist. Based at the University of Indonesia, Dr Supriatna is also editor-in chief of a new journal entitled *Tropical Biodiversity* which is published by The Indonesian Foundation for the Advancement of Biological Sciences.

Advisers
DR IVAN POLUNIN

Born in 1920 and educated in England, Ivan Polunin is a Doctor of Medicine from Oxford University. He has lived and worked in Southeast Asia since 1948 and taught for 30 years at the National University of Singapore in the Department of Social Medicine and Public Health. He has carried out extensive studies of the health of tribal and traditional populations and currently studies synchronous flashing fireflies and ancient ceramics of the region. He has travelled and photographed the length and breadth of Indonesia and contributed to a number of TV programmes for the BBC on people and the natural environment. He has a special interest in botany and has written books on the plant life of Singapore and Malaysia.

DR TONY WHITTEN

Dr Tony Whitten, an ecologist, has spent much of the last 20 years in Indonesia. He has lived in various parts of the archipelago and worked as an adviser to the Indonesian Ministry of the Environment. He is a freelance consultant and writer, currently based in Cambridge, UK. His numerous publications include: *Java and Bali: Ecology, Development and the Future, Wild Indonesia, Ecology of Sumatra* and *The Gibbons of Siberut*.

Project Consultant
PAUL SPENCER SOCHACZEWSKI

As Head of Creative Development for WWF, Paul Sochaczewski developed international public awareness and fundraising campaigns. He now runs the WWF Network on Conservation and Religions and Spiritual Beliefs. Prior to moving to Switzerland, he lived in Southeast Asia for 13 years, including eight in Indonesia, where he worked as creative director for an advertising agency and as a freelance journalist. He is co-author of *The Soul of the Tiger: People and Nature in Southeast Asia* and *Eco-Bluff: A Guide to Instant Environmental Credibility* and has recently retraced the Asian travels of Alfred Russel Wallace for a new book. He writes regularly for international publications.

Main Photographers
MICHAEL AW

Michael Aw is an underwater photographer who shares his time between Australia and Indonesia. He regularly contributes photographs and articles to marine life and diving publications and has recently produced *Beneath Bunaken*, a pictorial almanac documenting the life of the coral reef of North Sulawesi over a twenty-four hour period.

ALAIN COMPOST

Alain Compost is one of Indonesia's foremost wildlife photographers. He has lived in Indonesia for 20 years and has photographed the country's diverse natural history from Irian Jaya to Sumatra. His photographs have featured in many publications, including *Wild Indonesia* and *Green Indonesia*.

MIKE SEVERNS

Based in Hawaii, Mike Severns, a biologist, makes regular trips to Indonesia to photograph the region's stunning underwater life. He has contributed to numerous books and magazines and recently produced a book entitled *Indonesia's Magnificent Underwater Realm*. When not diving, he studies Hawaiian tree snails in the rain forest of the West Maui Mountains of Hawaii.

Bibliography

Behr, E., *Indonesia: A Voyage Through the Archipelago*, Archipelago Press, Singapore, 1990.

Campbell, J., *Irian Jaya: The Timeless Domain*, Tynron Press, Scotland, 1991.

Chou, L.M. and Alino, P.M., *An Underwater Guide to the South China Sea*, Times Editions, Singapore, 1992.

Ditlev, H., *A Field Guide to the Reef-building Corals of the Indo-Pacific*, Backhuys, Rotterdam, 1980.

Gray, W., *Coral Reefs and Islands: The Natural History of a Threatened Paradise*, David & Charles, Newton Abbot, England, 1993.

Gremli, M. and Newman, H., *Marine Life in the South China Sea*, APA Publications, Singapore, 1994.

Hall Brierley, J., *The Story of Indonesia's Spice Trade*, Oxford University Press, Kuala Lumpur, 1994.

Holliday, L., *Coral Reefs*, Salamander Books, London, 1989.

Holmes, D. and Nash, S., *The Birds of Sumatra and Kalimantan*, Oxford University Press, 1990.

Indonesia in Focus, Edu Actif, The Netherlands, 1990.

Johnsson, D. and Balkema, A.A.,(Ed.), *Palms for Human Needs in Asia*, Brookfield, Rotterdam, 1991.

Kuiter, R.H., *Tropical Reef Fishes of the Western Pacific Indonesia and Adjacent Waters*, Penerbit P.T. Gramedia Pustaka Utama, Jakarta, 1992.

MacKinnon, K., *Nature's Treasurehouse: The Wildlife of Indonesia*, Penerbit P.T. Gramedia Pustaka Utama, Jakarta, 1992.

MacKinnon, J. and Phillips, K., *A Field Guide to the Birds of Borneo, Sumatra, Java and Bali*, Oxford University Press, 1993.

Marsden, W., *The History of Sumatra*, Oxford University Press, Kuala Lumpur, reprinted 1966.

McNeely, J.A. and Wachtel, P.S., *Soul of the Tiger: Searching for Nature's Answers in Exotic Southeast Asia*, Doubleday, New York, 1988.

Ministry of National Planning/National Development Planning Agency, *Biodiversity Action Plan for Indonesia*, Jakarta, 1993.

Mitchell, A.W., *The Enchanted Canopy: Secrets from the Rainforest Roof*, Collins, 1986.

Muller, K., *Underwater Indonesia, A Guide to the World's Greatest Diving*, Periplus Editions, Singapore, 1992.

Payne, J., Francis, C.M. and Phillips, K., *A Field Guide to the Mammals of Borneo*, Sabah Society, Kota Kinabalu and WWF-Malaysia, Kuala Lumpur, 1985.

Periplus Editions, A series of travel guides on 'Sumatra', 'Kalimantan', 'Sulawesi', 'New Guinea', 'East of Bali', 'The Spice Islands', Periplus Editions, Singapore.

Rainforests: The Illustrated Library of the Earth, Myers, N. (Ed.), Weldon Owen Pty Ltd, Sydney, 1992.

Savage, Victor, R., *Western Impressions of Nature and Landscape in Southeast Asia*, Singapore University Press, 1984.

Severns, M. and Fiene-Severns, P., *Sulawesi Seas: Indonesia's Magnificent Underwater Realm*, Periplus Editions, Singapore, 1994.

Sharp, I. and Compost, A., *Green Indonesia: Tropical Forest Encounters*, Oxford University Press, Kuala Lumpur, 1994.

Vatikiois, M., *Over Indonesia*, Archipelago Press, Singapore, 1993.

Wallace, Alfred, R., *The Malay Archipelago*, Dover, New York, 1962, (1869).

Whitten, A.J., Damanik, S.J., Anwar, J. and Hisyam, N., *The Ecology of Sumatra*, Gadjah Mada University Press, Indonesia, 1984.

Whitten, A.J., Mustafa, M. and Henderson, G.S., *The Ecology of Sulawesi*, Gadjah Mada University Press, Indonesia, 1987.

Whitten, A.J. and Whitten J., *Wild Indonesia*, New Holland, UK, 1992.

Whitmore, T.C., *Tropical Rain Forests of the Far East*, Clarendon, Oxford, 1984.

Wilson, E.O., *The Diversity of Life*, Penguin, London, 1993.

World Conservation Monitoring Centre, *Global Biodiversity: Status of the Earth's Living Resources*, Chapman and Hall, London, 1992.

Glossary

ARCHIPELAGO
A scattered group of islands in the ocean. The Indonesian Archipelago – the largest such structure in the world – contains over 17,000 islands, the majority of which are uninhabited.

AUSTRALASIAN REALM
A geographical region distinguished by the presence of Australian and continental Asian fauna and flora.

BIOGEOGRAPHY
A scientific subject which focuses on the geographic distribution of plants and animals.

BIOLOGICAL DIVERSITY
A term used to describe the natural richness of the Earth at the species and gene level.

BIOSPHERE
The part of the Earth's surface, including the oceans and lower atmosphere, where living organisms occur.

BUTTRESS ROOT
Roots which grow from the base and trunk of a tree above ground and provide support for tall trees growing on shallow or waterlogged soils.

CAULIFLORY
A feature of certain rain forest trees whereby buds (and later fruit) are produced on the trunk as opposed to on the branches of the crown.

COMMENSALISM
A form of symbiosis in which one species benefits from an association with another without harming or benefiting the other.

COMPETITION
An interaction between individuals of the same species, or between different species within the same ecosystem, in which the growth or survival of one or all species or individuals is affected adversely.

CONTINENTAL SHELF
A gently seaward-sloping surface that extends out from the shoreline to the top of the continental slope at about 150-200 metres depth.

CRUSTACEANS
A group of largely marine species which includes crabs, lobsters, shrimps, barnacles and woodlice.

DEMERSAL
A term used to describe fish and other aquatic speices which live close to the sea floor.

DIPTEROCARP
Trees of the family *Dipterocarpaceae*, many of which are native to Southeast Asia. Dipterocarps are typified by large leathery leaves with bright coloured flowers. These trees flower infrequently, maybe once in every five years.

ECOSYSTEM
The organisms which live in a particular environment, such as a rain forest, and the physical part of the environment that impinges on them.

ENDEMIC
A species that is native to a particular site and is only found in that location.

EPIPHYTE
A plant which perches and grows on other kinds of plants in a neutral or beneficial manner, but which is not a parasite. In the rain forest, many orchids and ferns are epiphytes.

FOOD WEB
The pattern of links in an ecosystem whereby energy is transferred from the primary producers (green plants) through a series of other organisms that eat them and which are, in turn, consumed by other organisms.

GONDWANALAND
A former supercontinent of the southern hemisphere from which South America, Africa, Australia and Antarctica are derived.

HABITAT
The living space of an organism or community, characterised by its physical or biotic properties.

HUNTER-GATHERERS
People who obtain food and much else of their livelihood by hunting wildlife and gathering vegetable and animal materials from the forest.

INDO-MALAYAN REALM
A biogeographical region which spans from west India and Sri Lanka to Peninsular Southeast Asia and west and central Indonesia.

INVERTEBRATE
Any animal lacking a backbone of bony segments that enclose the central nerve cord.

KERANGAS
Forest-heath vegetation typical of poor nutrient soils of Southeast Asia. Much of the nutrient supply to these soils is derived from rainfall.

LAURASIA
A former circumpolar supercontinent embracing what are now North America, Europe and Asia.

MALESIA
A term used to describe the tropical flora of the Australasian region, specifically that on and between the Sunda and Sahul shelves; an area comprising Malaysia, Papua New Guinea, and the islands of Indonesia and The Philippines.

MANGROVE
A type of swamp forest which grows on tropical and sub-tropical tidal mudflats and estuaries.

MUTUALISM
A feature whereby two or more species live together, or in close association, to the benefit of each partner.

MYCORRHIZA
A symbiotic association between fungi and plant roots.

NEMATOCYST
A defensive and feeding mechanism of many coelenterates such as coral polyps, sea anenomes and jellyfish. The nematocyst consists of a microscopic pear-shaped sac with a lid, the outer end of which is extended to form a long, hollow thread, coiled within the sac. They are commonly known to sting fiercely and can cause severe skin irritations and even death in humans.

NICHE
A term used to describe the position and role occupied by a given species in its ecosystem.

PARASITISM
The interaction between two or more species whereby one (the parasite) extracts some benefit (for example, food and shelter) to the detriment of the other (the host).

PELAGIC
Species which inhabit the open water of the sea.

PHOTOSYNTHESIS
A term given to a series of chemical reactions by which plants, utilizing sunlight, combine carbon dioxide with water to make energy-rich glucose, releasing excess oxygen into the atmosphere.

PLANKTON
Minute aquatic organisms that drift with the water current, generally being unable to control their directional movement. Two types of plankton occur; zooplankton (animals) and phytoplankton (plants), the latter carry out photosynthesis and form the basis of the aquatic food chains of the oceans.

PLEISTOCENE
A period of the Earth's history which is thought to date from approximately 1.8 million years ago to some 10,000 years ago.

PNEUMATOPHORE
A specialized 'breathing' root developed in plants that grow in waterlogged soils, such as mangroves. The aerial part of the root contains many pores enabling the plant to exchange gases with the atmosphere.

POLLINATION
The transfer of pollen grains from the anther (male part of the plant) to the stigma (the female recipient) of a flowering plant, leading to fertilization and development of seeds and fruit. Many different mechanisms are used by plants – wind, insects, birds and mammals – to ensure pollination.

POLYP
The soft-bodied, sedentary form of coelenterates such as coral and sea anenomes, consisting of a cylindrical trunk which is usually attached to the substrate, with the mouth surrounded by tentacles. Polyps are the individual building blocks of a coral reef.

PROPAGULE
The name given to the seed of mangrove plants. These are usually spiked to stick in the soft sediment surrounding mangroves, preventing them from being washed out to sea.

RAIN FOREST
A forest which receives at least 200 centimetres of rain evenly spread throughout a year. Trees are usually arranged in several irregular layers, forming a dense canopy which traps most of the sunlight striking the forest.

SAHULAND
The name often given to the tropical portion of the combined Australia-New Guinea landmass (probably including Halmahera) that was exposed at times of low sea-level during the Pleistocene.

SLASH-AND-BURN CULTIVATION
A common form of agriculture practised in Southeast Asia, whereby vegetation is felled, dried and burnt, the ashes adding nutrients to the soil. Crops are grown for two to three years, before the area is left fallow for a further 5-30 years, before repeating the cycle. Also known as 'shifting cultivation' or 'swidden agriculture'.

SPECIES
The basic unit of classification, consisting of a population or series of populations of closely related and similar organisms.

SUNDALAND
A name commonly given to the unit made up of Peninsular Malaysia, Sumatra, Java and Borneo together with intervening islands which are linked by shallow water (less than 200 metres). In the Pleistocene epoch, this area formed a complete landmass with, what is today, the sea-bed exposed as land during periods of low sea-level.

SYMBIOSIS
A process whereby two or more species live together in a prolonged and intimate ecological relationship.

TAMBAK
Artificial, shallow warm water ponds constructed for aquaculture.

TRANSMIGRATION
A programme whereby agricultural workers (and their families) are officially encouraged by the government to move from a crowded or poor agricultural region to a more fertile zone, often a forested area, where they may practise agriculture.

WALLACE'S LINE
An important zoogeographical division first proposed by the British naturalist and explorer Alfred Russell Wallace to separate the fauna (and to a lesser extent the flora) of the Asian and Australian faunal regions.

WALLACEA
The zone of mixing between species of the Oriental and Australian regions, as separated by the Wallace Line, running east of Bali and Kalimantan.

ZOOXANTHALLAE
Tiny, single-celled plants that live in the tissues of coral polyps and giant clams, which are capable of photosynthesis.

Index

Page numbers in bold refer to illustrations.

Index

Index

Acknowledgements

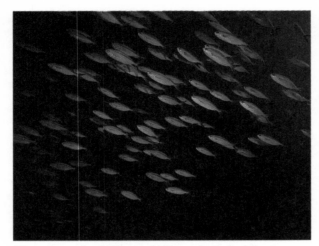

The author and publisher would like to thank the following people for their assistance and advice in producing this book:
Karl Ammann, Professor P N Avadhani, Tantyo Bangun, Claire Billington and Jonathan Rhind at the World Conservation Monitoring Centre, Cambridge, UK, Yvonne Byron, Jean-Paul Ferrero, Dr Margaret Gremli, Rio Helmi, Dr Sian Jay, Lystia Kusumawardani, Lee Hong Eng, Lim Yew Cheong, John McGlynn, Dr Øyvind Sandbukt, Christopher Smith, Morten Strange, Michael Sweet and Herwarth Voigtmann.

The author would like to extend his special thanks to Paul Spencer Sochaczewski for the enormous encouragement and advice provided throughout the project, to Alain Compost for his invaluable assistance, and to Ibu Seti-Arti Kailola for her help with research and arrangements in Indonesia.

Unless otherwise specified the photographs have been supplied by Alain Compost.

The endpapers show the Mahakam River, Kalimantan (Rio Helmi). The opening pages: page 1 forest, Kalimantan (Rio Helmi), pages 2-3 fallow coastal ricefields in Bali, pages 4-5 tidal swamp, Tanjung Puting, Kalimantan (Karl Ammann), pages 6-7 orang-utan (Karl Ammann), page 8 palm leaf (David Stone), whip coral (Michael Aw), page 9 rhinoceros hornbill (Auscape: Jean-Paul Ferrero), page 12 basketstar, fully extended at night (Michael Aw), page 13 forest, Sulawesi (Dominic Sansoni). The chapter openers – Contents: Mahakam River (Rio Helmi), yellow featherstar with trumpetfish (Michael Aw), lesser bird of paradise (Auscape: Jean-Paul Ferrero); Introduction: forest, Sumatra, Keli Mutu, Flores (Michael Freeman), lace coral (Michael Aw); Water: Bali (Raghu Rai), squid (Michael Aw), grouper (Herwarth Voigtmann); Land: forest, Gunung Leuser, orang-utan (Karl Ammann), milky stork; Parks: Segara Anakan crater lake, Lombok, green turtle, plumed egret. Page 208 br (Michael Aw).

Above: school of fusilierfish.

Right: bats at sunset, West Java.

Karl Ammann: p. 191, 197m.

Antiques of the Orient: p. 20, 21t, 29, 94t, 94b (two), 95t, 118t (two), 127, 139t (two), 140t, 145t, 168t, 168b, 171m, 185.

Auscape: John Cancalosi: p. 115m.

Auscape: Ben Cropp: p. 54b.

Auscape: Kev Deacon: p. 41t, 83.

Auscape: Jean-Paul Ferrero: p. 112br, 114, 115t, 137, 151, 152tl, 152br, 153 (two), 161tl.

Auscape: Krafft: p. 18.

Auscape: Wayne Lawler: p. 16, 100t, 100b, 108, 111, 126t.

Auscape: Becca Saunders: p. 61b, 66, 73tl, 74t, 78mr, 80, 82t.

Auscape: Alby Ziebell: p. 56.

Michael Aw: p. 32, 38tr, 38bl, 41m, 41b, 41r, 42t, 42b, 45r, 54t, 61tr, 65l, 65r, 67t, 67b, 68tr, 68m, 68br, 69t, 69mr, 69b, 72tl, 73tr, 73b, 75m, 76t, 77t, 78br, 81m.

Tantyo Bangun: p. 84t, 96, 101.

Bruno Barbey: p. 19t.

John Falconer: p. 28, 162.

Jill Gocher: p. 146m.

Leo Haks: p. 93m (two).

Rio Helmi: p. 36, 100, 147.

Robin Moyer: p. 24, 25, 163, 170tl, 170mr.

Ivan Polunin: p. 123t, 135tr.

Guido Alberto Rossi: p. 102.

Sejati: p. 88t, 88b (two), 89t, 89b, 90.

Mike Severns: p. 35, 38tl, 38br, 39 (three), 42m, 44t, 55, 60, 61tl, 64, 68tl, 68bl, 69ml, 70m, 74b, 75t, 75b, 76b, 77b (two), 78tr, 78mr, 79, 82bl, 82br, 86t, 199r.

Mahendra Sinh: p. 166, 167.

Morten Strange: p. 48l, 98b, 117, 135b.

Herwarth Voigtmann: p. 34t, 34b, 71, 72tr, 72b, 78bl.

Key: t (top), b (bottom), l (left), r (right), m (middle).